China
&
the U.S.
1964-72

China
&
the U.S.
1964-72

Edited by Kwan Ha Yim
Department of Political Science
Manhattanville College (Purchase, N.Y.)

FACTS ON FILE, INC.   NEW YORK, N.Y.

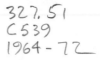

China
&
the U.S.
1964-72

Library of Congress Catalog Card No. 72-80832
ISBN 0-87196-207-1

9 8 7 6 5 4 3 2 1
PRINTED IN
THE UNITED STATES OF AMERICA

CONTENTS

FOREWORD

This volume is a sequel to the Facts on File publication *China and the U.S. 1955-63*. The narrative presented here covers the last phase of Sino-American relations during the Cold War era, from the beginning of the Johnson Administration to the change that followed President Nixon's historic visit to Peking in Feb. 1972. It is set against the background of the Vietnam War and of the manifold ramifications of the war for the domestic and international politics of both nations.

Ever since the establishment of the People's Republic on mainland China (1949), Sino-American relations had been frozen, as it were, in a sterile antagonism. The two great powers faced each other across the Pacific as adversaries, trading insults, diatribes and threats—all in full view of the public. In the absence of normal diplomatic relations, both parties were reduced to communication by signals rather than by polite words.

The Vietnam War proved to be the beginning of the end of this anomalous state of affairs. True, Communist China was not directly involved in the war. Nevertheless, the war provided a new medium by which China and the U.S. continued their contest of will. The U.S. increased its military build-up in South Vietnam in order to frustrate Peking's "war of national liberation" by proxy. This in turn confirmed Communist China's own image of "American imperialism" and hardened its anti-American stance. The war was fought with unparallelled brutality on all sides.

But it was in the intractability of the war that the adversaries came to terms with the need for embarking on a new course away from their antagonistic relationship. The war was costly in the heavy toll it took of human lives. It was no less costly in the disruption it caused the domestic structures of

1

China and the U.S. Both nations experienced internal turmoil
on a massive scale. Old stereotypes, convictions and policies
broke down under the mounting strain.

Events encompassed in this sweep of history are invariably
complex, and their turn often cataclysmic. It would be impossible to do them justice in this small volume and at this
distance in time from the events. What is attempted here is an
interim history, a rough sketching of the terrain on which
those events have moved. Thus, no pretense is made here either
of completeness or of profundity. Facts are presented with
minimum of editorial comments so they may speak for themselves. This factual material is drawn largely from the record
compiled by FACTS ON FILE in its weekly coverage of world
history.

WIDENING CONFLICT (1964)

U.S. Outlines Policy Toward Peking

Lyndon B. Johnson became the President of the U.S. Nov. 22, 1963 on the death of his predecessor, John F. Kennedy. By then, the U.S.-Communist Chinese relations had reached an impasse. The Warsaw ambassadorial talks, begun during the offshore island crisis of 1958, had become what appeared to be a ritualistic exercise unproductive of meaningful dialogue. The U.S. and Communist Chinese delegates traded well-worn polemics, each side blaming the other for the deadlocked relations. 1964 saw more of the same on the plane of bilateral relations between Washington and Peking. But there was added a new dimension: the Sino-U.S. conflict turned into a generalized ideological conflict around the world, from Asia to Africa and Latin America.

Still, at the heart of the Sino-U.S. conflict lay the unresolved status of Taiwan. The island, which provided a sanctuary for the Chinese Nationalists, was claimed by Communist China as an integral part of China to be "liberated," if necessary, by force. The U.S., which had signed a defense pact with the Nationalists on Taiwan in 1954, was determined to prevent the forcible seizure of the island by the Communist Chinese. The U.S. 7th Fleet patrolled the Taiwan Strait. Secure in their island bastion, the Chinese Nationalists kept up their claim to represent the legitimate government of China—and kept alive their dream of resuming their rule of the mainland.

Shortly after Johnson took office, Asst. State Secy. (for Far Eastern affairs) Roger Hilsman, in a speech at the Commonwealth Club of·San Francisco Dec. 13, 1963, declared that the U.S. was in favor of keeping the "door open" to negotiations with Communist China when the Peking government abandoned its "venomous hatred" of the U.S. The speech,

3

which originated from Hilsman's office and was delivered after a perfunctory clearance at the White House, made these points:

• Although China's hard stand was not likely to soften soon, there were signs of "evolutionary forces at work" among Chinese intellectuals and the more sophisticated "2d echelon of leadership" in the Chinese government. Communist Chinese toleration of other societies and other desired changes in the Peking government could best be promoted by a U.S. policy of firmness coupled with "a constant readiness to negotiate."

• The U.S. "maintain[ed] a policy of non-recognition of . . . Communist China at a time when we are willing to broaden contacts with the Soviet Union." The reasons for this difference were: (a) U.S.-Chinese relations could not improve as long as Peking insisted that the U.S. withdraw its commitment to guarantee the independence of Nationalist China; (b) the USSR regarded survival in the atomic age as of mutual interest to all nations whereas China believed there were no "common interests which cross ideological lines"; (c) the Soviet Union apparently understood that the West's willingness to negotiate was no sign of weakness whereas Communist China felt that "any conciliatory gesture" was a weakness to be exploited; (d) the West had to maintain a firm policy as long as China sought to exploit the weaknesses of its neighbors through aggression and subversion.

• The U.S. was not "ignoring China and its 700 million people." This "myth" was refuted by the fact that the U.S. and Chinese ambassadors met periodically in Warsaw to discuss matters of mutual interest.

• The Chinese were "dangerously overconfident" and "wedded to outdated theories but pragmatic when their existence is threatened. We have no reason to believe that there is a present likelihood that the Communist regime will be overthrown."

• The U.S. was "determined to keep the door open to the possibility of change [in the Peking government] and not to slam it shut against any developments which might advance our national good, serve the free world and benefit the people of China." The U.S., however, would not "betray" its "interests and those of" its "allies to appease the ambitions of Communist China's leaders."

Sino-Soviet Dispute Grows Worse

The Hilsman "open door" speech failed to elicit any significant change in Peking's attitude toward the U.S. (The Chinese Communist newspaper *Ta Kung Pao* Dec. 14, 1963 dismissed it as a continuation of the "aggressive policy" of the U.S. and charged that the "open door" policy was a call to China to "open the door to welcome the thief.") But the speech was delivered against the background of a growing split between Moscow and Peking, a split that was to become the most significant factor in Sino-American relations. 1964 saw the dispute taking on an increasingly acrimonious and open character.

A New Year's editorial published Jan. 1 by the Chinese Communist Party newspaper *Jenmin Jih Pao (People's Daily)* declared that in 1964 China would continue to "actively support revolutionary struggles of all oppressed peoples" and to "resolutely oppose the policy of war and aggression of imperialism headed by the United States." The editorial's attacks extended to the USSR, which, it said, had created difficulties for and harmed China's economy, and to Soviet bloc "revisionists," who were blamed for efforts to "isolate" China. The Chinese people, it said, had overcome all of these difficulties.

Jenmin Jih Pao Feb. 3 published an article under the heading "The Leaders of the Communist Party of the Soviet Union [CPSU] Are the Greatest Splitters of Our Time." The article, 7th in 2 series of Chinese attacks on the CPSU, took issue with Soviet Premier Nikita S. Khrushchev's foreign policy of "peaceful co-existence," "peaceful competition" and "peaceful transition." All of these goals were said to be the marks of "revisionism." The article argued: "Opportunism and revisionism are the political and ideological roots of splittism. And splittism is the organizational manifestation of opportunism and revisionism. It can also be said that opportunism and revisionism are the greatest and vilest splitters and sectarians in the Communist movement." It charged that the Soviet Union sought to dominate the world in collusion with the U.S. The Soviet leaders, it said, "reversed enemies and comrades."

The next month, Peking published its 8th attack on the Soviet Union, a 30,000-word statement that appeared in *Jenmin Jih Pao* and the Chinese Communist ideological journal *Hung Chi (Red Flag)* Mar. 31. This article, entitled "the Proletarian Revolution and Khrushchev's Revisionism," called on all Communist parties round the world to repudiate Khrushchev, "the greatest capitulationist in history," and to join the Chinese Communists in their efforts to press for a world revolution.

On his part, Khrushchev denounced the Chinese Communists, blaming the latter for the split in the international Communist movement. Addressing the plenary session of the CPSU central committee Feb. 14, the Soviet premier said that the Soviet Union was trying to restore "the monolithic unity of the world Socialist system" based on the consensus reached at the Moscow conference of 81 Communist parties in 1960. He said: "We have fought and will continue to fight against revisionists, dogmatists, the newly-based Trotskyists, who, while making highsounding revolutionary phrases about the struggle against imperialism, undermine in fact the unity of the world Communist movement by splitting their activities."

While touring in Hungary in the fiirst week of April, Khrushchev lashed out against the Chinese. In a speech in Budapest Apr. 1, he said: "There are people . . . who call themselves Marxists-Leninists and at the same time say there is no need to strive for a better life. According to them, only one thing is important—revolution." The Soviet premier expressed doubts as to whether revolution was more important than goulash. In later remarks during his Hungarian tour, Khrushchev referred to the Chinese Communists in such pejorative terms as "idiots" and "crazy." At the end of his tour, he delivered a speech in Budapest Apr. 9. In this speech, which was telecast throughout Europe, he declared that the Chinese Communists were "renegades and traitors" and that their "spasmodic efforts to subordinate world communism will end in shameful failure."

Chou En-lai Tours Africa

At odds alike with the U.S. and the USSR, Communist China found itself diplomatically isolated. In an effort to break out of this diplomatic isolation and to win friends in the "3d world," Communist Chinese Premier Chou En-lai made a 2-month tour of Africa during Dec. 1963-Feb. 1964. Chou's party included Foreign Min. Chen Yi and a 50-member government delegation. Chou's tour, begun Dec. 14 with visits to the United Arab Republic (Egypt), Algeria and Morocco, was interrupted Dec. 31, 1963 for a 9-day visit to Albania. He then returned to Africa to visit Tunisia, Ghana, Mali, Guinea, the Sudan, Ethiopia and Somalia. Chou had planned to stop in Kenya and Tanganyika, but these visits were canceled by the Chinese, apparently because of a recent British military intervention in those countries against mutinies of African troops.

The African countries Chou's party visited varied widely in their political and economic backgrounds and in their diplomatic relations with the West. They also differed in their receptivity to Chinese friendship. Chou, as one Western commentator noted, travelled wearing "the revolutionary's beret and the diplomat's toga." In the capitals he visited, Chou was seen to take a low-key posture as he explained his country's stand on the test-ban treaty, the UN, the Chinese-Indian border dispute. He expressed his hopes for another Afro-Asian conference like the Bandung Conference of 1955. His softspoken words and mild manners contrasted with the image of Communist China as a militantly revolutionary nation.

In Egypt, the recipient of aid from the U.S. and the USSR, Chou spoke mainly about "world peace" and about the world being divided between "imperialists" and "Afro-Asian" nations. After conferring with UAR Pres. Gamal Abdel Nasser, Chou declared in a joint communique Dec. 22, 1963 that he and the Egyptian leader had agreed on a "common ground." Peking's African policy, Chou said, was guided by the following principles:

"It supports the African peoples in the fight against imperialism and old and new colonialism and for winning and safeguarding of national independence;

"It supports the governments of African countries in their pursuance of a policy of peace, neutrality and non-alignment;

"It supports the African peoples in their desire to realize solidarity and unity in the form of their choice;

"It supports the African countries in their efforts to settle their differences through peaceful consultations;

"It maintains that the sovereignty of the African countries must be respected by all countries and that all encroachment and interference from whatever quarters should be opposed."

Following a visit to Algeria and Morocco and a side-trip to Albania, Chou and his party flew to Tunis, the capital of Tunisia, Jan. 9, 1964. Chou conferred with the Tunisian president, Habib Bourguiba. Bourguiba described his talks with Chou to a newsman as having been conducted "with the frankness of friendship." Bourguiba said: "I told him what shocked us in his manner, style and conceptions. I said, 'You come to Africa as the enemy of the capitalist states, of the West, of the neutralists and the non-aligned, of India, of Tito, of Khrushchev, of everybody. You have not chosen an easy policy. I'll say that. Don't expect to score much in Africa. Others won't tell you straight; I will—you won't get far in this continent." At the state banquet honoring the Chinese delegation, Bourguiba assured China of Tunisia's support for its admission to the UN, but he made clear his disquiet over China's use of force in the frontier dispute with India and over its refusal to sign the 1963 Moscow treaty curbing nuclear weapons tests. A joint communique issued Jan. 10 announced that Tunisia had recognized the Peking government and would establish diplomatic relations with it.

The Chinese delegation flew from Tunis to Accra Jan. 11 for a 5-day visit to Ghana. Ghana's welcome was described as warm, but the government-owned *Ghanaian Times* declared editorially Jan. 12 that Ghana would not take sides in the Chinese-Russian ideological dispute. Chou conferred with Ghanaian Pres. Kwame Nkrumah beginning Jan. 12 and combined the talks with visits to model farms and industrial plants. He was the guest of honor Jan. 13 at a presidential dinner at which Nkrumah hailed China's progress under communism. A joint communique issued Jan. 16, at the close of Chou's visit, expressed the 2 countries' backing for a 2d Afro-Asian solidarity conference, to which Latin Americans would be invited, and for economic and political action against South African racism.

Chou continued his African trip with visits to Mali (Jan. 16-20) and Guinea (Jan. 21-26) for meetings with Mali Pres. Modibo Keita and Guinea Pres. Sekou Toure. He flew to Khartoum Jan. 27 to visit the Sudan and confer with Pres. Ibrahim Abboud. From the Sudan he flew Jan. 30 to Addis Ababa for meetings with Emperor Haile Selassie of Ethiopia. A communique issued by Selassie and Chou Feb. 1, at the conclusion of the 3-day visit, pledged Ethiopia's support of Communist China's admission to the UN and announced, without clarification, that the 2 countries' relations would be "normalized."

Chou returned to Peking Feb. 5. The official Communist Chinese newspaper, *Jenmin Jih Pao,* commented editorially Feb. 6: "In the communiques issued after their talks, Premier Chou En-lai and the leaders of the African countries agreed: In order to prevent world war, it is necessary to wage an unremitting struggle against the imperialist policies of aggression and war; the contemporary national liberation movement is an important force in defense of world peace; imperialism and old and new colonialism must be completely liquidated in Africa;

Asian-African solidarity must be strengthened with the utmost effort, and, in the opinion of many countries, active preparations should be made for a second Asian-African conference; disputes among Asian-African countries should be settled through peaceful negotiations on the basis of Asian-African solidarity; national economies should be developed by mainly relying on one's own strength supplemented by foreign assistance.''

France Recognizes Communist China

While Chou En-lai was still on his African tour, Peking's effort to end its diplomatic isolation scored a significant breakthrough when France recognized Peking. The announcement, made simultaneously Jan. 23, 1964 in Peking and Paris, said: "The government of the People's Republic of China and the government of the French Republic have decided in mutual agreement to establish diplomatic relations. For this purpose, the 2 governments have agreed to appoint their ambassadors within 3 months.''

This new development was a *tour de force* in French foreign policy under Gen. Charles de Gaulle. De Gaulle had been known to entertain a grand vision of European nations forming an *entente* from the Atlantic to the Urals. In 1959 talks with Soviet Premier Khrushchev, the French president was reported to have declared that the "Yellow Peril" from the Chinese would cement Franco-Russian relations. Events belied de Gaulle's prediction. Far from pursuing the vision of a greater Europe, the Soviet government showed that it was much more interested in dealing with the U.S. and Great Britain (the "Anglo-Saxon powers") on a treaty banning nuclear tests in the atmosphere, under water and in space. The conclusion of the partial test-ban treaty in Aug.1963 by the U.S., UK and USSR provoked a denunciation from France and Communist China; it proved to be a catalyst in bringing about Franco-Chinese rapprochement. The 2 minor nuclear powers were united by their common interest in breaking what they considered a double-hegemony of the superpowers, the U.S. and USSR. A Paris *Match* writer described the new turn in French policy as "an almost desperate attempt to break the embrace of the 2 superpowers. . . ."

The Peking-Paris announcement of Jan. 27 made no mention of Taiwan. Apparently, the French government sought at first to normalize its relations with Peking without severing ties with Taipei. If successful, this would have brought about a "2 Chinas" solution. In Oct. 1963, Edgar Faure, a former French premier, went to Peking on a semi-official mission. The purpose of the trip was to persuade Peking to waive the requirement that France break diplomatic relations with Taipei. In an interview with a correspondent of *le Figaro,* Faure asserted in Jan. 1964 that there was no condition involved in the French agreement to normalize diplomatic relations with Communist China. The French Foreign Ministry announced Jan. 27 that French recognition of Communist China was not predicated on the break-off of diplomatic relations with Nationalist China.

The *de facto* "2 Chinas" solution was ruled out by the stand taken by Communist China. A statement by the Peking Foreign Office Jan. 28 said: "According to international practice, recognition of the new government of a country naturally implies ceasing to recognize the old ruling group overthrown by the people of that country. . . . Consequently, the representatives of the old ruling group can no longer be regarded as representatives of that country to be present side by side with the representatives of the new government in one and the same country or international organization. It was with this understanding that the government of the People's Republic of China reached agreement with the government of the French Republic on the establishment of diplomatic relations and the exchange of ambassadors between China and France."

Communist Chinese Premier Chou En-lai told newsmen Feb. 3: "The government of the People's Republic of China, as the only legal government of the entire Chinese people, is prepared to send its diplomatic representative to Paris. I emphatically declare that, apart from the diplomatic representative of the People's Republic of China, it is impossible for anyone to act as the diplomatic representative of China in Paris."

The Chinese Nationalist government in Taipei, apparently on a suggestion from Washington, did not immediately withdraw its diplomatic representative from Paris. Taipei protested but maintained its embassy in Paris until Feb. 13, 1964.

Gen. de Gaulle, at his news conference Jan. 31, commented on the French recognition of Communist China, linking it to the war in Indochina. De Gaulle said: "There is in Asia no political reality . . . that does not concern or affect China. There is . . . neither a war nor a peace imaginable on this continent without China being implicated in it. Thus, it would be . . . impossible to envisage, without China, a possible neutrality agreement relating to Southeast Asian states—a neutrality, which, by definition, must be accepted by all, guaranteed internationally; which should exclude all the varied forms of outside intervention; neutrality which seems in this period in which we are to be the only situation which can be compatible with a peaceful life and the progress of the peoples concerned."

The U.S. State Department Jan. 27 expressed regret at the French recognition of Communist China and reaffirmed the U.S. commitment to defend Nationalist China. The statement said that the French action was "an unfortunate step, particularly at a time when Chinese Communists are actively promoting aggression and subversion in Southeast Asia and elsewhere." Pres. Johnson, commenting on the French action, said at his news conference Feb. 1: "I do not agree with Gen. de Gaulle's proposals. I do not think that it would be in the interest of freedom to share his view."

Other governments reacted in differing ways Jan. 27 to the news of the French action. The USSR and Soviet bloc countries welcomed the French-Chinese announcement. The West German government expressed regret at the French action and said that it would have welcomed consultation and discussion of the

matter with other Western countries. The Portuguese government declined comment, but Lisbon officials made clear their
agreement with the French action. Indian spokesmen expressed
negative reactions to the news, but Pakistan Foreign Office officials said that it marked a step toward "peace" in Asia. Canadian officials said that their government would take no steps
to emulate the French action despite Canada's recent sales of
wheat to China.

The Nationalist Chinese government announced Feb. 10
that it had broken diplomatic relations with France because of
the French recognition of Communist China. The Nationalist
action ended a controversy over whether French diplomatic relations with both Chinese governments—the Communist regime
in Peking and the Nationalists in Taipei—would constitute
French recognition of the existence of "2 Chinas."

The Taiwan announcement came only hours after the French
Foreign Ministry had issued a statement in which it made clear
that the de Gaulle government would no longer consider the
Nationalist embassy in Paris to be the diplomatic representative
of China. The French government, although reluctant to initiate
the break with Taiwan, had sought the rupture in order to proceed with its plans for an exchange of diplomatic missions with
Peking. It was reported that the Peking regime had refused to
send its envoys to Paris until the Nationalist representation had
been ended. French sources continued to deny, however, that
Peking had demanded a French break with Taipei as a precondition to carrying out the recognition agreement.

The Nationalist action was made official Feb. 11 in a note
delivered to the French Foreign Ministry by Kao Shih-ming,
Nationalist charge d'affaires in Paris. (The Nationalist mission
in Paris had confirmed Feb. 6 that ownership of the Nationalist
embassy had been transferred to the Chinese delegation to
UNESCO. The transfer had been made to forestall a Communist Chinese attempt to lay legal claim to the embassy building,
a claim which the French government had indicated it would
support.)

A U.S. State Department statement issued in Washington Feb. 10 said that the Nationalist break had been understandable in view of the position taken by France. It rejected the French contention that Peking had not demanded that France end its ties with the Nationalists.

Chou En-lai Tours Southeast Asia

With the question of the Chinese representation at Paris settled, Premier Chou En-lai, accompanied by Foreign Minister Chen Yi, left Feb. 14, 1964 for a tour of Southeast Asia that took him to Burma, Pakistan and Ceylon. Among highlights of the tour:

Burma—Chou and Marshal Chen Yi arrived in Rangoon Feb. 14 for a 5-day visit at the invitation of Gen. Ne Win, chairman of Burma's ruling military Revolutionary Council. The 2 leaders left Rangoon Feb. 15 for Ngapali, a seaside resort on the Bay of Bengal, where they held their political talks. They remained in Ngapali until the Chinese delegation left for Pakistan.

A joint communique issued Feb. 18 by Chou and Ne Win confirmed reports that the 2 leaders had discussed the Chinese-Indian border dispute; it expressed the hope that China and India would enter direct negotiations toward a settlement of the problem on the basis of a Dec. 1962 peace plan advanced at a Colombo meeting of 6 Asian-African powers. The communique also expressed both leaders' wishes for peace and the liquidation of colonialism in Asia and pledged Burma's support for Communist Chinese admission to the UN.

(It was reported from Rangoon Feb. 18 that Ne Win, at a New Delhi meeting Feb. 8 with Indian Prime Min. Jawaharlal Nehru, had urged Nehru to come to Burma to confer with Chou on a settlement of a Sino-Indian border dispute. Ne Win was said to have informed Chou that Nehru had refused any such meeting while Chinese troops remained on territory traditionally considered to be Indian. Ne Win's New Delhi visit was said to have been undertaken at Chou's request.)

Pakistan—Chou's visit to Pakistan was marked by the most significant action of his Asia tour: the announcement that Communist China had abandoned its traditional neutrality toward the Kashmir dispute and in the future would support Pakistan's position against India's.

The Chinese delegation flew to Karachi Feb. 18 and to Rawalpindi (the temporary capital) Feb. 20 to begin its Pakistan visit. Chou was welcomed warmly in Rawalpindi by Pres. Mohammed Ayub Khan, and the 2 leaders began 3 days of political discussions.

(Ayub Khan, meeting with newsmen in Rawalpindi Feb. 21 before the conclusion of his talks with Chou, offered Pakistan's "good offices" to bring about a lessening of tensions between the U.S. and Communist China. Speaking of the clash between Indian and Chinese interests and U.S. and Chinese interests in Southeast Asia, Ayub Khan asserted that "the Chinese are prepared to be reasonable with anyone who is . . . reasonable with them." Ayub acknowledged, however, that the question of a Washington-Peking accord was complicated by the U.S.' "honorable commitment" to the Nationalist Chinese regime on Taiwan.)

China's reversal of policy on the Kashmir problem was disclosed in a joint communique issued by Chou and Ayub Khan Feb. 23. Made public by Pakistani Foreign Min. Zulfikar Ali Bhutto, the communique said that the 2 leaders had expressed "the hope that the Kashmir dispute would be resolved in accordance with the wishes of the people of Kashmir as pledged to them by India and Pakistan." The communique's wording referred to past pledges by India and Pakistan to abide by the result of a Kashmir plebiscite on the region's political future. India subsequently had refused to permit a plebiscite to be held; Pakistan had failed in attempts to bring UN pressure on India to carry out its pledge, partially because of the USSR's support of India in the dispute.

Chou and Chen Yi had ended their talks with Ayub and Pakistani officials in Rawalpindi Feb. 22; they went to Lahore Feb. 23 and flew across Indian territory Feb. 24 to Dacca, East Pakistan.

Interviewed in Dacca Feb. 25 by an AP of Pakistan reporter, Chou declared that he welcomed Ayub Khan's offer of "good offices between China and the United States." He said, however, that a lessening of U.S.-Chinese tensions depended exclusively on the U.S.' abandonment of its "hostile policy toward China." Questioned later Feb. 25 at a Dacca news conference, Chou made it clear that he meant abandonment of the U.S.' support for the Nationalist government on Taiwan and an end to U.S. involvement in South Vietnam, Laos and elsewhere in Asia. He denounced the U.S.' support of the Nationalists as a policy designed to lead to the creation of "2 Chinas." He called the U.S. the "most vicious exponent . . . of imperialist policies of war and aggression."

Chou left Dacca Feb. 27 for Ceylon.

Ceylon—The Chinese delegation arrived in Colombo, Ceylon Feb. 27 and received what was described as an unenthusiastic public reception. Chou and Mrs. Sirimavo Bandaranaike, Ceylon's prime minister, began their talks the same day and broke them only to address a sparsely-attended Colombo rally Feb. 28. A joint communique issued Feb. 29 disclosed that Mrs. Bandaranaike had urged, unsuccessfully, that China withdraw from some border posts it had occupied in Ladakh in 1962. Chou rejected the suggestion but renewed Chinese offers to negotiate with Indian leaders on a settlement of the border question. The communique also made clear that Ceylon supported India in its proposal to convene a 2d conference of non-aligned nations along the lines of the 1961 Belgrade conference, from which Communist China had been excluded. Chou countered that China believed the "time was ripe" for a 2d Afro-Asian conference similar to the 1955 Bandung meeting, at which China had been a major participant.

Chou and Chen Yi arrived in Kunming, China Mar. 1 on their way back to Peking.

U.S. Deepens Involvement in Southeast Asia

Meanwhile, political instability grew in South Vietnam. The military junta, which had overthrown Ngo Dinh Diem Nov. 1, 1963, was in turn overthrown in a bloodless coup Jan. 30, 1964 by Maj. Gen. Nguyen Khanh, commander of the Vietnamese army's First Corps.

The U.S. stepped up its efforts to shore up the new South Vietnamese government. Pres. Johnson, in a speech at the University of California at Los Angeles Feb. 21, sounded a warning indirectly against Communist China by saying that "those engaged in external direction and supply" of the Communists in South Vietnam were playing a "deeply dangerous game." The U.S. Defense Department Feb. 24 announced that Defense Secy. Robert McNamara would visit Saigon for the purpose of assessing the military effectiveness of the new government of Gen. Khanh.

State Secy. Dean Rusk, addressing an AFL-CIO-sponsored conference on world affairs Feb. 25, criticized Communist China for its involvement in Southeast Asia and its aggressive activities elsewhere in the world. He said: "Peiping continues to insist upon the surrender of Formosa as the *sine qua non* of any improvement whatever in the relations with the United States. We are loyal to our commitments to the government of the Republic of China; and we will not abandon the 12 million people of free China on Taiwan to Communist tyranny. Peiping incites and aggressively supports the aggression in Southeast Asia in violation of the Geneva Agreements of 1954 and the Geneva Accords of 1962. Peiping attacked India and occupies a position from which it continues to threaten the subcontinent of South Asia. Peiping is attempting to extend its tactics of terror and subversion into Africa and Latin America. In other words, Peiping flouts the first condition for peace: leave your neighbors alone. And we in the United States have not forgotten Peiping's aggressive intervention in Korea—an act for which it stands condemned by the United Nations. The American people cherished their close aud cordial ties with the people of the Chinese mainland. They look forward to the time when it will be possible to renew this historic friendship."

With political instability continuing, Viet Cong influence rapidly spread in the rural areas of South Vietnam. The Chinese Communist Party newspaper *Jenmin Jih Pao* commented Mar. 4 that the "U.S. paper tiger had been punctured and exposed."

Defense Secy. McNamara left for Saigon Mar. 8 on a 5-day inspection tour. Before leaving Washington, McNamara told newsmen that his trip affirmed "the U.S. commitment to furnish whatever military tiaining and logistical support is needed by the South Vietnamese to suppress their insurgency and to continue to furnish that support for whatever period is required." While in South Vietnam, McNamara visited several strategic hamlets in the Mekong River delta. At Hoa Hao, he said: "The thing which we want to emphasize is that Khanh has the full and complete support of Pres. Johnson and our whole government, and I want to let his people know this."

Following McNamara's return from his trip to Saigon, the White House convened the National Security Council Mar. 17. The statement issued by the White House after the NSC meeting admitted "setbacks" in South Vietnam but took note of the fact that Gen. Khanh's Saigon government had "produced a sound central plan for the prosecution of the war." This plan included the mobilization of manpower and the creation of military and para-military forces capable of conducting counterinsurgency warfare. The statement reaffirmed the U.S. pledge to aid Gen. Khanh's government "for as long as it is required to bring Communist aggression and terrorism under control."

Congressional reaction to Johnson's policy was mixed: Sen. Ernest Gruening (D., Alaska), in a speech on the U.S. Senate floor Mar. 10, called for the cessation of "the useless and senseless losses of American lives in an area not essential to the security of the U.S." Sen. Wayne Morse (D., Ore.), agreeing with Gruening, said: "We should never have gone in.

We should never have stayed in. We should get out." Sen. J. W. Fulbright (D., Ark.), on the senate floor Mar. 25, made a speech entitled "Old Myths and New Realities." He held that there were only 2 realistic alternatives: to expand the war or to "bolster the capacity of the South Vietnamese to prosecute the war on its present scale." Whichever the option, said Fulbright, "it should be clear to all concerned that the United States will continue to meet its obligations and fulfill its commitments with respect to Vietnam."

In April 1964, ex-Vice Pres. Richard M. Nixon travelled in Asia, ostensibly for the Pepsi-Cola Co. On his return from the trip, which had included a visit to Saigon, Nixon Apr. 15 told newsmen that the U.S. should strengthen its anti-Communist policy in Asia. Addressing the American Society of Newspaper Editors in Washington Apr. 18, Nixon reiterated his call for a stronger anti-Communist policy on the part of the U.S. In Southeast Asia, he said, the South Vietnamese should be allowed to enter Cambodia and Laos in "hot pursuit." Later, at his press conference Feb. 23, Pres. Johnson was asked if the Nixon statement was based on faulty information. Johnson answered: "No, I wouldn't make that comment. I don't know what it was based on. I haven't talked to Mr. Nixon. I assume that he spent a good deal of his time looking after Pepsi-Cola interest. I don't know how much information he got. But at least that is what he said he was doing."

State Secy. Rusk visited South Vietnam Apr. 17-20 to emphasize U.S. support of Premier Khanh and his regime's war against the Viet Cong. Before going to Saigon, Rusk had stopped in Formosa and had conferred with Chinese Nationalist Pres. Chiang Kai-shek. Rusk had assured Chiang that U.S. support of his government against Communist China remained unchanged.

On arriving in Saigon Apr. 17, Rusk declared in an airport statement: South Vietnam and its allies must defeat Communist efforts to "impose their own misery on you." "I am here to make it clear once again that we shall help you to do it." Peace would come to South Vietnam "when Hanoi and Peiping have been taught to leave their neighbors alone."

Rusk was briefed later by Amb. Henry Cabot Lodge, Gen. Paul D. Harkins, chief of the U.S. Military Assistance Command, and CIA and other U.S. officials. Rusk Apr. 18 discussed the Vietnamese and Southeast Asian situation during a meeting in Saigon with Khanh, Lodge, Gen. Earle G. Wheeler, Army chief of staff, and Asst. State Secy. (for Far Eastern affairs) William P. Bundy. Rusk, accompanied by Khanh, Lodge and Wheeler, later toured the northern province of Ninh Thuan. In a visit to the fortified hamlet of Phuoc Hung, Rusk told villagers that "we are comrades in your struggle" against the Viet Cong. "Some day that regime in Hanoi will disappear and you and your brothers in the north will be able to join in a free and democratic Vietnam."

Before leaving South Vietnam, Rusk said in an airport statement Apr. 20 that he and Khanh had discussed ways in which the U.S. could bolster its assistance to his regime. Rusk said he was "impressed by the military, economic and social programs instituted by Gen. Khanh."

Rusk returned to Washington Apr. 20 and reported to Pres. Johnson. After the White House meeting, Rusk said South Vietnam might ask several of the U.S.' allies for military advisers to assist in the war against the Viet Cong.

Pres. Johnson May 18 sent the Congress a new request for $125 million in economic and military assistance to South Vietnam; this was in addition to $500 million already requested. He went to Honolulu June 1 to attend a high-level conference convened to discuss the Southeast Asian situation. Among those who attended the meeting were State Secy. Dean Rusk, Defense Secy. Robert McNamara, Chairman of Joint Chiefs of Staff Maxwell D. Taylor, CIA Director John A. McCone and Amb.-to-Saigon Henry Cabot Lodge Jr. At the conclusion of the meeting June 2, Johnson said at a press conference: "It may be helpful to outline 4 basic themes that govern our policy in Southeast Asia. First, America keeps her word.

2d, the issue is the future of Southeast Asia as a whole. 3d, our purpose is peace. 4th, this is not a jungle war but a struggle for freedom on every front of human activity."

Johnson delivered an address the following day at the U.S. Coast Guard Academy at New London. Johnson asserted that the U.S. military power was greater than "the combined might of all the nations in the history of the world." The *Christian Science Monitor* interpreted this remark as a warning against Communist China.

The U.S.' determination to prevent a Communist take-over of Southeast Asia reportedly had been conveyed to French Pres. Charles de Gaulle by U.S. State Undersecy. George W. Ball in Paris June 5, to Communist China through British diplomatic channels and by Danish Premier Jens Otto Krag to Soviet Premier Khrushchev during a recent Khrushchev visit to Denmark. It was reported that U.S. officials had informally urged newsmen to stress that U.S. policy in Southeast Asia was tantamount to an unlimited commitment to bar Communist aggression in the area. This policy was seen as similar to the U.S. position on defending West Berlin.

Asst. State Secy. (for Far Eastern affairs) William P. Bundy warned that if Pathet Lao forces in Laos gained a decided military advantage, "the only response we would have would be to put our own forces in there." Bundy's statement was made in testimony May 4 (made public June 18) before the House Appropriations subcommittee that was holding hearings on Pres. Johnson's $3½ billion foreign aid program. Bundy predicted that the U.S. would "drive the Communists out of South Vietnam" even if it meant eventually "attacking the countries to the north."

Adm. Harry D. Felt, commander of U.S. forces in the Pacific, declared in Taipei June 20 that the U.S. was "willing to risk war with Communist China because we believe too strongly it cannot and must not win." Asked whether he believed the U.S. was ready to risk full-scale conflict to halt Chinese expansionism in Southeast Asia, Felt answered: China "will not risk going to war with the United States . . . because they know how strong we are. Now you asked if we were willing to risk—yes."

In the meantime, a new crisis developed in Laos. An American reconnaisance plane was shot down June 6, 1964 in northern Laos. Another plane was lost June 7. U.S. fighter jets retaliated by straffing Pathet Lao positions June 9. *Jenmin Jih Pao* June 10 called the air raids "direct military attacks on the Laotian people." The Chommunist Chinese Foreign Office June 13 addressed a note to the Soviet Union and Great Britain requesting that they, in their capacity as co-chairmen of the 1962 Geneva Conference on Laos, reconvene the 14-nation conference in Geneva. *Jenmin Jih Pao* June 15 observed that "the peace in Indochina and Southeast Asia is hanging by a thread."

A Communist Pathet Lao broadcast June 17 charged that planes of the "United States and its lackeys" June 15 had "spray[ed] poisonous chemicals over the area of Nhom Ma Lat, Cammon Province," and that "local inhabitants and a number of oxen were poisoned."

Western military sources in Vientiane June 17 said leftist reports of air raids were often exaggerated or false. According to these sources, a raid on Pathet Lao headquarters in Khang Khay June 11 had been made by a single Laotian air force piston-engine plane and not by 6 planes, as Communist China still charged.

It was reported during this period that the U.S. was strengthening its military posture in Southeast Asia by a series of moves that included (a) sending more arms and equipment to its military supply base in Thailand and (b) building a powerful forward air base in South Vietnam.

The reinforcement of U.S. supplies in Thailand was disclosed by the Defense Department June 20. A department spokesman said that tanks, armored personnel carriers, trucks and other military equipment were being sent to "resupply and replace" materiel that had been sent to Thailand during the 1962

Laotian crisis. The department spokesman described the shipment as routine. The U.S. reported June 22 that it was helping Thailand build 2 roads linking the strategic Laotian border area in the north with Thailand's principal road network. The $11 million project was being financed equally by Thailand and the U.S. Agency for International Development.

The *N.Y. Times* reported June 22 that the U.S. was building a huge Air Force base at Danang, South Vietnam to put the U.S. in a strategic position to cope with any possible full-scale military move by Communist China. The base was about 350 miles north of Saigon and 160 miles from the Chinese island of Hainan. It would be capable of handling the largest jet planes. Although unfinished, the base was already servicing F-100 jet fighters.

In a formal statement, the U.S. State Department asserted June 22: "There can be little doubt in the minds of the Communist leaders . . . that we are prepared to help the Vietnamese repel Communist aggression. Our support to Thailand is equally clear. We have provided military assistance to Thailand for some time, while also helping the Thai government build its military capacity. Our position with respect to Laos is equally clear."

This statement was designed to dispel any doubts as to the U.S. commitments in the area and, thereby, to avert "another Korea."

To these signals of hardening U.S. attitude, Peking responded by taking a similarly uncompromising stance. Peking made its views clear after North Vietnamese Foreign Min. Xuan Thuy sent a message June 25 to the 14 signers of the 1954 Geneva accords, including Communist China, calling on them to take "firm . . . action to demand that the U.S. government give up its design of intensifying provocation and sabotage" against North Vietnam. Communist Chinese Foreign Min. Chen Yi replied July 6 that "the Chinese people naturally cannot be expected to look on with folded arms" if North Vietnam were attacked. Marshal Chen committed Communist China to

defend North Vietnam against any U.S. attack, which he called
a potential threat to China's security.

The Chinese Communist Party newspaper *Jenmin Jih Pao*
called Chen's statement "a forceful warning from the Chinese
government to United States imperialism." The newspaper said
in an editorial: "The Chinese people have always maintained
that it is an unshirkable proletarian internationalist duty of all
Socialist countries to safeguard the peace and security of the
entire Socialist camp, to protect all its members from any imperialist invasion and to defend the Socialist camp."

Chen denounced the U.S. July 14 for "direct and undis-
guised military intervention in Laos" and charged the U.S. with
plotting "to expand its aggressive war in South Vietnam." He
warned of the danger of a war throughout Southeast Asia and
advocated reconvening of the 14-nation Geneva conference.

The Gulf of Tonkin Resolution

1964 was a Presidential election year in the U.S. The Republican Party (GOP) nominated Sen. Barry Goldwater (R.,
Ariz.) as its Presidential candidate. Goldwater ran on a strongly
anti-Communist platform. In his acceptance speech, Goldwater
July 16 charged that the Johnson Administration was misleading
the American people about Vietnam. "Make no bones about
this," he said. "Don't try to sweep this under the rug. We are
at war in Vietnam." The Administration, he charged, was "letting our finest men die on battlefields unarked by purpose, un-
marked by pride or the prospect of victory." "Communism and
the governments it now controls are enemies of every man on
earth who is or wants to be free," Goldwater warned.

Events that moved the U.S. toward a decisive action in
Indochina occurred in the first week of August in the Gulf of
Tonkin. The U.S. destroyer *Maddox* was attacked by North Vietnamese PT boats Aug. 2 approximately 30 miles off the shores
of North Vietnam. This took place near North Vietnamese
naval installation that had been shelled by South Vietnamese

vessels within the preceding 3 days. The destroyer *Maddox* fired back at the North Vietnamese and, joined by 4 U.S. aircraft, drove off the PT boats. Pres. Johnson Aug. 3 ordered the continuation of the naval patrol in the Gulf of Tonkin by adding another destroyer under cover of combat air patrol. The U.S. naval and air force was under Presidential order to attack the enemy, in the event of further unprovoked attacks, "with the object of not only driving off the force but of destroying it."

Another attack by North Vietnamese PT boats took place Aug. 4, this time 65 miles off the coast of North Vietnam. It involved 2 U.S. destroyers: the *Maddox* and the *C. Turner Joy*. In the clash 2 of the North Vietnamese boats were sunk. Johnson conferred with the National Security Council and Congressional leaders Aug. 4; shortly before midnight, he made a nationally televised speech annoucing his decision to bomb North Vietnam. Johnson the following day sent a message asking Congress for a resolution similar to the Formosa resolution of 1955.

Defense Secy. Robert McNamara disclosed at his news conference Aug. 5 that 60 sorties had been launched against North Vietnamese PT-boat bases and oil storage dumps. 25 North Vietnamese PT-boats were reported destroyed and 2 U.S. planes lost. The air raids commenced on North Vietnam approximately an hour after Johnson's nationally televised announcement.

Explaining why Johnson had publicly announced the U.S.' retaliatory action against North Vietnam before the first Communist target was actually struck by U.S. planes, McNamara said he had suggested that Johnson deliver his TV address at 11:40 p.m. (the first Communist base had been hit at 1:15 a.m.). His reason: "By that time U.S. naval aircraft had been in the air on their way to the targets approximately one hour"; by means of radar, the North Vietnamese "had then received indications of the attack"; "the time remaining before the aircraft arrived over their targets would not permit the North

Vietnamese to move their boats to sea or to alert their forces"; "it was important that" Americans learn of the attack from their government rather than from Hanoi; "it was desirable that the North Vietnamese government and others be told as soon as possible of the attack."

Other Defense Department sources said Pres. Johnson's speech and a subsequent one by McNamara had been aimed at letting Peking know that it was North Vietnam and not Communist China that the U.S. was attacking.

In U.S. House debate Aug. 7, Rep. Ed Foreman (R., Tex.) asked critically: "What kind of responsibility is this when the President goes on radio and TV and tells them [the Communists] one hour and a half in advance that the air strike is coming?"

Johnson defended the timing of his announcement of the U.S. attack at his news conference in Austin, Tex. Aug. 8. "When the strike got off the carrier," the President said, "they were in their [North Vietnamese] radar, and . . . it was very important that we say to the American people what was happening before Hanoi said it to them and that we say to all peoples what kind of an attack it was without any description."

The U.S. continued its military buildup in the Southeast Asian area as a precautionary move. The first planes of a 2-squadron force arrived in Thailand Aug. 6 and were sent to the northern part of the country within range of Communist-held sectors in Laos and North Vietnam. Other U.S. planes had begun arriving in Saigon Aug. 5 and were later sent to the huge Danang air base, about 50 miles south of the North Vietnamese frontier.

Asst. Defense Secy. Arthur Sylvester announced Aug. 11 that the U.S. had "indications that a number of Chinese Communist MIG-15s and MIG-17s have been introduced into North Vietnam." Sylvester said Chinese movement of their planes into North Vietnam had "been expected for some time because of known preparations such as lengthening of runways of airfields in the Hanoi area." In making the announcement,

Sylvester recalled that McNamara had "suggested last week [during his Aug. 6 press conference] that the Chinese Communists might introduce planes into North Vietnam."

In his message to Congress Aug. 5, Johnson said that the resolution he requested would "give convincing evidence to the aggressive Communist nations . . .that our policy in southeast Asia will be carried forward. . . ."

The U.S. Congress Aug. 7 approved the requested resolution giving Johnson its advance approval for any actions he might have to take in the Southeast Asia crisis. The House vote was 416-0, the Senate vote 88-2. Text of the joint resolution:

To promote the mainternance of international peace and security in southeast Asia.

Whereas naval units of the Communist regime in Vietnam, in violation of the principles of the Charter of the United Nations and of international law, have deliberately and repeatedly attacked United States naval vessels lawfully present in international waters, and have thereby created a serious threat to international peace; and

Whereas these attacks are part of a deliberate and systematic campaign of aggression that the Communist regime in North Vietnam has been waging against its neighbors and the nations joined with them in the collective defense of their freedom; and

Whereas the United States is assisting the peoples of southeast Asia to protect their freedom and has no territorial, military or political ambitions in that area, but desires only that these peoples should be left in peace to work out their own destinies in their own way: Now, therefore, be it

Resolved by the Senate and House of Representatives of the United States of America in Congress assembled, That the Congress approves and supports the determination of the President, as Commander in Chief, to take all necessary measures to repel any armed attack against the forces of the United States and to prevent further aggression.

SEC. 2. The United States regards as vital to its national interest and to world peace the maintenance of international peace and security in southest Asia. Consonant with the Constitution of the United States and the Charter of the United Nations and in accordance with its obligations under the Southeast Asia Collective Defense Treaty, the United States is, therefore, prepared, as the President determines, to take all necessary steps, including the use of armed force, to assist any member or protocol state of the Southeast Asia Collective Defense Treaty requesting assistance in defense of its freedom.

SEC. 3. This resolution shall expire when the President shall determine that the peace and security of the area is reasonably assured by international conditions created by action of the United Nations or otherwise, except that it may be terminated earlier by concurrent resolution of the Congress.

Senate debate on the resolution had lasted 9 hours Aug. 6-7. Sens. Wayne L. Morse (D., Ore.) and Ernest Gruening (D., Alaska), who cast the dissenting votes, contended that the resolution was unconstitutional as "a predated declaration of war power" reserved to Congress. Morse had charged Aug. 5 that the incident leading to the resolution was as much the U.S.' "doing" as North Vietnam's. He said the U.S. had been as much "a *provocateur*" in South Vietnam as North Vietnam had been.

Sen. George D. Aiken (R., Vt.), expressing a view held by many Senators, said Aug. 7: "I am still apprehensive of the outcome of the President's decision, but he felt that the interests of the United States required prompt action. As a citizen I feel I must support our President whether his decision is right or wrong. . . . I support the resolution with misgivings."

State Secy. Dean Rusk, Defense Secy. Robert S. Mc-Namara and Gen. Earle G. Wheeler, chairman of the Joint Chiefs of Staff, had testified Aug. 6 on behalf of the resolution at a combined session of the Senate Foreign Relations and Armed Services Committees and the House Armed Services Committee.

Rusk said that "in the face of the heightened aggression on the Communist side, exemplified by these latest North Vietnamese attacks, it has seemed clearly wise to seek in the most emphatic form a declaration of Congressional support both for the defense of our armed forces against similar attacks and for the carrying forward of whatever steps may become necessary to assist the free nations covered by the Southeast Asia Treaty. We cannot tell what steps may in the future be required to meet Communist aggression in Southeast Asia. The unity and determination of the American people, through their Congress, should be declared in terms so firm that they cannot possibly be mistaken by other nations. The world has learned over 50 years of history that aggression is invited if there is doubt about the response. Let us leave today's aggressors in no doubt whatever."

Rusk said later in his testimony: "The immediate action that was here does seem to be exclusively North Vietnamese, but the Chinese Communists have been giving strong public support to the position of North Vietnam, and they recently made a statement on the 6th of August: 'Aggression by the United States against North Vietnam means aggression against China. The U.S. government must stop its armed provocations against the democratic Republic of Vietnam. Otherwise it must be held responsible for all the grave consequences arising therefrom.' It is our impression that the Chinese would give at least very strong political and public support to the North Vietnamese in this situation. We just frankly do not know whether they will translate that into action of any sort. . . ."

McNamara added: " . . . there are Chinese bases on Hainan Island. Our destroyers were operating in this area as were our aircraft. During the period our destroyers and aircraft were operating on patrol in this area, during the time of the North Vietnamese attack on them, Chinese aircraft were operating out of Hainan Island in this direction. They did not approach our vessels or aircraft, and they did not in any way attack."

In debate, later Aug. 6, Senate majority leader Mike Mansfield (D., Mont.) declared: "He [the President] has weighted the degree of military response to the degree of military provocation. . . . He asks for and he will have, in this endeavor, the support of Congress and the people of the United States. . . . What needs to be done to defend ourselves will be done." Sen. Richard B. Russell (D., Ga.), chairman of the Armed Services Committee, said: "It is not our purpose to escalate the war, but if events require more vigorous response, I believe our nation has the will to use that power. There is much more danger to cut tail and run." Sen. John C. Stennis (D., Miss.) said: "I believe this firm course may be our last and our only chance to avoid what could quickly develop into a fullscale war."

Pres. Johnson signed the resolution Aug. 10. He declared at the signing ceremony: "Thus, today, our course is clearly known in every land. There can be no mistake—no miscalculation

—of where America stands or what this generation of Americans stands for. The unanimity of the Congress reflects the unanimity of the country."

A North Vietnamese government statement Aug. 6 denounced the U.S. raid on North Vietnam as "premeditated warlike acts." Reiterating charges that the U.S. "had fabricated the story of 2 American destroyers being attacked [by North Vietnamese PT-boats] for the 2d time," the Hanoi statement said the U.S. air attack "exposes even more clearly the design to invade North Vietnam and extend the war here as declared many times by the U.S." North Vietnam, in its statement, appealed to the nations that had participated in the 1954 Geneva Conference on Indochina, "the Socialist countries and the peace-loving countries in the world" to "take timely measures to check the United States warmongers' hands so as to defend peace in Indochina and Southeast Asia." A North Vietnamese note to the International Control Commission (ICC) Aug. 8 charged that the U.S.' reprisal raid on North Vietnam was an act of aggression.

Commenting publicly for the first time on the U.S. attack, North Vietnamese Pres. Ho Chi Minh Aug. 8 expressed the "indignation and wrath of our entire people at the United States government's deliberate act of aggression."

A Communist Chinese government statement Aug. 6 charged that the U.S. air strikes against North Vietnam had put the U.S. in the position of having "made the first step in extending the war in Indochina." Declaring that Peking "fully supports the just stand" of North Vietnam, the Chinese statement said "these United States acts of aggression are wholly premeditated." Peking said North Vietnam's Aug. 2 attack on "a United States warship [that] had intruded into Vietnamese territorial waters" was an act of "self-defense." The statement upheld Hanoi's contention that "the so-called 2d Tonkin Gulf incident of Aug. 4 never occurred," that the U.S. report that North Vietnamese PT-boats had attacked U.S. warships a 2d time "was a sheer fabrication" "in order to extend the war in Indochina."

The Chinese Communist Party newspaper *Jenminh Jih Pao* charged editorially Aug. 7 that the U.S. had committed "armed aggression" against North Vietnam to "retrieve its defeat in Indochina, to gain some political capital for the coming Presidential elections and to involve the allies of the United States in war." (The Chinese Communist news agency Hsinhua, reporting on UN Security Council debate on the U.S.-North Vietnam dispute, said Aug. 7 that the Soviet delegate had "refrained from refuting the lie fabricated by the U.S. government about U.S. warships having been attacked" by North Vietnam.)

Organized demonstrations protesting the U.S. attack on North Vietnam were held in Peking Aug. 9. In a speech to a crowd of 100,000 at a sports stadium rally, Liao Cheng-chih, a member of the Communist Party Central Committee, said: "The Chinese people are determined by practical deeds to volunteer aid to the Vietnamese people in their just struggle against United States aggression and in defense of their motherland."

Soviet Premier Khrushchev Aug. 8 denounced the U.S. attack on North Vietnam as "an attempt to restore the use of violence and piratical methods . . . in relations between states." Khrushchev warned "all types of wild men and semi-wild men to live in peace [and] to respect the independence of nations." Khrushchev warned that the USSR would "stand up for . . . other Socialist countries if the imperialists impose war on them." The USSR had assured Hanoi of its support Aug. 7 in a note sent by Foreign Min. Andrei Gromyko to Foreign Min. Tuan Tui. U.S. "intrusion into the airspace" of North Vietnam, Gromyko said, posed "a threat to the security of the peoples of other countries" and "can entail dangerous consequences."

NUCLEAR DEADLOCK (1964-5)

Peking Moves Toward Nuclear Arms

The American military involvement in Vietnam, according to U.S. government officials, was part of larger efforts to contain the growing power of Communist China. But a more serious threat to American national security, insofar as it emanated from Peking, was perceived in an entirely different field; it was the development by Communist China of nuclear weapons.

As early as 1960 informed sources in the U.S. had predicted the imminence of Communist China's emergence as a nuclear power. In a symposium on Communist Chinese science jointly sponsored by the National Science Foundation and the AAAS (Association of American Atomic Scientists), T. C. Tsao of Columbia University Dec. 26, 1960 stated that the world should not be surprised "if the Chinese explode an atomic bomb or launch a rocket soon."

The anticipated moment arrived within 2 months after the adoption by the U.S. Congress of the Gulf of Tonkin resolution giving Congressional support to the prosecution of war in Indochina by the Johnson Administration.

U.S. State Secy. Dean Rusk warned Sept. 29, 1964 that China might be on the verge of detonating its first nuclear device. Rusk's warning was reported to have been based on U.S. intelligence estimates that a Chinese nuclear test might take place within a few days, perhaps in conjunction with the celebration Oct. 1 of the 15th anniversary of the Peking Communist regime. Rusk's statement, issued by State Department spokesman Robert J. McCloskey, said: "For some time it has been known that the Chinese Communists were approaching the point where they might be able to detonate a first nuclear device. Such an explosion might occur in the near future. If it does occur, we shall know about it and will make the information

33

public." "Detonation of a first nuclear device does not mean a stockpile of nuclear weapons and the presence of modern delivery systems," the statement emphasized. The U.S., it added, "has fully anticipated the possibility of Peiping's entry into the nuclear weapons field and has taken it into full account" in U.S. military and nuclear planning.

Washington officials told newsmen that China appeared to have reached an advanced stage in preparations for a nuclear test. They said information on these preparations had come from many sources, among them foreign governments, and from U.S. conventional and technical espionage. Although China has plentiful supplies of uranium, according to unattributed scientific opinion, China would not be able to produce sufficient plutonium to build an effective nuclear weapons stockpile for another 5 to 10 years. Work on uranium enrichment—to increase the concentration of U-235—was said to have started only in about 1963, probably in Lanchow, in a plant built with some Soviet aid. The *N. Y. Times* reported from Paris Oct. 8 that China had informed some friendly Afro-Asian governments that it planned to explode a nuclear device after the end of October. Among the countries reportedly advised of this were Guinea, Mali, Cambodia and Burma. China's reasons for disclosing its atomic plans beforehand were said to be 2-fold: (1) It sought to allay criticism by contending that China's possession of an A-bomb would help restore the balance of power between the West and the Afro-Asian nations; (2) Peking sought to prepare friendly nations for fresh Chinese diplomatic initiatives in Africa and Asia.

Peking Boycotts Disarmament Talks

The anticipated entry of Communist China in the nuclear arms race brought an added urgency to arms control. The U.S., in the absence of normal diplomatic relations with Peking, was not in a position to initiate arms limitations talks directly with the nascent nuclear power. The problem was further complicated by the fact that Peking was not represented in the UN, the organization in which disarmament talks had been held. The U.S. government's wish to involve China in UN-sponsored disarmament talks had been expressed as early as Jan. 1960 in connection with the 10-nation disarmament committee meeting in Geneva. Testifying in a closed session of the Senate Foreign Relations Committee Jan. 21, 1960, U.S. State Secy. Christian Herter had maintained that Peking's participation in an East-West arms accord would be "inevitable." The State Department said in a statement later that day that if "substantial progress is made toward controlled disarmament" in forthcoming 10-nation arms talks in Geneva, "then it would be logical to consider participation in such a disarmament program by other countries, including Red China."

Pres. Eisenhower had reiterated this position at a news conference Mar. 16, 1960. He declared that as international disarmament developed, the world "unquestionably [would] have to take into account the armaments of Red China," although "there has to be a very great deal of progress before we are into the stage of worrying about Red China."

China linked its participation in the UN-sponsored disarmament talks with its representation in the world organization. Accordingly, it consistently refused to take part in the disarmament talks while it remained excluded from the UN. Moreover, it repeatedly declared that it would not be bound by any disarmament accord arrived at without its participation in the negotiations. Thus Foreign Min. Chen Yi, addressing a National People's Congress meeting in Peking, said Jan. 21: "China is ready . . . to commit itself to international obligations to which it agrees. However, any . . . disarmament agreement which is arrived at without [Chinese] . . . participation" "cannot . . . have any binding force on China."

In the same vein, the Standing Committee of the National People's Congress stated Jan. 21, 1960: "China has always favored universal disarmament and will unhesitatingly commit herself to international obligations to which she agrees.

However, it must be pointed out that any international agreement concerning disarmament, without the formal participation of the Chinese People's Republic and the signature of her delegate, cannot, of course, have any binding force on China."

Explaining the Chinese position on disarmament talks to a foreign newsman May 8, 1960, Premier Chou En-lai said: "If China were invited to take part in the big-power disarmament conference while the People's Republic of China [was] not recognized, we of course cannot consider the matter. How can one who is not recognized go to and attend a conference with those who do not recognize him? This is inconceivable."

The 10-nation arms talks in Geneva ended June 27, 1960 with a Communist walk-out. The U.S. and USSR opened bilateral negotiations, reaching an accord on "the statement of agreed principles." Acting jointly, the 2 super-powers introduced a resolution in the UN General Assembly in Dec. 1961 calling for an expanded disarmament conference of 18 nations, including 8 nonaligned ones. Again renewed interest in Communist China's participation was expressed by members of the UN, but this still did not change Peking's announced policy. *Jenmin Jih Pao* stated editorially Apr. 3, 1962: "But, just as the Chinese government has time and again emphatically stated, it will not undertake any obligation regarding any disarmament agreement or other international agreements in the discussion of which no Chinese representative has taken part and which no Chinese representative has signed."

U.S.-USSR Rapprochement Strains Sino-Soviet Relations

Apart from the question of conference participation, Communist China had maintained a common front with the Soviet Union on the general question of disarmament and arms control—that is, until the summer of 1962. As outlined by Liu Chang-sheng, Communist China's delegate to the World Federation of Trade Unions, June 8, 1960, Peking's disarmament policy had been framed as part of its anti-imperialist struggle. Liu explained:

We support the disarmament proposals put forward by the Soviet Union. It is of course inconceivable that imperialism will accept proposals for general and complete disarmament. The purpose of putting forward such proposals is to arouse the people throughout the world to unite and oppose the imperialist scheme for arms drive and war preparations, to unmask the aggressive and bellicose nature of imperialism before the people of the world in order to isolate the imperialistic bloc headed by the U.S. to the greatest extent, so that they will not dare unleash a war lightly. But there are people who believe that such proposals can be realized when imperialism still exists and that the "danger of war can be eliminated" by relying on such proposals. This is an unrealistic illusion. . . . Only when Socialist revolution is victorious throughout the world can there be a world free from war, a world without arms. Such a world is inconceivable while imperialism still exists. . . . To win world peace, the struggle of the world's peoples and diplomatic negotiations carried out by the Socialist countries should go hand in hand. It should not be supposed that since diplomatic negotiations are needed, the struggle of the peoples can thus be dispensed with. On the contrary, diplomatic negotiations must be backed up by the united struggle of the world's peoples. To win people, we should mainly rely on the struggles waged by the peoples of various countries, continuously develop the strength of the liberation movements in colonial and dependent countries, continuously expand the revolutionary forces of the people within the imperialist countries. . . .

The situation changed when the U.S. and USSR, the main protagonists in the arms race, began to move toward a rapprochement based on their common interest in preventing the proliferation of nuclear weapons. It was reported in Aug. 1962 that the 2 super-powers had reached an accord on the non-transfer of nuclear weapons to any non-nuclear power. Communist China, interpreting this accord as indicative of a super-power collusion, reacted with a bitter denunciation. *Jenmin Jin Pao*, in its editorial of Aug. 9, 1962, argued:

We hold, however, that when imperialism is stubbornly hindering and opposing agreement on the suspension of nuclear tests and the prohibition of nuclear weapons and is using such weapons to threaten the people of the world, the Socialist countries, to ensure the security of the Socialist camp and defend world peace, naturally must possess nuclear weapons and, moreover, nuclear weapons of better quality than those of U.S. imperialism.

The Socialist countries love peace; nuclear weapons in their hands and nuclear tests conducted by them are entirely different in nature from nuclear weapons in the hands of the imperialist bloc and nuclear tests conducted by that bloc. The possession of nuclear weapons and the carrying out of nuclear tests by the Socialist countries can only be a telling blow against the imperialist policy of the nuclear arms drive and nuclear blackmail and therefore helps to prevent war; it will help force imperialism to accept some kind of agreement on the discontinuance of nuclear testing and the prohibition of nuclear weapons and so will help the cause of world peace.

Jenmin Jih Pao broadened its criticism of the Soviet policy for a detente with the West. In a year-end statement published Dec. 31, 1962, the official Chinese Communist newspaper mounted a broad-gauged attack on Soviet Premier Khrushchev and his policy of "peaceful coexistence." Ostensibly written to answer criticism from the Italian Communist Party head, Palmiro Togliatti, the *Jenmin Jih Pao* article did not mention Khrushchev by name. However, it was clear from the context —and from the fact that Khrushchev's remarks were quoted and criticized although not attributed to him—that these "others" were Khrushchev. *Points made by the Chinese statement, entitled "The Differences Between Comrade Togliatti and Us":*

Imperialism a 'paper tiger'—"Comrade Togliatti and certain other comrades have strongly opposed the Marxist-Leninist proposition of the Chinese Communist Party that 'imperialism and all reactionaries are paper tigers.' . . . Togliatti said that it 'is wrong to state that imperialism is simply a paper tiger which can be overthrown by a mere push of the shoulder.' Then there are other persons who assert that today imperialism has nuclear teeth, so how can it be called a paper tiger? [Khrushchev's words in his Dec. 12, 1962 speech] . . .

"The possession of nuclear weapons by imperialism has not changed by one iota the nature of imperialism, which is rotten to the core and declining, inwardly weak though outwardly strong. . . . When in his talk with Anna Louise Strong Comrade Mao Tse-tung first put forward the proposition that imperialism and all reactionaries are paper tigers, the imperialists already had nuclear weapons. In this talk Comrade Mao Tse-tung pointed out: 'The atom bomb is a paper tiger which the U.S. reactionaries use to scare people. It looks terrible, but in fact it is not. Of course, the atom bomb is a weapon of mass slaughter, but the outcome of a war is decided by the people, not by one or 2 types of weapons.' . . .

"In the final analysis, neither nuclear teeth nor any other kind of teeth can save imperialism from its fate of inevitable extinction."

Coexistence & imperialism—"Even more absurd is the allegation that 'a world without war' can be achieved through peaceful coexistence. In the present situation, it is possible to prevent imperialism from launching a new world war if all the peace-loving forces of the world unite . . . and fight together.

But it is one thing to prevent a world war and another to eliminate all wars. . . .

"The principle of peaceful coexistence can apply only to relations between countries with different social systems, not to relations between oppressed and oppressor nations, nor to relations between oppressed and oppressing classes. . . .

"But Togliatti and those attacking China extend their idea of 'peaceful coexistence' to cover relations between the colonial and semicolonial people . . . and the imperialists. . . .

"They do not like the sparks of revolution among the oppressed nations and peoples. They say that a tiny spark may lead to a world war. Such a way of speaking is really asking the oppressed nations to 'coexist peacefully' with their colonial rulers . . . rather than to resist or wage struggles for independence, much less to fight wars of national liberation."

Soviet policy toward Cuba—"Those who accuse China of opposing peaceful coexistence also attack the Chinese people for supporting the just stand of the Cuban people in their struggle against U.S. imperialism. . . .

". . . On more than one occasion we have made it clear that we neither called for the establishment of missile bases in Cuba nor obstructed the withdrawal of the so-called 'offensive weapons' from Cuba. We have never considered that it was a Marxist-Leninist attitude to brandish nuclear weapons as a way of settling international disputes. . . . What we did strongly oppose . . . is the sacrifice of another country's sovereignty as a means of reaching a compromise with imperialism. A compromise of this sort can only be regarded as 100% appeasement, a 'Munich' pure and simple."

Need for revolution—"Marxist-Leninists, while favoring struggle for reforms, resolutely oppose reformism."

"Whenever the possibility for peaceful transition appears in a given country, the Communists should strive for its realization. After all, possibility and reality . . . are 2 different things. Hitherto, history has not witnessed a single example of peaceful transition from capitalism to socialism. Communists should not pin all their hopes for the victory of the revolution on peaceful transition. The bourgeoisie will never step down from the stage of history of its own accord."

"Communists must . . . be prepared to repel the assaults of counterrevolution and to overthrow the bourgeoisie by armed force at the critical juncture of the revolution. . . ."

The Soviet Communist Party rejected the Chinese ideological thesis and political attack Jan. 7, 1963. It warned that if China continued its attack on Soviet-bloc policies, it could split the world Communist movement. The Soviet reply to China was made in an article published by the Moscow Communist

Party newspaper *Pravda* and given prominent publicity in other major Soviet newspapers and broadcasts. As the Chinese article had done, *Pravda* began by excoriating secondary Communist leaders rather than its true target (*Pravda* attacked the Albanians) but ended by condemning positions whose more powerful advocates were clearly identifiable.

Experts considered the following Soviet warning the most important part of the statement: "Communists cannot but feel gravely concerned over the thesis launched recently that there is a 'temporary majority' in the international movement which 'persists in its mistakes,' and a 'temporary minority' which 'boldly and resolutely upholds the truth.' . . . To insist on this thesis would in effect mean to lead matters to the fragmentation of the international Communist movement, to undermine the ideology on which it is built. . . . This thesis only serves to substantiate the split of the Communist movement and renunciation of the common positions of the Marxist-Leninist parties."

The statement rejected Chinese contentions that Soviet actions during the Cuban crisis constituted a Communist-bloc "Munich." It denounced the "home-made thesis on the 'paper tiger,' which is an underestimation of the forces of imperialism."

Albania (by implication, China) had rejected the principles of peaceful coexistence, *Pravda* said. "But what, then, is the general line? War? If so, where, then, is the difference between such an approach . . . and the viewpoint of the adventurist circles of imperialism." "Which Marxist-Leninist would agree that the way to the victory of communism lies through a thermonuclear war? The dogmatists . . . do not understand that competition in peaceful conditions is one of the most important battlegrounds between socialism and capitalism. As regards the struggle against imperialism proclaimed by the dogmatists, it boils down to mere high-sounding phrases and foul language."

The Russian-Chinese differences were debated Jan. 15-21, 1963 by Khrushchev and other high-ranking Communists, including representatives of Peking, at a gathering in East Berlin of delegations from 70 national Communist parties. The East Berlin gathering technically was held for the 6th Congress of the East German Socialist Unity (Communist) Party. But the guest delegations transformed the congress into a forum for discussing the Sino-Soviet disagreements. The congress' purpose was confirmed Jan. 15, when East German Communist Party First Secy. Walter Ulbricht convened the meeting with an address in which he attacked China for invading India. Ulbricht's address was followed by major speeches by Khrushchev Jan. 16.

Addressing the congress' participants for $2\frac{1}{2}$ hours Jan. 16, Khrushchev appealed for an end to the ideological debate. Although he defended his views on peaceful coexistence and again warned of the dangers of nuclear war, Khrushchev urged other Communist leaders to agree to an ideological truce and avert a split in the Communist movement. His words were directed at Albania, but in the context, China was his target.

As reported by the USSR's Tass news agency, Khrushchev's speech included the following statements:

● "No doubt that as a result of a world thermonuclear war, . . . the warbreeding capitalists would inevitably perish. But would the Socialist countries . . . benefit by a worldwide thermonuclear catastrophe? . . . [Marxists-Leninists] cannot conceive the creation of a Communist civilization on the ruins of the world cultural centers, upon an earth deserted and poisoned by thermonuclear fallout."

● "I will tell you a secret: Our scientists have worked out a 100-megaton bomb. But according to our scientists' calculations, a 100-megaton bomb must not be used in Europe. Should our probable enemy unleash war, then where should we drop it? Over West Germany or France? But the explosion of such a bomb . . . would affect you [East Germany] and several other countries. Therefore we can use such a weapon only outside the confines of Europe. . . . And a 100-megaton bomb is not the limit." "Comrades, to put it in a nutshell, . . . it is not advisable to be in a hurry for the other world."

• "As it is said, blessed is he who chatters about war and does not understand what he is chattering about. The Albanian leaders chatter much about rocket-nuclear war. . . . Except for chatter they have nothing to their name and . . . do not dispose of any real means. As you see, in these matters we have different positions and different responsibilities."

Wu Hsiu-chuan, Communist Chinese delegate, delivered his speech Jan. 18. Wu's speech was jeered and reviled from the floor of the congress. Delegates shouted, whistled and stamped their feet as Wu assailed Yugoslavia's "revision" of Marxist doctrine in terms that were recognized as directed at the USSR. According to Reuters correspondent Jack Altman, the only Western reporter permitted to attend the congress after Jan. 16, the Chinese spokesman was subjected to public humiliation unprecedented in recent Communist history. Wu was silenced several times by the reaction from the floor. His address was concluded in silence, without applause. Key points of Wu's address:

• "More and more people in the world have come to realize that U.S. imperialism is the center of world reaction, the most ferocious enemy of the people of the world, and the most ferocious enemy of world peace."

• "The Communist Party of China is consistent in safeguarding the unity of the socialist camp. . . . This is why, when the practice of publicly attacking another fraternal party by name —the Albanian Party of Labor—first emerged more than a year ago, . . . the Communist Party of China expressed its resolute opposition. . . ."

• "The modern revisionists represented by the renegades to the working class, the Tito group of Yugoslavia, have surrendered to imperialist pressure, are willingly serving imperialism and are . . . undermining the international unity of the working class. . . ."

The Chinese Communist Party Central Committee assailed Khrushchev and the Soviet leadership publicly June 16 for pursuing policies of "peaceful coexistence" at the expense of the revolutionary aims of the world Communist movement. The new attack came in a 60,000-word letter addressed to the Soviet party's Central Committee June 14 and publicized 2 days later by the Peking press and radio.

The letter warned that over-emphasis on policies of peaceful coexistence had led "certain persons in the international Communist movement" to neglect their duty to advance communism by whatever means were necessary: "peaceful and armed, open and secret, legal and illegal, parliamentary struggle and mass struggle." If this error was perpetuated, Peking warned, the "proletarian party will paralyze the revolutionary will of the proletariat, disarm itself ideologically and sink into a totally passive state of unpreparedness . . . and . . . bury the proletarian revolutionary cause."

The Chinese declared that the peaceful-coexistence theme already had led some Communist leaders to take a "passive or scornful or negative attitude toward the struggles of the oppressed peoples for liberation." "Certain persons," they charged, "now go so far as to deny the great international significance of anti-imperialist, revolutionary struggles of Asian, African and Latin American peoples . . . and to hold down those struggles." The letter declared that coexistence "cannot replace the revolutionary struggles of the people." There was "no historical precedent for a peaceful transition" to socialism, the document warned.

The letter denounced as "erroneous" the view that (1) "the contradiction between the proletariat and the bourgeoisie can be resolved without proletarian revolution in each country," and (2) "the contradiction between oppressed nations and imperialism can be resolved without revolution by the oppressed nations."

The Soviet Communist Party replied July 14 in an open letter from the Central Committee to all party members and organizations in the Soviet Union. The letter was published in the Soviet press together with the text of the original Chinese letter, considered the most violent Marxist critique of Russian policy published in the USSR since the 1920s. The open letter rejected the Chinese message's attacks on Khrushchev's coexistence policies and denounced the Chinese leaders for their apparent willingness to see millions die in a nuclear war if this would advance their own aims. The committee declared: "We are sure that all of our party and the entire Soviet people support us in that we can not share the views of the Chinese leadership on the creation of a '1,000 times higher civilization' on the corpses of hundreds of millions of people."

Delegations representing the central committees of the Soviet and Chinese Communist parties began talks in Moscow July 5 on the 2 parties' differences on Communist policy and ideology. The talks were opened amidst an exchange of propaganda attacks in which the 2 sides accused each other of political and ideological betrayal and of attempts to use the world Communist movement for national ends.

The Chinese delegation, headed by Central Committee Secy. Gen. Teng Hsiao-ping, arrived in Moscow by plane July 5. Met at the airport by CPSU Central Committee Secy. Mikhail A. Suslov, the leader of the Soviet delegation, the Chinese emissaries were driven into Moscow, where the 2 sides opened their conference. The talks were recessed July 20 without having lessened the ideological differences separating the 2 powers.

Following the final session July 20, the Chinese went to the Kremlin, where they were received by Khrushchev (for the first time since the talks were opened) for a farewell dinner in what Moscow radio described as "a friendly atmosphere." After the Kremlin dinner, the Chinese were escorted to the Moscow airport by the Soviet delegation. According to Western newsmen, the 2 delegations remained "frigidly" apart except for a perfunctory handshake and a few words exchanged by Suslov and Teng immediately before the Chinese boarded their plane for home.

A joint communique published in Moscow and Peking July 21 indicated that the 2 sides had failed even to begin negotiations of the differences between them. The communique said only that the delegations had "set forth their views and positions" on "important questions of principles concerning contemporary world developments, the international Communist movement and Soviet-Chinese relations."

A Chinese government statement broadcast Aug. 15 by Peking radio charged that the USSR had offered in 1957 to help China produce nuclear bombs but had withdrawn its offer in 1959 to placate the U.S. The Chinese statement said, in part: "It is no new story that Soviet leaders, in collusion with American imperialism, plot to bind China hand and foot." "On June 20, 1959, when there was no hint of the so-called nuclear test ban treaty, the Soviet government unilaterally scrapped the Oct. 15, 1957 agreement concerning new defense technology [and] refused to supply China with atomic bomb samples and technical materials for the manufacture of atomic bombs, apparently as a gift for . . . [Khrushchev] to take to Eisenhower when visiting the United States in September."

Peking Denounces Test-Ban Treaty

Shortly after the Moscow meeting failed to produce an accord on Sino-Soviet ideological differences, the Soviet Union concluded with Great Britain and the U.S. the treaty banning nuclear tests in the atmosphere, under water and in outer space. Peking denounced the treaty even before it was initialed.

The Chinese Communist Party newspaper *Jenmin Jih Pao* declared July 20 that "such talks [as those in Moscow] amount to saying that there is no alternative to capitulation in the face of imperialist nuclear blackmail." Reiterating Communist China's rejection of Soviet fears of nuclear war, the paper said: "Some people believe that if nuclear war breaks out all mankind will perish"; but Mao Tse-tung had "pointed out that mankind will definitely not be destroyed even if the imperialists insist on a nuclear war with the sacrifice of hundreds of millions of people"; "the future of mankind will nevertheless be a bright one [under communism]."

A Communist Chinese government statement issued July 31, after the treaty had been initialed, called for an immediate summit meeting by all heads of government to "discuss the . . . complete prohibition and thorough destruction of nuclear weapons," the dismantling of all foreign bases and the creation of nuclear-free zones covering most of the world. The Chinese statement denounced the Moscow treaty as a "dirty fraud" perpetrated by the U.S., Britain and USSR to "consolidate their nuclear monopoly and bind the hands of all peace-loving countries subjected to the nuclear treaty." It charged that the Soviet government had made an "about face" in accepting the treaty and had "sold out" the interests of the Soviet bloc.

A Soviet government statement Aug. 3 denounced the July 31 Chinese attack on the treaty and charged that the Chinese were "trying to cover up their refusal to sign a nuclear test-ban treaty." It said: "Trying to discredit . . . the assured success in the struggle for diminishing the war danger, to vilify the peace-loving foreign policy of the Soviet Union, the leaders of China have shown . . . that their policy leads . . . to the further stepping up of the nuclear arms race. . . . This position is tantamount to actual connivance with those who advocate world thermonuclear war."

Jenmin Jih Pao countered in an Aug. 3 editorial that the test-ban treaty was "a U.S.-Soviet alliance against China, pure and simple." It charged that Khrushchev had betrayed the Soviet people by agreeing to the treaty, and it predicted that he would be overthrown.

Chinese Premier Chou En-lai warned Aug. 6, in a message to the 9th World Conference Against Nuclear Weapons, that "the danger of nuclear war, instead of being reduced, has [been] increased" by the pact. The conference, which had opened in Hiroshima, Japan Aug. 5, served as a forum for the competing Soviet and Chinese views. The 14-member Soviet delegation and delegates from India, Czechoslovakia, Hungary, Rumania and Yugoslavia walked out Aug. 5 when Chao Pu-chu, leader of the Chinese delegation, rose to speak. Chao charged that the test-ban treaty "allows the aggressor the right of massacre and denies the victims the right of self-defense."

China Detonates Nuclear Device

A year later, in the fall of 1964, Communist China emerged as the 5th nation to join the ranks of nuclear powers. It detonated its first nuclear device at 3 a.m. EST Oct. 16 at a test site reported to be in the Taklamakan Desert area of the Central Asian province of Sinkiang. The test was announced later the same day in a statement made public by Peking's Hsinhua news agency. Confirmation was provided within a few hours by a statement issued by U.S. Pres. Johnson.

The official Chinese announcement gave no details of the test. It said only that "China exploded an atom bomb at 1500 hours on Oct. 16, 1964, and thereby conducted successfully its first nuclear test." The announcement was devoted principally to Peking's explanation of its reasons for developing a nuclear bomb and to a demand that a world summit conference be convened to outlaw atomic weapons and destroy existing nuclear stockpiles. It repeated China's past contentions that the July 1963 U.S.-British-Soviet treaty curtailing nuclear tests was "a big fraud to fool the people of the world, that it tried to consolidate the nuclear monopoly held by the 3 nuclear powers and tie up the hands and feet of all peace-loving countries" and that it increased, rather than decreased, the danger of nuclear war.

The Chinese statement said:

"China cannot remain idle and do nothing in the face of the ever-increasing threat posed by the United States. China is forced to conduct nuclear tests and develop nuclear weapons." China proceeded from the view that "the atom bomb is a paper tiger." "China is developing nuclear weapons not because we believe in the omnipotence of nuclear weapons. . . . The truth is exactly to the contrary. . . . China's aim is to break the nuclear monopoly of the nuclear powers and to eliminate nuclear weapons."

"The development of nuclear weapons by China is for defense and for protecting the Chinese people from the danger of the United States launching a nuclear war." "The Chinese government hereby solemnly declares that China will never at any time and under any circumstances be the first to use nuclear weapons." "On the question of nuclear weapons, China will commit neither the error of adventurism nor the error of capitulationism. The Chinese people can be trusted."

"The Chinese government hereby formally proposes to the governments of the world that a summit conference of all the countries of the world be convened to discuss the question of the complete prohibition and thorough destruction of nuclear weapons, and that, as a first step, the summit conference should reach an agreement to the effect that nuclear powers and those countries which will soon become nuclear powers undertake not to use nuclear weapons, neither . . . against non-nuclear countries and nuclear-free zones, nor against each other."

China celebrated the nuclear test Oct. 18 with street rallies in Peking and with a special message, distributed nationally, in which its scientists and military and technical personnel were honored for having brought China to "a new stage of modernization of its national defense." The message, which referred to the detonation as a nuclear test rather than as the explosion of an atomic bomb, was signed by Communist Party Chairman Mao Tse-tung, by the party's Central Committee and by China's State Council.

The Chinese government Oct. 20 released the text of a note in which Premier Chou En-lai was said to have called on world leaders to join in a summit meeting to ban nuclear weapons. The text was modelled on China's initial announcement that it had exploded a nuclear bomb and would seek such a conference. The U.S. State Department confirmed Oct. 21 that the note had been transmitted to Pres. Johnson through the U.S.

embassy in Warsaw. It made clear that the Chinese proposal was unacceptable to the U.S.

U.S. Responses to the Chinese Nuclear Test

The U.S. government criticized China for its nuclear test but sought to allay apprehensions in the U.S. aroused by the test.

Pres. Johnson said Oct. 16 that the Chinese test came "as no surprise" to the U.S. government and that "it has been fully taken into account in planning" the U.S.' defense program and nuclear capability. In a prepared statement on the event, Johnson said that the "military significance" of the atomic blast "should not be overestimated." China was still a long way "from having a stockpile of reliable weapons with effective delivery systems," he said. Johnson stressed the U.S.' "readiness to respond to requests from Asian nations for help in dealing with Chinese Communist aggression" should Peking "eventually develop an effective nuclear capability."

Johnson deplored China's "nuclear weapons program" as "a tragedy for the Chinese people, who have suffered so much under the Communist regime." "Scarce economic resources which could have been used to improve the well-being of the Chinese people have been used to produce a crude nuclear device which can only increase the sense of insecurity of the Chinese people," he declared.

Although assailing the Chinese test as contrary "to the cause of peace," Johnson said that "there is no reason to fear that it will lead to immediate war." "Regretting the contamination of the atmosphere caused by the Chinese Communist test," Johnson pledged continued U.S. "efforts to keep the atmosphere clear" and to strive for "concrete, practical steps away from nuclear armaments and war."

In a nationwide TV and radio address Oct. 18, Johnson said: China's atomic test should not be treated "lightly." "Until this week only 4 powers had entered the dangerous world of nuclear explosions. Whatever their differences, all are sober and serious states, with long experience as major powers in the modern world. Communist China has no such experience."

Johnson cited 4 ways in which the U.S. would work to minimize "the danger of nuclear war": "First, we will continue to support the limited test ban treaty. . . . We call on the world —especially Red China—to join the nations which have signed it. 2d, we will continue to work for ending of all nuclear tests of every kind, by solid and verified agreement. 3d, we continue to believe that the struggle against nuclear spread is as much in the Soviet interest as in our own. We will be ready to join with them and all the world—in working to avoid it. And 4th, the nations that do not seek . . . nuclear weapons can be sure that if they need our strong support against some threat of nuclear blackmail, then they will have it."

Communist China, in an editorial Oct. 22 in *Jenmin Jih Pao,* rejected Pres. Johnson's Oct. 18 suggestion that Peking sign the test-ban treaty and help prevent the spread of nuclear weapons. The editorial asserted that Johnson's criticism of the Chinese test "boiled down to this: the United States alone can have nuclear weapons, China should not. . . . This is 100% tyrant's language and gangster logic." The editorial warned that Communist China had "finally gained the means of resisting the United States nuclear threat."

State Secy. Dean Rusk had predicted Oct. 18 that the Chinese would explode another atomic device as soon as it was capable of doing so in order to score propaganda advantage. Rusk said Peking had "upset the effort . . . of every nation . . . to end atmosphere testing." He said that in embarking on a nuclear program of their own the Chinese had "set back the hopes of mankind significantly."

A statement issued Oct. 21 by the U.S. Atomic Energy Commission said that the Chinese had detonated "a fission device employing U-235 [enriched uranium]" rather than the simpler type of device that used plutonium as its explosive material. The AEC said that preliminary analysis of the radioactive debris carried by the cloud of fallout produced by the test confirmed that the Chinese test was of low yield, "roughly equivalent" to the 20-kiloton bomb the U.S. had used against Hiroshima in World War II. It added that "the low yield of the test coupled with other information obtained from the radioactive debris indicates that the technology of the device is that which we would associate with an early nuclear test."

AEC officials conceded later Oct. 21 that the Chinese bomb had been more sophisticated in design than the Hiroshima weapon and had employed an advanced form of implosion trigger to detonate the fission materials. Most of the AEC information came from air samples taken from the bomb-produced fallout cloud as it drifted eastward over Japan Oct. 17, the Aleutians Oct. 18, the northern Pacific Oct. 19 and Canada and the western U.S. Oct. 20.

Rep. Harris McDowell (D., Del.) reported Oct. 21 that he had been informed by State Secy. Rusk that much of the U.S.' information on the Chinese test and test site came from military reconnaissance satellites. He said Rusk had reported that satellite photos had showed clearly the erection of the tower on which the Chinese nuclear device was detonated.

U.S. Defense Secy. Robert S. McNamara stressed at a news conference Oct. 22 that the Chinese had tested only a primitive nuclear device that posed no military threat. He said: It would be "many years" before the Chinese Communists "obtain the capability to inflict nuclear damage on this country or our allies"; the main point illustrated by the test was the "dangers of nuclear spread" as more nations obtained the capability to develop nuclear weapons. McNamara had warned in a Chicago radio interview Oct. 3 that "tens of nations" would be able to develop nuclear weapons in 10 to 20 years. He explained that lower costs of production and delivery systems would permit such a situation. He called the spread of nuclear weapons "one of the most important problems we face."

Test Ban Vs. 5-Power Summit Talks

UN Secy. Gen. U Thant proposed at a news conference Oct. 22, 1964 that the U.S., USSR, Britain, France and Communist China meet in 1965 to discuss the banning of nuclear testing. He suggested that a "dialogue" between the 5 nuclear powers might be "very worthwhile."

"Of course, there are protocol and diplomatic considerations," Thant conceded, "but I feel very strongly that they should be secondary. The primary consideration should be that of nuclear destructibility and radioactivity." He called the Chinese nuclear test "particularly regrettable" in view of (a) the 1963 agreement by the U.S., USSR and Britain to refrain from above-ground nuclear tests and (b) a 1962 UN General Assembly resolution condemning "all tests, including underground tests."

Thant said he saw "some merit" in a proposal by ex-Kansas Gov. Alfred M. Landon, the 1936 U.S. Republican Presidential candidate, that the 5 nuclear powers meet. Landon had made the suggestion in a speech in Columbus, O. Oct. 20. "Since 1948 I have urged the recognition of Red China and its admission to the United Nations," Landon declared. "I have said that discussions of limitation of world armament, a World Court, even the United Nations, were useless without including China, with 1/4 of the world's population."

The Johnson Administration indicated Oct. 23 that it was not interested in either China's suggestion for a world summit conference to ban nuclear weapons or in U Thant's proposal of a 1965 meeting of the 5 nuclear powers. State Department officials called Peking's suggestion a "sucker" proposal that was neither serious nor constructive. If China really wanted to show serious interest in talks, the State Department spokesman said, it could communicate with British, French and Soviet diplomats in Peking or with the U.S. ambassador in Warsaw. The U.S. spokesman conceded that Peking would have to be a party to negotiations and agreements "at some stage . . . if such agreements are to have any real meaning. In this sense, we never have precluded the participation of any country in disarmament negotiations." But State Department officials expressed continued opposition to Communist Chinese membership in the UN or participation in the Geneva disarmament conference. They asserted that such recognition of Communist China would be tantamount to rewarding Peking for a nuclear test, and they complained that some of the nations proposing such a prize were the very ones that had consistently condemned Western nuclear tests. They warned that such rewards would convince Communist China of the efficiency of aggressive deeds and thereby put the world in greater danger of Chinese belligerence.

U.S. Amb.-to-UN Adlai E. Stevenson speculated in Louisville, Ky. Oct. 23 that the U.S. might be more willing to consider 5-power nuclear test ban talks if Communist China signed the 1963 nuclear test ban treaty.

British Foreign Secy. Patrick Gordon Walker said at a UN news conference Oct. 27 that Britain "would consider very favorably" any suggestion advanced by Thant for halting the spread of nuclear weapons. Speaking after a talk with Thant, Gordon Walker asserted that there was "a good deal to be said" for having Communist China join the Geneva disarmament talks.

French Pres. Charles de Gaulle declared in a message to Chou En-lai Oct. 30 that France was prepared to participate "at any moment" in "any serious negotiations" among the 5 nuclear powers. De Gaulle promised to "study with attention" Chou's Oct. 16 proposal for nuclear disarmament talks. De Gaulle's message also said: "France has not ceased during all of the past years to pronounce herself in favor of genuine disarmament, which naturally means that priority should be given to nuclear disarmament. . . . [W]henever the occasion has arisen she has made detailed propositions concerning, first, the elimination of vehicles serving, or liable to serve, in the transportation of nuclear arms. Those propositions have taken into account the existing difficulty in assessing stockpiles of such devices. It is evident that disarmament cannot be conceived and cannot be put into practice if it is not accompanied by efficient control. . . . The French government remained ready to participate fully in any serious negotiations that could be organized among competent and responsible powers to discuss the problems of disarmament on a constructive and practical basis."

Communist Chinese Pres. Liu Shao-chi warned Oct. 30 that the U.S. faced a "serious test" in deciding whether to agree to Peking's proposal of a 5-power conference. Speaking at a Peking dinner in honor of King Mohammed Zahir and Queen Homaira of Afghanistan, Liu said the first step in China's proposal would be for nuclear powers and nations about to become nuclear powers to foreswear the use of atomic weapons. He vowed that Peking would "unswervingly carry through to the end the struggle to oppose United States imperialist policies of aggression and war, smash nuclear blackmail and the nuclear threat of United States imperialism and realize the noble aim of the complete prohibition and thorough destruction of nuclear weapons."

An editorial in *Jenmin Jih Pao* declared Nov. 22 that Communist China would not participate in the 18-nation Geneva disarmament talks. "Now that China has nuclear weapons, the United States wants to drag her into the affairs of the United Nations," the editorial said. It also rejected U Thant's proposal of a 5-power conference on banning nuclear testing.

British Prime Min. Harold Wilson Dec. 23 rejected Peking's Oct. 17 suggestion of a world summit conference to ban nuclear weapons. He called for detailed discussion and negotiation on disarmament first.

Tass reported Jan. 3, 1965 that Soviet Premier Aleksei N. Kosygin had informed Communist China of the USSR's support of its summit conference proposal. Kosygin said that even though the USSR favored a "radical" agreement on nuclear weapons, it also approved of measures to "limit" and "slow down" the nuclear arms race. He suggested that the adoption of a pact denouncing the use of nuclear weapons could precede an agreement on banning and destroying atomic weapons.

Communist China Explodes 2d Nuclear Device

While the diplomatic impasse resulting from the U.S. support of the test ban and Peking's insistence on the summit conference of nuclear powers continued, Communist China, in the spring of 1965, exploded another nuclear device.

The U.S. State Department had warned Feb. 16 that Communist China was readying its 2d nuclear test. The department declared in a statement: "The United States has reason to believe that Communist China is preparing for another nuclear test. The United States government deplores this indication that the leaders of Communist China are, in the face of worldwide condemnation of atmospheric nuclear testing, continuing such tests." A U.S. State Department spokesman May 14 called it "deeply regrettable" that China had tested a 2d nuclear device "in total disregard of the test-ban treaty."

Peking announced May 14 that it had "exploded another atom bomb over its western areas" at 10 a.m. that day and thus had "successfully concluded its 2d nuclear test." The Chinese communique continued: "Following on the explosion of China's first atom bomb . . . . this nuclear test is another important achievement scored by the Chinese people in strengthening their national defense and safeguarding the security of their motherland and world peace. . . . It is a great victory for the party's general line of Socialist construction. It is a great victory for Mao Tse-tung's thinking. . . . China is conducting necessary nuclear tests within defined limits and is developing the nuclear weapon for the purpose of coping with the nuclear blackmail and threats of the United States and for the purpose of abolishing all nuclear weapons. . . . China will never be the first to use nuclear weapons. . . . Together with all the peace-loving countries and people of the world, the Chinese government and people will, as always, continue to strive for the noble aim of the complete prohibition and thorough destruction of nuclear weapons."

The Chinese announcement indicated that the nuclear device had been dropped from a plane. U.S. sources estimated the force of the detonation as equivalent to that produced by the explosion of perhaps a little more than 20 kilotons (20,000 tons) of TNT—a yield generally described as in the low-intermediate range.

The Communist Chinese nuclear buildup continued. The *Wall Street Journal* reported from Washington July 13 that China was building a fleet of long-range submarines capable of launching missiles armed with atomic warheads. The report said that Communist China might be able to mount a sub-marine-launched nuclear attack within 2 to 3 years. China, according to the report, was building Soviet-designed G-class diesel-electric submarines equipped with 3 vertical tubes in the conning tower for missile launching. The Soviet G-class submarine had a range of 44,000 miles.

At the NATO Council meeting in Paris Dec. 15, U.S. Defense Secy. McNamara stressed the growing nuclear capability of China. He made these estimates: By 1967, Peking would have enough fissionable material to begin a small stockpile of atomic weapons. By 1967, it would also have developed a medium-range ballistic missile with an atomic warhead. It would have several launchers for medium-range missiles deployed by 1968 or 1969 and possibly "several dozen" by 1975. And by 1975, China would have deployed intercontinental ballistic missiles armed with atomic warheads and capable of hitting targets in the U.S. and Western Europe. China then (Dec. 1965) had an army of 2,300,000 plus a large trained militia. China spent about 10% of its gross national product (GNP) on defense as compared with about 2% of GNP spent on defense in India, Pakistan and Brazil. Judging by China's current declarations, Peking planned to use military force to support "revolutionary wars." China's next target would be Thailand.

COLLISION COURSE IN VIETNAM (1965)

U.S. Escalates Air War

While the Chinese intransigence in nuclear arms control compounded the problems of national security for the U.S., the deepening involvement by the U.S. in the war in Vietnam posed a direct threat to Communist China. During 1965-6, 2 years after the incumbent Lyndon B. Johnson won the 1964 Presidential election by a landslide, the U.S. intensified its war effort in Vietnam, first in the air and afterwards on land. This profoundly affected not only the course of U.S.-Chinese relations but also the internal situation in each country.

The escalation of U.S. military activities in Vietnam coincided with further demonstrations of the chronic political instability in the Saigon government. Gen. Nguyen Khanh, who had ousted the military junta Jan. 30, 1964, was himself forced to relinquish control of the government in October of the same year. The succeeding civilian regime, headed by Premier Tran Van Huong, stayed in office for less than 3 months before it, too, was overthrown by the Armed Forces Council Jan. 27, 1965. The faction-ridden Vietnamese Armed Forces Council then installed as premier the physician Phan Huy Quat, 56. In the meantime, the Viet Cong (Vietnamese Communist) forces, taking advantage of the political instability, rapidly expanded their control over rural areas of South Vietnam.

In an effort to stabilize the political situation in Saigon and to bolster the South Vietnamese will to resist Communist expansion, the U.S. resorted to the escalation of air attacks against North Vietnam and the Viet Cong in the South.

U.S. planes launched Feb. 7, 1965 heavy air attacks on North Vietnamese territory. Carrier-based planes bombed and strafed the southern military base of Donghoi. South Vietnamese planes, escorted by U.S. jets, carried out a follow-up attack

Feb. 8 against the North Vietnamese military communications center in the Vinhlinh area. Both air strikes were in retaliation for a Viet Cong ground attack earlier Feb. 7 on the U.S.' Camp Holloway airbase at Pleiku, 240 miles northeast of Saigon. 8 Americans were killed and 126 others wounded when a barracks was blown up in the Communist attack. The Viet Cong also destroyed 9 helicopters and a transport plane and damaged at least 9 helicopters and 6 light observation planes.

A White House statement revealing the air attacks Feb. 7 said that North Vietnamese "barracks and staging areas" hit by the U.S. planes had been "actively used by Hanoi for training and infiltration of Viet Cong personnel into South Vietnam." U.S. Presidential aide McGeorge Bundy said Feb. 8 that the air strikes against North Vietnam were "right and necessary" but that "the primary contest is in South Vietnam." Bundy made the statement at a news conference after reporting to Pres. Johnson and the National Security Council on a fact-finding mission he had conducted in South Vietnam Feb. 4-6. Bundy said the air-strike decision was made "after the Pleiku incident."

About 160 U.S. and South Vietnamese land-based and carrier-based planes Feb. 11 carried out the 3d and severest retaliatory air strike in a week against North Vietnamese targets. The 3½-hour attack was in reprisal for a series of Viet Cong terrorist assaults that had followed the 2 earlier air raids on North Vietnam. In one incident, the Viet Cong Feb. 10 blew up a U.S. barracks at Quinhon, killing at least 23 Americans. Pres. Johnson decided on the retaliatory air strike after discussing the Quinhon bombing at a National Security Council meeting later Feb. 10. In the Feb. 11 air strike, the attacking planes hit 2 separate areas—Chan Hoa and Chaple, 160 miles and 40 miles, respectively, north of the 17th Parallel, which divided North and South Vietnam. Barracks and staging areas were heavily bombed by planes from the U.S. aircraft carriers *Ranger, Hancock* and *Coral Sea* and by U.S. and South Vietnamese planes from Danang and Saigon. The Chaple area had been hit by South Vietnamese planes in the Feb. 8 raid. A

U.S. spokesman said Chaple was hit again because there were remaining targets in the center, which comprised 125 building and motor-pool areas. He said half of the base had been destroyed in the first raid. The Chaple installations, the spokesman said, were "adjacent to routes that lead into South Vietnam."

The Feb. 11 raid was announced simultaneously in Washington and Saigon. A statement issued by the White House Feb. 11 said the air strikes were "against military facilities in North Vietnam used by Hanoi for the training and infiltration of Viet Cong personnel into South Vietnam." The air assaults, the statement said, "were in response to further direct provocations by the Hanoi regime" since Feb. 8. The White House then cited: the Quinhon incident; an attack on a Phuoc Long Province district town, "resulting in further Vietnamese and United States casualties"; "a number of mining and other attacks on the railway in South Vietnam as well as assassinations and ambushes involving South Vietnamese civil and military officials."

U.S. Amb. Maxwell Taylor said in a Mutual Broadcasting System radio interview Feb. 13 that the retaliatory air strikes against North Vietnam undercut Viet Cong sanctuary in that country and served to make Hanoi reconsider its role in the war in South Vietnam. Asserting that North Vietnam could halt guerrilla attacks, Taylor said: "Hanoi has been directing the Viet Cong for years, and the Viet Cong have been responding to that direction. There is no reason to believe that Hanoi cannot issue an order and not get obedience from the disciplined Viet Cong." Taylor said the air strikes had "a very good effect" on the South Vietnamese morale. The U.S. objective, the ambassador said, remained "a South Vietnam free to determine its own government and its own future without Communist interference." Taylor said the over-all situation in South Vietnam "remains reasonably favorable in a purely military sense, but the problem of governmental stability is still with us."

In a CBS-TV interview Feb. 14, Taylor said future air attacks on North Vietnam would be determined "by the behavior of the Hanoi government." "Our objective," Taylor said, "is limited—namely . . . to persuade Hanoi to desist in its efforts to maintain the insurgency in this country." Asserting that the advantages of the air strikes against North Vietnam were largely psychological, Taylor warned that they had been "deliberately planned . . . to suggest the possibility of other and bigger forms of reaction."

The U.S. Air Force, joined by South Vietnamese, carried out what was reported as the heaviest air attack yet on North Vietnam Mar. 2. 100 U.S. and 60 South Vietnamese planes took part in the raid.

A denunciation of the Mar. 2 attack on North Vietnam was issued Mar. 3 by 19 Communist parties holding an international conference in Moscow. They charged that the U.S. was guilty of "open aggression" and "barbarous acts."

Soviet Premier Aleksei N. Kosygin had warned the U.S. against its "aggressive actions" in Vietnam. In a TV report Feb. 26 on a recently-completed tour of North Vietnam, North Korea and Communist China, Kosygin said that if the U.S. did not halt its military attacks, the conflict in Vietnam "will inevitably transcend its original boundaries." Such attacks, Kosygin declared, must stop in order to "create conditions for the exploration of avenues leading to the normalization of the situation in Indochina."

The National Liberation Front, the Viet Cong's political arm, had pledged Feb. 12 that its forces would launch an all-out attack on U.S. military installations in South Vietnam in retaliation for the raids on North Vietnam. The front declared in a radio broadcast that the U.S. "must know that any aggression against our heroic Vietnam will be punished appropriately." The broadcast urged the guerrillas to "fight the enemy with all means and weapons: Weaken their forces as much as possible . . . Destroy the strategic hamlets, and force the United States imperialists to pay more blood debts."

Hanoi announced Feb. 14 that it had asked the International Control Commission to withdraw its observers from North Vietnam because it could not guarantee their safety in view of the U.S. and South Vietnamese air strikes. The withdrawal order affected 5 observation posts: at Dondang, an entry point for a main railway and highway from Chinese military bases at Nanking and Canton; at Laokay, a secondary post alongside railroad and highways from China's Mengtzu air bases; at the port of Haiphong, and at Donhoi and Vinh. North Vietnam did not request the removal of the ICC office in Hanoi.

Chinese Reaction

Peking also denounced the U.S. action. A Chinese government statement warned Feb. 13 that North Vietnam had the right to deal "counterblows" to South Vietnam "now that" Pres. Johnson "has twice personally directed the aircraft of the South Vietnamese puppets to bomb" North Vietnam. Peking reiterated its previous assertions that "aggression" against North Vietnam "by the United States means aggression against China, and . . . the Chinese people . . . know how to aid the people of Vietnam in driving out U.S. aggressors."

Accusing the U.S. of having "invaded South Vietnam in violation of the Geneva agreements," the statement said Washington "has now further taken the lead in breaking up the line of demarcation between Southern and Northern Vietnam." Recalling China's military role in the Korean War, Peking said, "you have been taught a lesson on this score. . . . Do you want to have the lesson repeated in Indochina?"

Chinese Foreign Min. Chen Yi declared Feb. 15 that "peaceful coexistence with United States imperialism . . . was out of the question." Repeating Peking's charges that Pres. Johnson had "personally ordered the bombing" of North Vietnam, "expanding the war in Indochina," Chen said it was "imperative to wage tit-for-tat struggle against" U.S. attacks. Chen spoke at a Peking reception, given by Soviet Amb.

Stepan V. Chervonenko, marking the 15th anniversary of the Soviet-Chinese Treaty of Friendship, Alliance & Mutual Assistance.

Chinese Communist Party Chairman Mao Tse-tung was reported Feb. 11 to have told U.S. journalist Edgar Snow that the U.S. and China would not become involved in a war over Vietnam unless China itself were attacked. In an interview with Snow (published Feb. 15 in the West German magazine *Der Stern*), given several weeks before the current crisis erupted, Mao said that since State Secy. Dean Rusk had expressed U.S. unwillingness to attack China, such a conflict was unlikely. Mao predicted that in one or 2 years "the Americans will lose interest" in South Vietnam and the Viet Cong would emerge victorious.

Chinese Premier Chou En-lai declared Feb. 24 that U.S. forces must withdraw from Indochina "completely, immediately and unconditionally" before there could be a peace agreement in the conflict.

Communist China Feb. 28 denounced the U.S. statement on Hanoi as a "pretext" for carrying out fresh attacks on North Vietnam. Peking charged in a Hsinhua broadcast that the U.S. had long been "busy inventing excuses and preparing for new aggression" against North Vietnam.

U Thant Proposes Peace Settlement

UN Secy. Gen. U Thant proposed a Vietnam peace plan Feb. 24, 1965. At a news conference, Thant said he had presented his plan for a settlement to "some of the principal parties directly involved in the question of Vietnam." His plan called for a settlement by preliminary negotiations followed by a full-scale peace conference among the parties directly involved.

It was reported from UN headquarters in New York Feb. 25 that North Vietnam had informed Thant that it was sympathetic to the proposals he had outlined Feb. 24. Hanoi was said to have told Thant of its position before he made his plan public. Thant's proposals were formally submitted to the U.S., France, Britain and the Soviet Union but apparently not to Communist China.

The U.S. was cool to Thant's suggestion. George Reedy, Pres. Johnson's press secretary, said Feb. 25 that Thant's proposals had not been brought to the President's attention. State Secy. Dean Rusk said at a Washington news conference Feb. 25 that the U.S. would not enter negotiations to end the Vietnam War until North Vietnam gave some "indication" that it was "prepared to stop what it is doing and what it knows it is doing against its neighbors." Rusk insisted that this was the basic condition, "the missing link" necessary before talks could be held. Rusk ruled out U.S. participation in "a negotiation aimed at the acceptance or confirmation of aggression." Such negotiation, he said, "simply ends in bitterness and hostility" and "merely adds to the danger." In reference to domestic and international appeals for negotiations, Rusk pointed out the availability of channels of communication with Communist governments. He cited talks held in Warsaw Feb. 24 by U.S. Amb.-to-Poland John Moors Cabot and Communist Chinese Amb. Wang Kuo-chuan. The discussions centered on Vietnam and were one of a periodic series of conferences held by the 2 ambassadors.

Ex-Vice Pres. Richard M. Nixon proposed Feb. 25 that "we use our naval and air power," "short of atomic weapons," "to cut off all supplies from North Vietnam to South Vietnam." Nixon said Pres. Johnson should reject suggestions that the U.S. participate in peace talks that required American troop withdrawal from South Vietnam. The U.S. should "avoid being forced into negotiations when at the bottom of a totem pole," he said.

The U.S. State Department Mar. 9 formally rejected U Thant's proposals. Pres. Johnson said at press conference Mar. 13: "We have not had any indication from anyone that Hanoi is prepared or willing or ready to drop what it is doing to its neighbors."

Meanwhile, the U.S. State Department Feb. 27 issued a white paper saying "North Vietnam is carrying out a carefully conceived plan of aggression against" South Vietnam. The 14,000-word document was entitled "Aggression from the North —the Record of North Vietnam's Campaign to Conquer South Vietnam." It charged that Hanoi's military assistance to the Viet Cong was in violation of the UN Charter and the 1954 Geneva conference agreements on Indochina and was "a fundamental threat to the freedom and security of South Vietnam." The report cited testimony of North Vietnamese soldiers who either had defected or had been captured after being sent South by Hanoi. Among major accusations made in the white paper:

• "The hard core of the Communist forces attacking South Vietnam were trained in the North. . . . They are ordered into the South [by Hanoi] and remain under the military discipline of the military command in Hanoi. Special training camps operated by the North Vietnamese army give political and military training to the infiltrators."
• "Since 1959 nearly 20,000 Viet Cong officers, soldiers and technicians are known to have entered South Vietnam" through Hanoi's "infiltration pipeline" "under orders from Hanoi." These infiltrators were "well-trained officers, cadres and specialists." Viet Cong forces had increased from less than 20,000 in 1961 to 35,000.
• The Vietnam War was "a totally new brand of aggression." It was "not a spontaneous and local rebellion against the established government" in Saigon. The conflict represented efforts by "a Communist government" to "deliberately . . . conquer a sovereign people in a neighboring state."

In conclusion the white paper said: "If peace can be restored in South Vietnam, the United States will be ready at once to reduce its military involvement. But it will not abandon friends who want to remain free. It will do what must be done to help them. The choice now between peace and continued and increasingly destructive conflict is one for the authorities in Hanoi to make.''

U.S. Offers to Negotiate

The determination on the part of the U.S., Communist China and North Vietnam to persit in conflict increased the danger of further escalation of war. Communist Chinese Premier Chou En-lai, in an interview with a correspondent of the Manila *Times,* said Mar. 20 that Peking was "against world war and would never provoke it.'' China had "shown restraint'' in Vietnam, but "our restraint has limits,'' he declared. Peking's Foreign Min. Chen Yi, in an interview with an Italian journalist Mar. 21, indicated that Communist China would send troops to North Vietnam *if* U.S. troops invaded North Vietnam and *if* North Vietnam requested Chinese intervention.

Chen said: "The United States began its aggression in 1954. Since then we have prepared to participate some day in this war, when the course of events would oblige us. . . . We have no right to take the initiative. We cannot decide to send our troops today. It would be possible for us, but we do not want to send our troops into Southeast Asia beyond our frontiers, to give the imperialists the pretext to shout that the Communist threat is knocking at the door. It is only in case of legitimate defense that we use our forces and fight. But if the countries which are our friends ask for our help, we will not fail to do it.''

The National Liberation Front, the political arm of the Viet Cong, appealed Mar. 24 for assistance from "friends in the 5 continents'' for "weapons and other war materials.'' The appeal, broadcast over Hanoi radio, warned: "If the United State imperialists continue to commit United States combat troops and those of their satellites to South Vietnam and continue to extend the war to North Vietnam and Laos, the South Vietnam National Liberation Front will call on the people of various

countries to send youth and army men to South Vietnam to side
with the South Vietnamese people in annihilating the common
enemy." Responding to this appeal, *Jenmin Jih Pao* said Mar.
25 that China was ready to send men "whenever the South
Vietnamese people want them." The paper added: "All negotiations with the United States imperialists at this moment are
utterly useless if they still refuse to withdraw from South
Vietnam."

On its part, the U.S. was equally firm in its determination
to sustain the non-Communist regime in South Vietnam. Pres.
Johnson, at his press conference Mar. 20, quoting the statement
he had made Mar. 17, 1964, said: "For 10 years, under 3 Presidents, this nation has been determined to help a brave people
to resist aggression and terror. It is and will remain the policy
of the United States to furnish assistance to support South
Vietnam for as long as it is required to bring Communist aggression and terrorism under control." He underscored the con-
tinuity of the American policy by referring to the press report
saying that he had made the policy statement 47 times. "Well,
I want to repeat it again this morning for your information and
for emphasis."

Johnson reiterated his position Mar. 25 in a White House
press release, explaining what the U.S. would consider an honorable peace. The settlement should ensure "the return to the
essentials of the agreements of 1954" (the Geneva accords), "a
reliable arrangement to guarantee the independence and security
of all in Southeast Asia." Johnson said: "The United States
will never be 2d in seeking a settlement in Vietnam that is based
on an end to Communist aggression. . . . I am ready to go
anywhere at any time and meet with anyone whenever there is
promise of progress toward an honorable peace."

In the face of the intransigence on both sides, 17 non-
aligned nations (Afghanistan, Algeria, Cyprus, Ceylon, Ethiopia,
Ghana, Guinea, India, Iraq, Kenya, Nepal, Syria, Tunisia,
Uganda, United Arab Republic, Yugoslavia and Zambia)
joined in an appeal to "the parties concerned" to start

negotiations "without posing any preconditions" for a political settlement. The appeal signed by the heads of state and governments of these countries Mar. 15, 1965, was delivered to State Secy. Rusk Apr. 1. A copy of the statement was also delivered the same day to UN Secy. Gen. U Thant and the governments of Canada, Communist China, France, Poland, the USSR, the United Kingdom, North and South Vietnam.

Preceding the formal U.S. reply to the 17 nations, Pres. Johnson stated the U.S. position in a speech at Johns Hopkins University the night of Apr. 7. The main points of the speech were:

• American troops were in South Vietnam to help the country maintain its independence. It was North Vietnam that started the war of "unparalled brutality." ("Simple farmers are the targets of assassination and kidnapping. Women and children are strangled in the night because their men are loyal to their government.")

• The rulers of Hanoi are being "urged on" by Communist China, "a nation which is helping the forces of violence in almost every continent. The contest in Vietnam is part of a wider pattern of aggressive purposes."

• The U.S. had promised to defend South Vietnam and intended to keep that promise. To abandon the small nation to its enemies and terror would be "an unforgiveable wrong." By upholding the commitment, the U.S. sought to strengthen "world order" and to deny the aggressor a new aggression. The U.S. would not be defeated, grow tired or withdraw.

• The U.S. objective was the independence of South Vietnam ("an independent South Vietnam—securely guaranteed and able to shape its relationships to all others—free from outside interference—tied to no alliance—a military base for no other country"). The United States was ready for "unconditional discussions" with the governments concerned, in large or small groups.

• Until peace was attained, the U.S. would use its power "with restraint and with all the wisdom that we can command."

• The U.S. proposed an international undertaking for Mekong River development, comparable to the TVA, which would bring to the peoples of Indochina, including the North Vietnamese, "an end to bondage of material misery." The U.S. proposed that all industrialized nations, including the Soviet Union, join the effort. Johnson would ask Congress to join in "a billion-dollar American investment" for this purpose.

Johnson's speech left Communist capitals completely unmoved. The Peking radio characterized it as "full of lies and deception," expressing a "dream to strike a political bargain with a billion dollars." *Pravda,* the Soviet Communist Party organ, commented Apr. 10 that the speech was a "noisy propaganda." *Nhan Dan,* the North Vietnamese Communist Party paper, dismissed Johnson's offer of economic aid, saying that it had the "smells of poison gas."

The White House Apr. 8 released the text of Johnson's reply to the 17 non-aligned nations. Describing their plea as "a constructive contribution to the effort of peace," Johnson said the U.S. fully supported the document's view that all people were entitled to the right to self-determination and "that recourse to force is contrary to the rights of the people of Vietnam to peace, freedom and independence." The President, however, reiterated the U.S. view that "the basic cause of the conflict in Vietnam is the attack by North Vietnam on . . . South Vietnam. The object of that attack is total conquest."

Johnson held that the "essentials" of any final settlement was "an independent South Vietnam—securely guaranteed and able to shape its own relationships to all others—free from outside interference—tied to no alliance—a military base for no country." He suggested several ways in which a peaceful settlement could be reached: "in discussion or negotiation with the governments concerned, in large groups or in small ones, in the reaffirmation of old agreements or their strengthening with new ones."

"We believe," the President said, "that peace can be achieved in Southeast Asia the moment that aggression from North Vietnam is eliminated." Citing the "campaign of terror and military action" against South Vietnam, "externally supported and directed," Johnson said that "when these things stop and the obstacles to security and stability are removed, the need for American supporting military action will also come to an end." Conceding the difficulties in securing an agreement once it had been achieved, the President said "new ways and means of assurance that aggression has in fact been stopped" would have to be devised.

Johnson reiterated Apr. 10 that the U.S. was determined to stand by its commitment to defend South Vietnam. He warned that "no men in any land at any time" should "misjudge our course by our cause." Speaking at the dedication of a new Job Corps center at the former Gary Air Force Training Base at San Marcos, Tex., Johnson asserted: "We love peace and we hate war, but our course is charted always by the compass of honor."

Meanwhile, the dangers of direct U.S.-Chinese military clashes grew with repeated incidents involving U.S. military aircraft shot down by Communist China. Peking had reported Apr. 2, 1965 that its forces Mar. 31 had shot down the 3d U.S. pilotless reconnaissance plane to fly over China. The Peking report said that one of the 3 drones that had been brought down "by the air force" over south-central China Jan. 2 had been put on display in a Peking museum. The Chinese asserted that the shooting down of the 3 aircraft was "a serious warning to United States marauders who are now extending the flames of their aggressive war in Indochina and conducting constant military provocations against China."

Communist China asserted Apr. 9 that its MiG fighter planes had clashed that day with U.S. jets over the Chinese island of Hainan. U.S. authorities acknowledged an American aerial engagement with MiGs over the South China Sea but said they did not know whether the planes were North Vietnamese or Chinese. The U.S. aircraft were patrolling the area to prevent possible MiG interference with a scheduled U.S. bombing raid on 3 North Vietnamese bridges. According to Peking's version of the incident, Chinese MiGs had intercepted 2 flights of 8 U.S. jets engaged in "provocative activities" over Hainan. The Chinese said that before fleeing, some of the U.S. planes "fired 2 guided missiles at random," striking one of their own jets and causing it to crash. *Jenmin Jih Pao* charged Apr. 12 that the U.S. planes had violated Hainan air space and "blatantly attacked Chinese planes." The U.S. mission in Saigon said Apr. 9 that 4 U.S. carrier-based F-4 Phantom jets had clashed with MiGs off Hainan and that one of the Communist planes was hit and set on fire. Insisting that the planes had not invaded Hainan air space, a U.S. Defense Department spokesman said the jets were at least 35 miles from the island. U.S. military officials in Saigon admitted Apr. 12 that one F-54 Phantom and its 2 pilots had been lost in the Hainan clash.

In Vietnam, the U.S. stepped up its air attacks on suspected enemy positions in the South and North, apparently in an effort to force the North Vietnamese to negotiate. The air raids intensified domestic opposition in the U.S. to the American involvement in Vietnam. (An estimated 15,000 people marched in Washington Apr. 17 in protest). The critics of the American policy called for the suspension of the bombing as a preferred method of inducing the North Vietnamese to negotiate. State Secy. Rusk, in a statement issued Apr. 17, rejected the call by saying that the suspension "would only encourage the aggressor and dishearten our friends." A stronger rejection was voiced by Pres. Johnson the same day at the L.B.J. ranch, Johnson City, Texas: "The infiltrations continue. The terror continues. Death in the night continues. And we must also continue. . . . To those governments who doubt our willingness to talk, the answer is simple—agree to discussion, come to the meeting room. We will be there."

Senate Foreign Relations Committee Chairman J. W. Fulbright (D., Ark.) said Apr. 18 that if a truce in Vietnam could not be achieved, "then I believe there might be some value in stopping the bombings temporarily." The raids were "inclined to keep the atmosphere very tense," encourage the North Vietnamese to "dig in" and discourage Soviet participation in peace talks, Fulbright said.

Canadian Prime Min. Lester B. Pearson had suggested Apr. 2 a "pause" in U.S. air strikes on North Vietnam. In an address in Philadelphia, where he accepted Temple University's 2d annual World Peace Award, Pearson said that if the raids were halted it "might provide the Hanoi authorities with an opportunity . . . to inject some flexibility into [their] policy without appearing to do so as the direct result of military pressure," and thus "the stalemate might be broken." Pearson discussed his proposal with Pres. Johnson at Camp David, Md. Apr. 3. In a report to the Canadian House of Commons, Pearson said Apr. 6 that Johnson had been "very interested" in his suggestions for a pause in the air strikes.

Johnson Apr. 27 reiterated his offer of "unconditional discussions" "with any government concerned." He said: "This offer may be rejected, as it has been in the past, but it will remain open, waiting for the day when it becomes clear to all that armed attack will not" lead to "domination over others." Reviewing the period after the Aug. 1964 incident in which U.S. planes first bombed North Vietnam in retaliation for an attack on U.S. warships in the Gulf of Tonkin, the President said: "For the next 6 months we took no action against North Vietnam. We warned of danger. . . . Their answer was attack and explosion and indiscriminate murder. So, it soon became clear that our restraint was viewed as weakness. . . . We could no longer stand by while attack mounted and while the bases of the attackers were immune from reply. And, therefore, we began to strike back."

U.S. Uses Force to Induce Hanoi to Negotiate

The air strikes against North Vietnam were continued intermittently but with mounting intensity during the last week of April and the beginning of May. In one of these assaults, more than 200 U.S. and South Vietnamese planes roamed the skies of North Vietnam Apr. 24, destroying bridges and ferries in a coordinated effort to wreck Communist supply routes to the south.

Additional American military and economic aid to intensify the war against the Viet Cong was agreed on Apr. 2 in Washington at a meeting of the National Security Council presided over by Pres. Jonnson and attended by Amb.-to-Vietnam Maxwell D. Taylor. Among the decisions taken: (1) Several thousand more U.S. troops would be sent to Vietnam. (2) U.S. planes would continue attacks on North Vietnam, probably increasing their intensity and extending the raids further north. (3) The U.S. would help increase South Vietnam's 557,000-man armed force by 160,000 men. (4) The Saigon government would get additional U.S. economic aid. After the NSC meeting, Taylor said at a news conference that the chances of Chinese Communist intervention in the Vietnam fighting were "very slight at the present time."

The new series of measures to intensify the U.S. war effort in Vietnam were elaborated at a high-level military-civilian strategy meeting held in Honolulu Apr. 19-20. Defense Secy. Robert S. McNamara, who attended the talks, returned to Washington Apr. 21 and reported to Johnson. The secretary said at a news conference later that U.S. military aid to South Vietnam would be increased from $207 million to $330 million a year. He said U.S. air and logistical support for the Vietnamese forces also would be raised. More helicopter and air support would be provided to help the South Vietnamese troops counter greater infiltration from North Vietnam, McNamara said.

Johnson asked Congress May 4 to appropriate an additional $700 million for fiscal 1965 "to meet mounting military requirements in Vietnam." Congress began affirmative action on the request immediately as an indication of its support of Administration policy in Vietnam. The President could have obtained the money by transferral of Defense Department funds, but, as he said in his special message to the Congress, "this is not a routine appropriation." Those supporting his request, he said, were "also voting to persist in our effort to halt Communist aggression in South Vietnam. Each is saying that the Congress and the President stand united before the world in joint determination that the independence of South Vietnam shall be preserved and Communist attack will not succeed."

(Congressional action on the President's request began immediately May 4: the House Armed Services Committee voted unanimously to give full jurisdiction over it to the Appropriations Committee, where it was approved by a subcommittee that day. The next day the request was unanimously approved by the Appropriations Committees of both the House and the Senate, and the House passed it later May 5 by 408-7 vote.)

The May 4 message reviewed the history of the U.S. involvement in Vietnam and reaffirmed the U.S. commitment there. In reference to U.S. air raids of North Vietnam, Johnson said: "Let us also remember when we began the bombings there was little talk of negotiations" but that "our firmness may well have already brought us closer to peace." "Wherever we have stood firm, aggression has been halted, peace restored and liberty maintained. This was true in Iran," Greece, Turkey, Korea, the Formosa Straits, Lebanon and in the Cuban missile crisis. It "will be true again in Southeast Asia." His request was "for prompt support of our basic course: resistance to aggression, moderation in the use of power, and a constant search for peace."

In his review of the Vietnam situation, the President said: The Communist aim in Vietnam "is not simply the conquest of the South, tragic as that would be," but "to show that the American commitment is worthless." "Thus, we cannot, and will not withdraw or be defeated. The stakes are too high, the commitment too deep, the lessons of history too plain."

Johnson reasserted the U.S. desire for peace and negotiations. He would not heed "those who urge us to use our great power in a reckless or casual manner," he said. "We have no desire to expand the conflict. We will do what must be done. And we will do only what must be done. For, in the long run, there can be no military solution to the problems of Vietnam. We must find the path to peaceful settlement. . . . We are still ready to talk, without conditions, to any government. We will go anywhere, discuss any subject, listen to any point of view in the interests of a peaceful solution."

The President expressed regret for "the necessity of bombing North Vietnam." He said: "We have no desire to destroy human life." "Our attacks have all been aimed at strictly military targets—not hotels and movie theaters and embassy buildings. . . . Who among us can feel confident that we should allow our soldiers to be killed, while the aggressor sits smiling and secure in his sanctuary, protected by a border which he has violated a thousand times? . . . However, the bombing is not an end in itself. Its purpose is to bring us closer to the day of peace. And wherever it will serve the interests of peace to do so, we will end it."

Summing up, Johnson said: "Our conclusions are plain. We will not surrender. We do not wish to enlarge the conflict. We desire peaceful settlement and talks. And the aggression continues. Therefore I see no choice but to continue the course we are on, filled as it is with peril and uncertainty."

The U.S. air attacks on North Vietnam were suspended temporarily May 13. Johnson declared May 13 that Communist China "apparently" wanted to continue the war despite the fact that "it would clearly be in the interest of North Vietnam to now come to the conference table." For North Vietnam, he said, "continuation of war without talks means only damage without conquest." However, he said, Communist China's target, "whatever the cost to their allies," was "not merely South Vietnam" nor "fulfillment of Vietnamese nationalism" but the domination of "all of Asia." "In this domination they shall never succeed," Johnson asserted. These remarks were made in a nationally televised address before the Association of American Editorial Cartoonists. The President said that "there is no purely military solution in sight for either side" and that the U.S. was "ready for unconditional discussions."

A report from Washington said that the U.S., through the International Control Commission's Canadian delegate, had informed the North Vietnamese government that the U.S. had suspended the bombings for an indefinite period. The North Vietnamese were said to have displayed no interest in peace talks. State Department press chief Robert J. McCloskey said May 18 that the Administration was "disappointed at the fact that there was no reaction" by Hanoi to the suspension of the bombings. He said "we must assume that the other side was aware that the strikes had not been carried out for a number of days, and we have seen no reaction to that fact."

The North Vietnamese Foreign Ministry charged May 18 that the air strike halt was "an effort to camouflage American intensification of the war and deceive world opinion." The Chinese Communist news agency Hsinhua contended May 18 that the U.S. had not halted its air attacks at all. Hsinhua claimed that during the weekend "many waves of reconnaissance and fighter aircraft" from Thailand bases had attacked North Vietnam.

The air raids were resumed May 18.

China Opposes Unconditional Negotiations

Johnson's peace strategy combined the carrot and stick. His Johns Hopkins speech offered the prospect of a Southeast Asia on the road to prosperity through American economic aid; on the other hand, the intensified air raids were intended to bring home to the North Vietnamese—and the Chinese—the consequences of defying U.S. power. In its outline, at least, the Johnson strategy was clear. To most Americans it seemed reasonable, as shown by the ease with which it commanded support from the U.S. Congress.

But from the Chinese—and North Vietnamese—the Johnson strategy failed to elicit the kind of response that had been sought. The Communist Chinese were particularly vociferous in denouncing the U.S. policy. *Jenmin Jih Pao,* in its editorial of Apr. 22, 1965, called Johnson's Apr. 17 statement a "war blackmail" and characterized his offers to negotiate as a "smokescreen" to conceal new military adventures. "It is clear," the editorial said, "in resorting to such tactics, U.S. imperialism wants to subdue the Vietnamese people by force and make them surrender to their bombing. . . . It wants them to accept the kind of 'peace' that would permit U.S. occupation of South Vietnam and reduce the South Vietnamese people to permanent slavery."

The *Jenmin Jih Pao* editorial further charged: "We have pointed out long ago that every time the Johnson Administration spreads the smokescreen of "seeking peace" it goes a step further along the path of war escalation. Now, people have seen more clearly that since Johnson put forward his proposal for 'unconditional discussion' on Apr. 7, the United States has quickened the tempo of escalation."

Similarly, *Jenmin Jih Pao* rejected the appeal by the 17 non-aligned nations, which appeal the paper credited to "the Tito clique of Yugoslavia." In its editorial of Apr. 22, *Jenmin Jih Pao* criticized the appeal by the non-aligned nations, because (1) the appeal failed to single out "the U.S. imperialist intervention and aggression" as "the source of tension in Vietnam," and (2) it called for negotiations "without any precondition." The latter "amounts to legalizing the U.S. imperialist aggression and compelling the Vietnamese people to recognize that U.S. imperialism has a right to scrap the Geneva agreements at will, to enslave and slaughter the South Vietnamese people and to expand the war to North Vietnam.

The *Jenmin Jih Pao* editorial referred to the official position of North Vietnam as stated by Pres. Ho Chi Minh to a correspondent of the Japanese Communist Party organ, *Akahata (Red Flag):* "To settle the south Vietnam question, the United States must, first of all, withdraw from south Vietnam, let the south Vietnamese people decide for themselves their own affairs, and stop its provocative attacks against the Democratic

Republic of [North] Vietnam. The carrying out of these basic points will bring about favorable conditions for a conference along the pattern of the 1954 Geneva Conference."

Johnson Apr. 24 issued an executive order designating Vietnam and the waters adjacent to it a "combat zone." The "combat zone," according to Peking's reading, included part of China's territorial waters in the vicinity of Hsisha Island. *Jenmin Jih Pao* May 2 charged that the U.S. action constituted "an act of piracy in flagrant violation of international law." The "combat zone," which was seen by Peking as a threat to Chinese sovereignty, according to the White House press release of Apr. 22, was meant to give the U.S. servicemen in Vietnam and the adjacent waters the same income tax relief as was extended to the members of the armed forces who had served in Korea during the Korean War.

U.S. Military Build-Up Continues

In the summer of 1965, with the Vietnamese situation continuously deteriorating, the U.S. took steps to escalate military operations in Vietnam. Gen. William C. Westmoreland, commander of U.S. forces in South Vietnam, was authorized to commit U.S. ground troops to direct combat against Viet Cong guerrillas if requested by the Saigon government, according to a State Department announcement of June 8. A month later, Pres. Johnson said at his press conference July 9 that the Administration was contemplating a limited mobilization of military manpower. The Defense Department revealed Aug. 3 that it had increased the monthly draft quotas to 27,400 men in September (up 10,400 over August's) and to 33,600 men in October. It also announced that for the first time since 1956 the Navy would get draftees—4,600 men.

Johnson announced at his news conference July 28 that he had ordered several military units dispatched to Vietnam, among them the Airmobile (First Cavalry) Division. This action "almost immediately" would raise U.S. military manpower in that country by 50,000. He coupled his announcement with a reaffirmation of the U.S.' readiness to negotiate an end the Vietnam conflict. He said that several attempts had been made to win agreement to negotiations but that all had been rejected by Communist China and North Vietnam. The U.S.' aim, he declared, was not to expand the struggle but to frustrate Communist aggression and force the instigators of the war to the negotiating table. The U.S., he said, would persist until "death and desolation" had brought the same peaceful solution that currently could be had at much lower cost. He appealed for the intercession of the UN and any of its 114 member states to bring about peace talks and announced that the U.S. had begun a major initiative to stimulate UN action in this direction.

Johnson's announcement evoked violent denunciations from Peking. A Chinese government statement referred to it Aug. 7 as "a wholesale exposure of the counterrevolutionary dual tactics used by the U.S. imperialists." In the same vein, a *Jenmin Jih Pao* editorial Aug. 7 disputed Johnson's plea to the UN: "The United Nations, the international organization under American control, has dared not utter a word against the U.S. crimes of aggression; only in time of Washington's need has it adopted resolution after resolution which serve the interests of the U.S. aggressors. The United Nations has written pages of its own ugly history. Washington's attempt to extricate itself from its Vietnam predicament by getting the United Nations to meddle in the Vietnam question can never be realized."

U.S. Army soldiers participated in their first major attack of the Vietnam War June 28 by joining South Vietnamese and Australian troops in what turned out to be a futile assault against the Viet Cong's Zone D area 20 miles northeast of Saigon. The zone was long regarded as the guerrillas' major stronghold in South Vietnam. In the Zone D operation, about 3,000 U.S. 173d Airborne Division troops teamed up with Vietnamese airborne units and an Australian battalion in a probing attack in a jungle area 18 miles wide and 36 miles long. The operation was called off June 30 after the attackers failed to make substantial contact with the enemy. During the 3-day operation, one American was killed and 9 other Americans wounded. A U.S. military statement said June 29 that Westmoreland had ordered the U.S. troops from their defensive positions at the nearby Bienhoa air base into Zone D "under the authority previously granted him" and "at the request of the government of Vietnam."

The expansion of U.S. military action in Vietnam was heightened June 17 when, for the first time, an attack was mounted by B-52 heavy jet bombers from the U.S. Strategic Air Command in Guam, 4,300 miles away. 27 of the planes bombed a suspected Viet Cong concentration north of the Binhduong Province town of Bencat, 30 miles north of Saigon. The B-52s carried out intermittent raids against Viet Cong targets through July and August. Starting in September and through the remainder of 1965, the heavy jet bombers carried out the strike missions at the rate of about one a day. Through the remainder of the summer and the fall of 1965, the ground fighting intensified— with increasing numbers of U.S. troops participating in combat.

Defense Secy. Robert S. McNamara announced Nov. 11 that the U.S. Administration "believe[d] it will be necessary to add further to the strength of United States combat forces in Vietnam." McNamara announced the decision after discussing the matter earlier in the day with Johnson, State Secy. Rusk and other Administration officials at the President's Texas ranch. McNamara said that in the previous 4 weeks he had received requests from U.S. commanders in Vietnam for more men. McNamara said U.S. forces in Vietnam then totaled 160,000 men. McNamara said U.S. and South Vietnamese forces had defeated the Viet Cong's monsoon offensive, which, he claimed, was intended to cut South Vietnam in half at its narrow waist and to destroy the South Vietnamese force. The Viet Cong, McNamara said, thus far in 1965 had suffered 100% higher losses than for a comparable period in 1964. But despite the rising casualties, McNamara disclosed, Viet Cong forces, had continued to increase.

The bloodiest battle of the war so far was fought Nov. 14-21, 1965 by U.S. and North Vietnamese troops in the Iadrang Valley between the Cambodian border and Pleime. The fighting was an extension of a bitter engagement that had been waged around the U.S. Special Forces camp at Pleime since Oct. 19. North Vietnamese units that had sought to elude the search-and-destroy operation of the First Cavalry Division had decided to hold their ground in the Iadrang Valley; they offered stiff resistance. U.S. intelligence officers speculated that the North Vietnamese had halted their withdrawal to protect a possible major staging and supply base in the valley. About 2,000 troops of the North Vietnamese 66th Regiment were reportedly involved in the engagement. First Cavalry troops suffered their heaviest casualties Nov. 17 in a 500-man North Vietnamese ambush. The Communists broke off the fight after being pounded by U.S. planes. U.S. military authorities said 300 North Vietnamese had been slain, but the effectiveness of the U.S. battalion as a fighting unit was said to have been destroyed. B-52s from Guam flew missions against the Communists throughout the Iadrang fighting. A U.S. military spokesman in Saigon reported Nov. 20 that 1,186 North Vietnamese troops had been killed in the Iadrang Valley.

A U.S. official was quoted as saying that "a significant increase in [U.S.] troop numbers is necessary just to keep up with the game." U.S. military authorities cited the need to reinforce the First Cavalry Division with another division or 2 to secure the Central Highlands area, scene of fierce fighting in the previous 3 months. McNamara, addressing reporters in Saigon Nov. 29, asserted that the "decision by the Viet Cong to stand and fight" despite powerful U.S. attacks "expressed a determination to carry on the conflict which can lead to only one conclusion—that it will be a long war." McNamara added that the recent fighting in the Central Highlands and the killing of thousands of Viet Cong and North Vietnamese troops there represented a "clear decision on the part of Hanoi to escalate the level of infiltration and to raise the level of the conflict."

Advance elements of the U.S. 25th Infantry Division arrived in Pleiku by plane Dec. 29 from their base in Hawaii. U.S. officials described the 14-hour 7,000-mile flight as the longest combat airlift in history. The rest of the division's 20,000 troops were scheduled to reach South Vietnam in 1966. The division's arrival would bring to more than 200,000 the number of U.S. military personnel in Vietnam, exclusive of 7th Fleet units stationed in the South China Sea.

Chinese Communist Premier Chou En-lai said Dec. 20 that the U.S. was "making preparations" for extending the war in Vietnam to all of Indochina and to China. Chou warned that if the U.S. decided on "going along the road of war expansion and on having another trial of strength with the Chinese people," then the Chinese would "take up the challenge and fight to the end." Chou spoke at a Peking reception marking the 5th anniversary of the Viet Cong's National Liberation Front.

GROWING U.S. DISSENT (1965-6)

America Divided

The deepening involvement by the U.S. in the Vietnam War increased the prospect of Sino-American confrontation. The prospect was disquieting. As the war continued to escalate, a growing number of Americans began questioning Pres. Johnson's war policy.

In Feb. 1965, when he ordered air raids against North Vietnam, Johnson was able to do so with a solid Congressional support. Senate majority leader Mike Mansfield (D., Mont.) said: It was Johnson's aim "to achieve stability if possible so that the Vietnamese government can manage its own affairs within South Vietnam. I think he is proceeding cautiously and carefully, and he has a very full appreciation of all the elements involved in any move he directs." Senate GOP leader Everett M. Dirksen (Ill.) said that "If we hadn't given an adequate response, we might have given the impression we might pull out" of South Vietnam.

At that time only a very small minority of Senators and Congressmen dissented from the Administration's new ventures in Vietnam. Prominent among these dissenters were Sen. Ernest Gruening (D., Alaska) and Sen. Wayne Morse (D., Ore.). Sen. Morse called the attacks "a black page in American history." They were soon joined by others.

In April, a call for a halt in the bombing was sounded by Sen. George Aiken (R., Vt.) and Sen. Joseph S. Clark (D., Pa.). Aiken said Apr. 23 that the air raids "will not put the North Vietnamese in a mood to negotiate." On the contrary, they might stiffen North Vietnamese resistance. He and Clark said that the mail from their constituents expressed opposition to the Administration's war policy.

Chairman J. William Fulbright (D., Ark.) of the Senate Foreign Relations Committee declared in a Senate speech June

15 that U.S. policy in Vietnam "should remain one of determination to end the war at the earliest possible time by a negotiated settlement involving major concessions by both sides." Fulbright said such negotiations were vital because "it is clear to all reasonable Americans that a complete military victory in Vietnam, though theoretically attainable, can in fact be attained only at a cost far exceeding the requirements of our interest and our honor." Fulbright expressed opposition to "unconditional withdrawal of American support from South Vietnam." He said "such action would betray our obligation to people we have promised to defend" and "would have disastrous consequences, including but by no means confined to the victory of the Viet Cong in South Vietnam." Fulbright voiced equal objection to escalation of the war. Contending that the air strikes against North Vietnam had thus far "failed to weaken the military capacity of the Viet Cong," Fulbright said escalating the conflict would provoke a large-scale North Vietnamese invasion of South Vietnam, which in turn "would probably draw the United States into a bloody and protracted jungle war" and eventually would precipitate "either massive Chinese military intervention in many vulnerable areas in Southeast Asia or general nuclear war."

Heartened by the division on Vietnam among U.S. political leaders, the opponents of the war sought to carry their views to the public through "teach-ins" and protest rallies and marches. Although generally leftist, the movement was diverse politically. It included religious and doctrinaire pacifist elements.

A student peace march was staged in Washington by Students for a Democratic Society, a leftwing non-Communist group with chapters at 63 universities. The rally, held Apr. 17, was supported by such groups as Women Strike for Peace and the Student Nonviolent Coordinating Committee. An estimated 15,000 demonstrators first picketed the White House and later marched to the Washington Monument for a series of addresses.

About 500 persons led by Protestant, Roman Catholic and Jewish clergymen held a silent vigil before the Pentagon in Washington May 12 to protest U.S. policy in Vietnam. Defense Secy. Robert S. McNamara met for about 75 minutes with the leaders, who included Dr. Edwin T. Dahlberg, ex-president of the National Council of Churches; Dr. A. Dudley Ward, general secretary of the Methodist Board of Christian Social Concerns; the Right Rev. Daniel Corrigan, director of the Home Department of the Episcopal Church, New York; and Rabbi Leon I. Feuer, president of the Central Conference of American Rabbis.

Several extreme opponents of the war—most of them youthful pacifists—burned their Selective Service cards publicly to dramatize their defiance of the Administration's policies and of a new law making it a crime to "knowingly" destroy or mutilate a draft card. The law, signed by the President Aug. 31, carried penalties of up to 5 years in prison and a $10,000 fine for violators. It had been submitted specifically to deal with an expected outbreak of draft-card burnings.

Nationwide demonstrations against U.S. policy in Vietnam were held Oct. 15-16 in about 40 U.S. cities. The demonstrations were organized by the National Coordinating Committee to End the War in Vietnam, a student-run organization set up in August with headquarters in Madison, Wis. near the University of Wisconsin campus. Major demonstrations took place in New York and Berkeley, Calif. In New York, a parade was held Oct. 16, and more than 10,000 demonstrators marched despite heckling and threats from counter-demonstrators. In Berkeley, several thousand students attempted to march Oct. 15 and again Oct. 16 to the Oakland Army Base for a mass "sleep-out"; on both occasions they were turned back at the Oakland city limits by Oakland police. The Berkeley marches were directed by the Vietnam Day Committee, a university-centered group that had organized similar demonstrations near the Oakland base earlier in the year. Frank Emspak, 22, a zoology graduate of the University of Wisconsin and chairman of the National Coordinating Committee to End the War in Vietnam, said in Madison Oct. 17 that 70,000-100,000 persons had taken part in the demonstrations.

Marchers estimated to number from 15,000 to 35,000 converged on the White House Nov. 27 in a "March on Washington for Peace in Vietnam." The demonstration had been initiated by the National Committee for a Sane Nuclear Policy (SANE), under the sponsorship of an *ad hoc* committee that included prominent American authors, artists, churchmen and civil rights leaders. After circling the White House for 2 hours, carrying placards with such slogans as "Respect the 1954 Geneva Accords" and "Stop the Bombing," the demonstrators marched to the Washington Monument to hear speakers, among them Dr. Benjamin Spock, Norman Thomas, Mrs. Martin Luther King Jr. and Rep. George E. Brown Jr. (D., Calif.). 17 authorized march slogans had been issued, but members of the leftist Youth Against War & Fascism joined the march with placards bearing such unauthorized slogans as "Bring the GIs Home Now." A few Viet Cong flags, also unauthorized, were carried by members of the Committee to Aid the National Liberation Front.

Sen. Robert F. Kennedy (D., N.Y.) Nov. 5, 1965 defended "the right to criticize and the right to dissent" from Administration policy on Vietnam. Speaking at a news conference in Los Angeles, Kennedy said he favored donating blood to North Vietnam because it would be "in the oldest tradition of this country." "I'm willing to give blood to anybody who needs it," he asserted. But he said such blood donations to Hanoi should be given only "with concurrence of the government and the supervision of the Red Cross."

With the possible exception of the civil rights issue, no problem was debated more widely or with more heat during 1966 than the issue of the war in Vietnam. The subject opened deep divisions in both political parties and in groups as varied as church organizations and labor unions. The extremes ranged from (a) the "hawks," who called for the U.S. to pour more men and materiel into Vietnam in an all-out drive to win a military victory, to (b) the "doves," whose varied proposals included demands that the U.S. stop bombing North Vietnam, that the U.S. stop fighting in Vietnam altogether and either pull out of the country completely or withdraw to defensible "enclaves," that the U.S. negotiate peace and/or that the U.S. bring the National Liberation Front, the Viet Cong's political arm, into a South Vietnamese coalition government.

In his State-of-the-Union message Jan. 12, 1966, Pres. Johnson pledged that the U.S. would stay in Vietnam "until aggression has stopped." He promised to "give our fighting men [in Vietnam] what they must have." But "we will strive to limit conflict," he declared, "for we wish neither increased destruction nor increased danger." He asserted that "there are no arbitrary limits to our search for peace." Johnson said: "We may have to face long, hard combat or a long hard conference, or even both at once. . . . The days may become months and the months may become years, but we will stay as long as aggression commands us to battle." "We will meet at any conference table, we will discuss any proposals . . . we will consider the views of any group. We will work for a cease-fire now or once discussions have begun. We'll respond if others reduce their use of force; and we will withdraw our soldiers once South Vietnam is securely guaranteed the right to shape its own future."

Peace Drive Fails

Caught between Communist intransigence and growing domestic dissent, the Johnson Administration launched a concerted peace drive toward the end of 1965. The bombing of North Vietnam was halted Dec. 24 as part of a Christmas cease-fire, but the suspension continued through Jan. 1966. As special Presidential emissaries, Amb.-to-UN Arthur Goldberg, Amb.-at-large W. Averell Harriman, Vice Pres. Hubert Humphrey and Presidential Asst. McGeorge Bundy were sent to various capitals.

Vice Pres. Humphrey left Washington Dec. 27, 1965 on a 5-day tour of Japan, Nationalist China, South Korea and the Philippines. He arrive in Tokyo Dec. 28 and conferred the following day with Japanese Premier Eisaku Sato. He left later Dec. 29 for Manila. Humphrey met later in Manila with Thai Foreign Min. Thant Khoman and conferred with Philippine Pres. Ferdinand Marcos Dec. 31.

On the first leg of his mission, Goldberg conferred with Pope Paul VI in Rome Dec. 29. Goldberg transmitted a message from Pres. Johnson describing the pontiff's pleas Dec. 19 and 24 for a cease-fire as "helpful in bringing about a Christmas truce." (The pope was reported to have sent messages Dec. 24 thanking Johnson, North Vietnamese Pres. Ho Chi Minh and South Vietnamese Chief of State Nguyen Van Thieu for accepting the Christmas truce. In a reply to the pope, sent Dec. 28 and made public Dec. 29, Ho thanked him "for the interest you show in the problem of peace in Vietnam." The remainder of Ho's reply was largely a reiteration of Hanoi's accusation against the U.S.) Goldberg Dec. 30 discussed Vietnam with Premier Aldo Moro and other Italian leaders. Goldberg then flew to Paris and met with French Pres. Charles de Gaulle Dec. 31. Goldberg said at a news briefing later that he had told de Gaulle of Johnson's conviction that the conflict "can only be settled at the conference table without prior conditions."

The U.S.' position on Vietnam was explained by Harriman in Warsaw Dec. 29 in talks with Polish Foreign Min. Adam Rapacki. Harriman flew to Yugoslavia Dec. 30 to confer with Pres. Tito. Bundy met with Canadian Prime Min. Lester B. Pearson in Ottawa Dec. 29. A statement issued by Pearson Dec. 30 expressed "appreciation and support for the latest American effort to find a peaceful solution to the conflict in Vietnam."

Washington's year-end peace drive failed to persuade Communist countries. As State Secy. Dean Rusk told newsmen in Washington Jan. 21, 1966, the American peace overtures had elicited "an overwhelmingly favorable response" "except from those who could, in fact, sit down and make peace."

The Chinese Communist Party newspaper *Jenmin Jih Pao,* in a Jan. 1 editorial, described the U.S. emissaries visiting various capitals as "monsters" and "freaks" who were raising "a lot of dust with their sinister activities." The editorial said: "Paralleled with its frenzied preparation for expanding its war of agression against Vietnam," the U.S. "has lately been chanting its worn-out tune of 'peace' more loudly than ever before"; the U.S. was the "common enemy of the people of the whole world"; Soviet policies were "Khrushchev revisionism." In a further comment on the U.S. peace efforts, *Jenmin Jih Pao* Jan. 5 urged "the well-intentioned people" visited by the American emissaries not to be taken in by Washington's "peace-talks hoax." The newspaper said the U.S.' peace overtures were a prelude to expansion of the war and the eventual permanent occupation by the U.S. of South Vietnam.

The Communist Chinese news agency, Hsinhua, said Jan. 1 that North Vietnam had rejected Washington's latest peace overtures. Quoting Hanoi radio and *Nhan Dan,* North Vietnam's Communist Party newspaper, Hsinhua said North Vietnam had "scuttled the conspiratorial schemes of United States imperialists and reiterated the solemn stand for the withdrawal of United States aggressors from South Vietnam." The U.S.' Vietnam peace missions were denounced by *Nhan Dan* Jan. 3 as "a noisy propaganda campaign" and "a trick aimed at screening their plans of war intensification and expansion."

A more detailed response to the U.S.' peace drive and Hanoi's first reaction to the pause in air strikes against North Vietnam were made in a statement issued Jan. 4 by the North Vietnamese Foreign Ministry. The Hanoi statement said: The U.S. moves were "a largescale deceptive peace campaign coupled with the trick of 'temporary suspension of air attacks' on North Vietnam." The "new 'peace proposals' " carried by Washington's emissaries were "actually a mere repetition of

old themes." Despite the halt in the raids, the U.S. "still bra-
zenly gives itself the right to launch air attacks" on North
Vietnam. The U.S. "has no right to impose" on North Vietnam "any condition whatsoever in exchange for stopping its
air raids on North Vietnam." The U.S.' "real purpose" in
calling for "unconditional discussions" was "to carry out the
plot of conducting negotiations from a position of strength and
attempting to force on the Vietnamese people acceptance of
United States terms." Hanoi's 4-point peace formula for Vietnam remained the "concentrated expression of the essential
military and political provisions" of the Geneva agreements
on Vietnam. The U.S., "with the puppet regime rigged up by
itself in Saigon," was "clinging to South Vietnam and perpetu-
ating the partition of Vietnam." "While making a noise about
its 'peace efforts,' the United States is making feverish preparations to double the United States strength in South Vietnam."
The U.S. had "intensified its air attacks on the liberated areas
in Laos and impudently authorized United States troops to intrude into central Laos and into Cambodian territory, thus
extending the war from South Vietnam to these 2 countries."

The U.S.' peace offensive was described Jan. 5 by the
National Liberation Front (NLF), political arm of the Viet
Cong, as a "smokescreen" to "cover up" a "crazy and adven-
turous policy of military build-up and to hoodwink public
opinion." The NLF statement, broadcast Jan. 7 by North
Vietnam radio, said U.S. diplomats were being sent to world
capitals to "stage buffoonery of U.S. 'peace efforts,' to adver-
tise the 'suspension' of bombing raids on North Vietnam as a
gesture of goodwill."

The Soviet Union had charged Jan. 2 that the U.S. planned to extend the war to Laos and Cambodia. The accusation
was made by *Pravda,* which asked: "How can this be reconciled
with Washington's notorious attempts to achieve peace in Vietnam about which American propaganda has now raised such
an outcry?" A 5-man Soviet mission led by Communist Party
Central Committee Secy. Aleksandr N. Shelepin visited Hanoi

Jan. 7-12 and paved the way for a Soviet pledge of increased military aid to North Vietnam. The military assistance pledge was made in a communique issued in Moscow Jan. 14, one day after Shelepin had returned to the Soviet capital. Citing Soviet support of North Vietnam's 4-point peace formula and the NLF's prerequisites for negotiations, the communique asserted that "these positions are the only correct basis for solving the Vietnamese problem."

The 4-point peace formula referred to in the Moscow communique had been set forth earlier by North Vietnamese Premier Phan Van Dong in a speech to the North Vietnamese National Assembly Apr. 8, 1965 and repeated Apr. 20, 1965 in the North Vietnamese reply to the peace plea by 17 non-aligned nations. It called for the withdrawal of American troops, the cessation of U.S. support to the Saigon government and the settlement of South Vietnamese internal affairs on the NLF's terms. *Text of the North Vietnamese 4-point formula:*

1. Recognition of the basic national rights of the Vietnamese people—peace, independence, sovereignty, unity, and territorial integrity. In accordance with the Geneva Agreements, the U.S. government must withdraw from South Vietnam U.S. troops, military personnel, and weapons of all kinds, dismantle all U.S. military bases there, and cancel its military alliance with South Vietnam. It must end its policy of intervention and aggression in South Vietnam. In accordance with the Geneva Agreements, the U.S. government must stop its acts of war against North Vietnam, and completely cease all encroachments on the territory and sovereignty of the Democratic Republic of Vietnam.

2. Pending the peaceful reunification of Vietnam, while Vietnam is still temporarily divided into two zones, the military provisions of the 1954 Geneva Agreements on Vietnam must be strictly respected. The two zones must refrain from joining any military alliance with foreign countries. There must be no foreign military bases, troops or military personnel in the respective territories.

3. The internal affairs of South Vietnam must be settled by the South Vietnamese people themselves, in accordance with the program of the National Front for the Liberation of South Vietnam, without any foreign interference.

4. The peaceful reunification of Vietnam is to be settled by the Vietnamese people in both zones, without any foreign interference. . . .

As against the North Vietnamese 4-point formula the U.S. offered a 14-point proposal for peace, which was announced by Vice Pres. Humphrey Jan. 3, 1966 at the White House as "elements which the U.S. believes can go into peace in Southeast Asia." *The proposal:*

1. The Geneva Agreements of 1954 and 1962 are an adequate basis for peace in Southeast Asia;

2. We would welcome a conference on Southeast Asia or on any part thereof;

3. We would welcome "negotiations without preconditions" as the 17 nations put it;

4. We would welcome unconditional discussions as Pres. Johnson put it;

5. A cessation of hostilities could be the first order of business at a conference or could be the subject of preliminary discussions;

6. Hanoi's 4 points could be discussed along with other points which others might wish to propose;

7. We want no U.S. bases in Southeast Asia;

8. We do not desire to retain U.S. troops in South Vietnam after peace is assured;

9. We support free elections in South Vietnam to give the South Vietnamese a government of their own choice;

10. The question of reunification of Vietnam should be determined by the Vietnamese through their own free decision;

11. The countries of Southeast Asia can be non-aligned or neutral if that be their option;

12. We would much prefer to use our resources for the economic reconstruction of Southeast Asia than in war. If there is peace, North Vietnam could participate in a regional effort to which we would be prepared to contribute at least $1 billion;

13. The President has said: "The Viet Cong would not have difficulty being represented and having their views represented if for a moment Hanoi decided she wanted to cease aggression. I don't think that would be an insurmountable problem."

14. We have said publicly and privately that we could stop the bombing of North Vietnam as a step toward peace although there has not been the slightest hint or suggestion from the other side as to what they would do if the bombing stopped.

Many Congress members had commented on Vietnam as Congress convened Jan. 10, 1966. Among remarks made in interviews or in statements: Sen. John Sherman Cooper (R.,Ky.) —"Negotiation, not escalation, should be the dominant theme of our activity now"; the President should "make clear, without reservation, that negotiations could include the Viet Cong, because it is obvious that neither negotiations nor a settlement

are possible without their inclusion." . . . Sen. Joseph S. Clark
(D., Pa.)—The President should have "complete freedom to
play out the string for peace"; the people did not want "the
reckless and impatient bomb throwers to force the President's
hand or limit his flexibility of action." . . . Sen. Bourke B. Hick-
enlooper (R., Ia.)—"I don't see that the [U.S.] suspension [of
the bombing] has accomplished anything"; "I think it is a
mistake to stop the pressure." . . . Rep. Leslie C. Arends (Ill.),
assistant GOP House leader—"There's a limit how long we
can keep this [suspension] up"; "something" would have to
be done unless North Vietnam indicated agreement "to talk
things over." . . . Rep. L. Mendel Rivers (D., S.C.). chairman of the House Armed Services Committee—Resumption
of the bombing "should start yesterday—no, make it the day
before."

Resumption of Bombing

With peace overtures failing to elicit cooperative response
from the other side, the Johnson Administration prepared the
American public for the resumption of bombing. Gen. Earle
G. Wheeler, chairman of the Joint Chiefs of Staff, testifying
Jan. 20, 1966 before a joint session of the Senate Armed Services and Appropriations subcommittees for defense, cautioned
against a permanent halt in air raids on North Vietnam. His
testimony was made public Jan. 22. Wheeler said that the U.S.
had "3 blue chips" in possible negotiations: the bombing of
North Vietnam, the presence of U.S. troops in South Vietnam
and the time of an ultimate American withdrawal.

Johnson Jan. 25 strongly indicated his decision to resume
the bombing. He did so at a joint White House meeting of the
National Security Council and a bi-partisan group of Congressional leaders. The meeting was described as a briefing, and the
lawmakers reportedly were given intelligence accounts of North
Vietnamese military activity during the bombing pause.

Simultaneously, the Administration released to the press an
intelligence report that said: According to aerial reconnaissance

photos and reports from Laotian refugees, North Vietnam had increased its shipments of war supplies to the Viet Cong in South Vietnam via the Ho Chi Minh Trail through Laos. U.S. reconnaissance planes had taken pictures of more than 200 trucks in southern North Vietnam between Dec. 31, 1965 and Jan. 13. Most of these vehicles had been sighted on Routes 1A and 15, which ran west to Laos and were principal connecting routes to the Ho Chi Minh Trail. The infiltration of men from North Vietnam to South Vietnam was increasing, and about 1,000 infiltrators had moved into South Vietnam's northernmost Quangtri Province Dec. 24, 1965, the day the bombing lull had started. North Vietnam was repairing bridges and other installations damaged by U.S. bombings.

Among those attending the White House conference were Vice Pres. Humphrey, Amb.-at-Large W. Averell Harriman. Gen. Earle G. Wheeler, Senate majority leader Mike Mansfield (D., Mont.), Senate Foreign Relations Committee Chrmn. J. W. Fulbright (D., Ark.), Senate minority leader Everett M. Dirksen (R., Ill.) and House minority leader Gerald Ford (R., Mich.).

Gen. Maxwell D. Taylor, a special adviser to Johnson, said Jan. 26 that the reasons for suspending the air raids had been "exhausted" and that, therefore, the bombings should be resumed. Speaking in New York at the annual luncheon of the Pilgrims of the United States, Taylor said that by halting the air attacks "we have shown friends and foes the sincerity of our peaceful purposes."

In testimony before the House Foreign Affairs Committee Jan. 26, State Secy. Rusk said that since the U.S. had stopped bombing North Vietnam, Washington had extended its peace efforts "from A to Z and almost through Z." Rusk described the clamor for continuation of the bombing pause a "curious double standard." While U.S. raids remained suspended, Viet Cong terrorists were carrying out bombings and assassinations in South Vietnam, Rusk said. Rusk restated Administration opposition to including the NLF in peace talks. Asserting that this matter was "directly related to what the fighting is all about," Rusk said: The NLF was "organized in Hanoi in 1960, specifically for the purpose of taking over South Vietnam by force. Now, if the Viet Cong come to the conference table as full partners, they will in a sense have been victorious in the very aims that South Vietnam and the United States are pledged to prevent."

The impending move toward the resumption of bombing further polarized the Congress. An Associated Press poll of 50 (of 100) Senators willing to express their views showed Jan. 26 that 25 favored and 25 opposed a resumption of bombing of North Vietnam. Among those listed as against the renewed raids were Sens. Mansfield, Fulbright, Aiken, Cooper, Thruston Morton (R., Ky.) and Robert F. Kennedy. Among the 25 for resuming the air strikes were Sens. Richard B. Russell (D., Ga.), Henry Jackson (D., Wash.) and John Stennis (D., Miss.).

A letter calling for continued suspension of the air strikes was signed by 15 Democratic Senators and presented to Pres. Johnson Jan. 27. The message said: "We believe we understand in some small degree the agony you must suffer when called upon by our Constitutional system to make judgements which may involve war or peace. We believe you should have our collective judgement before you when you make your decision." The letter had been drafted by Sens. Vance Hartke (Ind.), Eugene McCarthy (Minn.), George McGovern (S.D.), Quentin Burdick (N.D.), Lee Metcalf (Mont.), Frank E. Moss (Utah). (Moss was in London and was unable to sign the letter.) The other signers were Sens. Edward L. Bartlett (Alaska), Maurine Neuberger (Ore.), Frank Church (Ida.), William Proxmire (Wis.), Stephen M. Young (O.), Joseph S. Clark (Pa.), Ernest Gruening (Alaska) and Harrison A. Williams Jr. (N.J.).

The Senators' appeal was answered by Johnson Jan. 28 in a letter to Hartke. Johnson reminded Hartke that he (the President) was being "guided" in his actions on Vietnam in accordance with the joint Congressional resolution of Aug. 10, 1964, which gave the President broad powers to make decisions on the Vietnam situation. Johnson said his "views of the present situation remain as stated in my recent reply" to 76 House Democrats who had urged him Jan. 21 not to renew the air strikes.

Johnson Jan. 31 finally announced his decision to resume the bombing of North Vietnam. The announcement was made several hours after the bombing had actually started. For the first time in 37 days, U.S. bombers struck at North Vietnamese targets. Navy carrier-based planes and Air Force jets attacked ferries, bridges, roads and trucks.

Johnson simultaneously instructed Amb.-to-UN Arthur Goldberg to ask the UN Security Council to intervene in the crisis and seek an international conference to end the war and establish peace in Southeast Asia. The Council opened its deliberation Feb. 1.

Honolulu Conference

While the UN Security Council deliberated on the U.S. proposal, Johnson flew to Honolulu, Hawaii, accompanied by his military and political advisers, to confer with South Vietnamese Premier Nguyen Cao Key and other Saigon officials. The conference lasted from Feb. 6 to Feb. 8, 1966.

At the end of the conference the participants issued a "Declaration of Honolulu" outlining future U.S.-South Vietnamese political and military policy. The joint communique said that the 2 governments had "reached full agreement on a policy of growing military effectiveness and of still closer cooperation between [their] military forces." The conferees had "noted with regret the total absence of a present interest in peace on the part" of North Vietnam. Despite Hanoi's negative reaction, the U.S. and South Vietnam had "agreed upon continued diplomatic efforts for peace," the communique said.

(Among major economic and social goals outlined in the communique: The U.S. and South Vietnam would "take further concrete steps to combat inflation in Vietnam"; Johnson pledged full support for Saigon's "intensified program of rural construction"; the U.S. would help Vietnam develop "enlarged programs of agriculture cooperation"; U.S. assistance in the fields of health and education "would be intensified"; Vietnamese refugees who "come over from the enemy side must be adequately cared for and prepared to resume a useful role in society.")

Johnson Feb. 8 gave an optimistic report on the Honolulu conference. The President delivered his statement in Los Angeles, where he stopped briefly on his way back to Washington. Johnson said that the U.S. and South Vietnamese leaders in Honolulu had reached an understanding that "the war we are helping them fight must be won on 2 fronts." "One front is military," he said. "The other front is the struggle against social injustice: against hunger, disease, and ignorance, against political apathy and indifference." The President said the conferees had discussed the problems "of how to build the basis for a democratic constitution and free elections; of how to seek the peace; of how to conduct the war." Asserting that the solutions to these problems "will not be easy," Johnson said U.S. and South Vietnamese leaders "would meet again in the months ahead to measure that progress." "This revolutionary transformation cannot wait until the guns grow silent and the terrorism stops," the President declared. Johnson said Agriculture Secy. Orville L. Freeman was going to Saigon with Vice Pres. Humphrey "to see how we can help with food and rural development." Health, Education & Welfare Secy. John W. Gardner also would go to Saigon to advise the Vietnamese on education and health, the President said. Humphrey's assignment in Saigon, Johnson said, would be "to assure that our representatives there get to work rapidly and effectively on the tasks we laid out at Honolulu."

The President returned to Washington Feb. 9 and said at his news conference Feb. 11 that U.S. military forces in South Vietnam would be expanded; but he indicated that the build-up would be gradual. Johnson said "there will be additional men needed and they will be supplied as Gen. [William C.]

Westmoreland is able to use them and as he may require them."
(The U.S. force in South Vietnam then totaled about 205,000
men.) The President indicated a desire to correct what he considered the widely held but inaccurate view that U.S. activity
in Vietnam "is just a military effort." He pointed out that "we
distributed 8 million textbooks" and "doubled the rice production" in South Vietnam. He said he "thought it was good that
we could go" to Honolulu and "try to expose to the world . . .
what this country is trying to do to feed the hungry, and to
educate the people, and to improve the life span for people
who just live to be 35 now. . . ."

Senate Hearings on Vietnam

Opponents of the war tried to bring their case before the
American public. The Senate Foreigh Relations Committee,
headed by Chairman William Fulbright, decided to hold hearings on Vietnam in Feb. 1966 with national TV coverage. Prior
to the hearings, Fulbright told newsmen Feb. 7 that China
might intervene in Vietnam. He said that he was "fearful that
if the war in Vietnam is not handled extremely well, the Chinese
Communists will come in." Fulbright said that in his committee's hearings on Vietnam, the Administration's "policies
beyond Vietnam" were involved: "Communist China over-
shadowed the whole thing. There are rumors of very drastic
action." Fulbright said his latter statement referred to statements that had been made publicly by some Congress members
and privately by some military officials on possible actions the
U.S. would take if Communist China intervened in the war in
response to an extension of air strikes against North Vietnam.

The hearings took place in Washington Feb. 8, 10, 17 and
18, with testimony from James M. Gavin (Feb. 8), George F.
Kennan of the Institute for Advanced Study (Feb. 10), Gen.
Maxwell D. Taylor (Feb. 17) and State Secy. Rusk (Feb. 18).
Fulbright reported Feb. 8 that State Undersecy. George Ball
had declined, as had Defense Secy. McNamara and Gen. Earle
G. Wheeler, to appear at the inquiry in public session.

In his testimony, Gavin favored keeping U.S. troops in South Vietnam but opposed escalation of the war. He said: The U.S. had become "mesmerized" with Vietnam, and its policy there had become "alarmingly out of balance." "We have been escalating at the will of our opponents rather than on our own judgment." Additional large increases in U.S. troop strength in Vietnam would bring the U.S. "into another kind of confrontation" and raise the likelihood of intervention by China, which would further raise the possibility of Soviet involvement and of a reopening of the Korean front. The U.S. was "slowly creeping" toward "urban bombing," which had only dubious military value but evoked adverse "world opinion." Concerning his previously expressed opinion that the U.S. should limit its Vietnam military operations to defensible "enclaves" along Vietnam's coast, the use of the word "coast" was unfortunate, and he would include any enclave currently held by U.S. forces. These positions should be maintained while the U.S. took stock of the entire situation.

The hearings were climaxed by a 7-hour appearance of State Secy. Rusk Feb. 18. Rusk reiterated the Administrations's oft-stated position that the U.S. was in Vietnam "to check the extension of Communist power in order to maintain a reasonable stability in a precarious world." He said: U.S. soldiers were fighting there because "South Vietnam had, under the language of the SEATO treaty, been the victim of 'aggression by means of armed attack.'" "These are moments when toughness is absolutely essential for peace. If we don't make clear where we stand, then the prospect for peace disappears." "If there is doubt in Congress about the policy, let us vote, let us find out, let's have that decision considered in 1966." But before the vote, members of Congress should ponder "on what basis we have any chance to organize peace in the world."

Fulbright said the failure of most of the Asian members of SEATO to supply forces for the war indicated their belief that the war was a civil war and not "truly an example of Communist aggression." Fulbright also questioned Rusk's contention that the National Liberation Front was an "agent" of Hanoi. He said the U.S.' pledge to leave Vietnam after peace was attained was contradicted by the seemingly permanent U.S. military installations in Vietnam. Rusk replied that the bases were necessary to sustain the current effort and that the U.S. had built and left such bases before.

Fulbright said the Vietnamese conflict was not the kind "that warrants escalation" because it did not involve the vital security of the U.S., yet it could be a "trigger for world war." He said the U.S. had not stressed that it would accept the results of free supervised elections in which the NLF would be permitted to participate and that he had the impression "that we are in an unlimited war and the only kind of settlement is unconditional surrender." "Unconditional surrender of what?" Rusk asked. "That they give up and . . . come to the conference at your mercy, and we have total victory," Fulbright answered. "I see no occasion of any disposition to compromise."

Denying that the U.S. was asking for "unconditional surrender," Rusk said: "We are not asking anything from Hanoi except to stop shooting their neighbors in Laos and South Vietnam. We are not asking them to give up an acre of territory. We are not asking them to surrender a single individual, nor to change the form of government. . . . We are not asking them to surrender a thing except their appetite to take over South Vietnam by force."

Fulbright contended that the Communists should be given convincing assurances "that if an election is held in Vietnam, that we will abide by it regardless of the outcome." Rusk replied: "The only convincing way in which you could say that to the other side apparently is to let them have the government to start with that would conduct the elections." Asked by Sen. Albert Gore (D., Tenn.) if the U.S. would agree to elections and abide by their results, Rusk said, "Yes."

The full Senate debated on the war for 2 weeks in the latter part of Feb. 1966. Fulbright, addressing that body at the end of the debate Mar. 1, said that unless the U.S. was prepared to

fight a general war in Asia over South Vietnam, it had "no alternative but to seek a general accommodation" with China
for the "neutralization" of all Southeast Asia. "If the issue
between Chinese and American power in Southeast Asia can be
resolved," he said, "the future of Vietnam should not be too
difficult to arrange; but if the issue of Chinese and American
power is left unresolved, even a total victory in South Vietnam
is unlikely to solve very much."

Fulbright said: "It would seem to be highly advisable that
. . . we indicate to the Chinese that we are prepared to remove
American military power not only from Vietnam but from all
of Southeast Asia in return for a similar withdrawal on her
part." A "general neutralization agreement for Southeast Asia
could be enforced" (1) by "the prospect that the reintroduction
of Chinese power would be followed by the reintroduction of
American power," and (2) by placing the neutralization agreement "under the guarantee of the major powers with interests
in Southeast Asia, notably the United States, China, the Soviet
Union, Great Britain, France, India and Japan."

To get China's consent to the neutralization pact, Fulbright proposed "entrench[ing] ourselves in powerful bases on
the coast of Vietnam" and thus confronting the Chinese "with
a perfectly credible threat of permanent American bases on
their periphery." "History . . . suggests," Fulbright said, "that
the military solution that seems so promising today is likely to
result in disaster tomorrow, whereas the course of accommodation, which always seems so difficult, is the only course with
demonstrated promise of being able to bring about a lasting
and honorable peace."

Chinese Reaction

Peking reacted to the resumption of bombing with its customary denunciations. *Jenmin Jih Pao,* in an editorial Feb. 1,
1966, asserted that the U.S. action showed that the "peace
offensive" was a smokescreen to cover up the expansion of
war—something that "clear-sighted people" had seen all along.

The following day the same paper criticized the U.S. for bringing the issue before the UN Security Council, which, the Chinese argued, lacked jurisdiction in view of the Geneva Agreements. The war should be settled on the basis of the North Vietnamese 4-point formula and the Viet Cong 5-point proposal, both of which were in accord with the principles of the Geneva Agreements, the editorial asserted. *Jenmin Jih Pao* concluded: "All U.S. aggressors must quit South Vietnam without exception; Vietnam's affairs must be settled by Vietnamese themselves."

Communist China directed its criticism to other countries as well. An article that appeared in *Jenmin Jih Pao* Feb. 1 attacked Soviet diplomatic activities in Vietnam. Referring to Soviet Communist Party Central Committee Secy. Aleksandr N. Shelepin, who had visited Hanoi. Jan. 7-12, the article charged that the purpose of the trip was to "say clearly that the Vietnamese people must sit down around a conference table with the American aggressors." Soviet Premier Aleksei N. Kosygin was scored for his dealings with "Indian reactionaries" and a meeting he had held Jan. 13 in New Delhi with U.S. Vice Pres. Humphrey. Soviet Communist Party First Secy. Leonid I. Breznev's trip to Mongolia Jan. 11-15 to sign a mutual defense treaty was also assailed. *Jenmin Jih Pao* Feb. 1 also commented critically on Japanese Foreign Min. Etsusaburo Shiina's visit to the USSR Jan. 19-22. It charged that Japanese Premier Eisaku Sato was "following the United States and aligning itself with the Soviet Union to oppose China."

More verbal attacks on the U.S. followed.

Chinese sources assailed statements in which State Secy. Dean Rusk and Asst. State Secy. (for Far Eastern affairs) William P. Bundy had warned of Peking's expansionist policies. The Chinese news agency Hsinhua charged Feb. 20 that Rusk's testimony to the Senate Foreign Relations Committee Feb. 18 had been in effect a "declaration that United States imperialism will not lay down its butcher's knife and that it is determined to seize South Vietnam by force." Hsinhua said that Rusk had "tried to threaten the Vietnamese and Chinese people with a 'big war' '' but that the Chinese and Vietnamese would not be intimidated by Washington's "brinkmanship." Hsinhua asserted that China was determined to "give all-out support to the Vietnamese in their struggle against United States aggressors until their ultimate victory, whatever the cost may be." It warned that Peking was "fully prepared to take up the challenge and fight to the end if United States imperialism insists on carrying the war into their country."

Bundy's speech (delivered Feb. 12 in Pomona, Calif.) was assailed Jan. 20 by *Jenmin Jih Pao* as expressing the U.S.' determination to "remain the enemy of the Chinese people to the very end." The newspaper quoted Bundy as having said that the U.S. would continue its policy of containment of China until a new generation of Chinese leaders arrived on the political scene more disposed to pursuing a peaceful policy. *Jenmin Jih Pao* took issue with Bundy's remark that Communist China advocated "change through revolution and violence throughout the world." According to the newspaper, it was the U.S., and not China, that had embarked on the path of "aggression, intervention and enslavement" and thus had "kindled the flames of the people's anti-U.S. struggle on the Asian continent."

Jenmin Jih Pao Mar. 3 discounted the domestic debate in the U.S. as a "camouflage to hoodwink the people." The article described both the "hawks" (hardliners) and the "doves" (opponents of the war) as a "bunch of fools" who refused to "abandon the United States policy of aggression in Vietnam and Asia." Both sides in the debate actually were in fundamental agreement, the article said, because neither proposed immediate withdrawal of U.S. forces from South Vietnam and recognition of the National Liberation Front as the only representative of the South Vietnamese people.

Jenmin Jih Pao Mar. 6 denounced the British and Soviet governments as "2 pals" in collaboration to end the Vietnamese war by supporting Johnson's " 'peace talks' hoax." The newspaper attack was made in an article commenting on

British Prime Min. Harold Wilson's talks with Soviet leaders in Moscow Feb. 22-24. It said: "Despite the strict silence maintained by Soviet leaders, it is not difficult to perceive what they have been up to in the light of Harold Wilson's activities and reactions in Moscow." Soviet policy, the Peking statement contended, was aimed at bringing the Vietnamese Communists to peace talks by "hook or crook" "so as to bring about another Munich." And London was "energetically serving as the faithful lackey of U.S. imperialism on the Vietnam question," *Jenmin Jih Pao* added. British and Soviet policy on Vietnam, the article claimed, was based on narrow political motives: Wilson envisioned himself as a mediator between East and West, thus raising the prestige of his Labor Party; the USSR sought to bring the Vietnamese question "into the orbit of U.S.-USSR collaboration."

Senate Hearings on China

The Johnson Administration was concerned that its escalation of military activities in Vietnam might lead to direct military confrontation with Communist China. To avert such a danger, the Administration sought for ways to improve relations with Peking. In Feb. 1966, following the resumption of bombing, the U.S. government, through its ambassador at Warsaw, extended an invitation for Chinese journalists to visit the U.S. According to the State Department spokesman Feb. 14, Peking had "neither taken up the offer nor rejected it."

Johnson, in a speech in New York at Freedom House's Freedom Award dinner Feb. 23, said that the U.S. was determined to avoid escalation of the conflict into war with Communist China but would reply to any armed attack. Otherwise, the President's speech was entirely devoted to the Vietnam War.

The possibility of war with China was discussed by Defense Secy. Robert McNamara Mar. 3. After meeting with the Senate Foreign Relations Committee, McNamara told newsmen: "The risk of a major land war in Asia would increase significantly if our military strategy in Vietnam were such as to threaten the destruction of the North Vietnamese regime or the occupancy of its territory. . . . This is not in any sense [our] objective." "It would be irresponsible for me to say that we run no risk" of war with China. "That risk was created by our treaty commitments." While U.S. policy in Vietnam was "essentially defense—to protect South Vietnam from attack," if Hanoi continued to attempt to take over South Vietnam by force, the U.S. and South Vietnamese forces would have "to continue the effort in South Vietnam to destroy the main force units of the North Vietnamese army and of the Viet Cong." U.S. deployment of troops in Vietnam was "in direct response to the step-up in the military activity by Hanoi and the Viet Cong," but the U.S.' "basic strategy" was to stay "ahead of the anticipated enemy force buildup."

Committee chairman J.W. Fulbright later expressed unease at McNamara's views. Fulbright said he was concerned about the possibility of Chinese intervention to bar a military defeat of North Vietnam. Fulbright said that despite McNamara's insistence that the U.S. did not face "an unlimited, open-ended commitment to a major land war in Asia," "our objective seems to be the surrender of North Vietnam, and that means we will do anything necessary for victory rather than compromise."

Fulbright announced Mar. 6 that his committee would conduct hearing on China. The purpose of the hearings was to provide the American people with an education on China and to lessen the danger of war. He said: "The danger of war is real . . . because China is ruled by ideological dogmatists who will soon have nuclear weapons at their disposal and who, though far more ferocious in words than in actions, nonetheless are intensely hostile to the United States." "An 'open-ended' war in Vietnam can bring the 2 great powers [China and the U.S.] into conflict with each other, by accident or by design, at almost any time." "Some of our military experts are confident that China will not enter the war in Vietnam; their confidence would be more reassuring if it did not bring to mind the predictions of military experts in 1950 that China would not enter the Korean War, as well as more recent predictions about an early victory in Vietnam." "Certain China experts in our government" held the view "that the Chinese leaders themselves expect to be at war with the United States within a year, and it is clear that some of our own officials also expect a war with China." This "fatal expectancy" made war more likely.

The Senate hearings on China opened Mar. 8 with testimony by Prof. A. Doak Barnett, acting director of Columbia University's East Asian Institute. Barnett urged that the U.S. "alter" its "basic posture toward the Chinese Communist regime from one of containment plus isolation to one of containment without isolation." This meant "checking military or subversive threats and pressures emanating from Peking" while attempting "maximum contacts with and maximum involvement of the Chinese Communists in the international community." "In general," Barnett backed the Administration's Vietnam policy, but he advocated intensified economic, political and peace efforts. "If we began to back off our policy, we would tend to confirm the Viet Cong and Chinese approach, and this would not induce them to consider optional policies," he warned. "It might well confirm them in the course on which they are now embarked." He opposed neutralization of Southeast Asia, as proposed recently by Fulbright, because "there needs to be a stable power balance [in Southeast Asia] that in the long run we and China can accept." He also opposed the "enclave" policy advocated by Gen. James M. Gavin. "In regard to the bombing of North Vietnam, we should de-escalate" rather than escalate, he declared. While he did not think that a build-up of U.S. forces in Vietnam to 600,000 men would "automatically" bring Chinese intervention, Barnett said, "it is likely that if the Chinese concluded there was a major threat to the existence of the North Vietnamese regime, the result could be largescale, direct Chinese intervention."

Dr. John K. Fairbank, director of the East Asian Research Center at Harvard University, held Mar. 10 that the U.S.

should promote Chinese participation in international conferences while the U.S. pursued the containment policy—"an attitude of firmness backed by force." China should be permitted into the UN, he said, "even if they said they would dynamite the place." He thought it unlikely, though, that China would enter the international scene with its current leader, Mao Tse-tung. He said the U.S. should "hold the line," militarily, on the Korean border, the Formosa Straits and "somehow in Vietnam." He said: "I do not wish to dissociate myself with the Administration's [Vietnam] policy, nor do I wish to underwrite it. It's a fact." He was "not happy about our being there," but "perhaps power has to be used in smaller wars if we are to avoid bigger wars." Asked about the possibility of Chinese intervention, Fairbank said that as China had intervened in Korea, "China would have to defend the state on their southern border" to bar the establishment there of a "non-Communist-type state." Fairbank said the U.S. should not expect the fighting to end before negotiations were begun, because the Chinese way was to do both at once. The larger contest in Vietnam, he said, was "nationbuilding"; "the real test is not whether we can fight but whether we can be more constructive than destructive while we are fighting."

Dr. John H.M. Lindbeck, associate director of the East Asian Research Center at Harvard, and Benjamin J. Schwartz, a Harvard history professor, agreed Mar. 16 with previous witnesses that efforts should be made to bring Communist China into more normal participation in international affairs.

Lindbeck said that the U.S. policy of isolating China had no purpose that he could see "as a political scientist." He said the current Chinese leaders, preoccupied with internal problems, were not "thinking about promoting revolutions around the world and plotting to extend their control over China's neighbors." Currently, he said, China was "more isolationist than internationalist." As for Vietnam, Lindbeck said: While China "would be very cautious" about committing its own troops, China's reaction would be an "open question" if the

Viet Cong and North Vietnamese faced defeat; he was "horrified by the thought that the manpower available to Hanoi and the Viet Cong might reach the point where they might have to call on others."

Schwartz said: "There would be a great danger of confrontation" with Communist China in the event of a Viet Cong-North Vietnamese defeat in South Vietnam; "my hopes would lie in the direction of de-escalation." He thought China would scale down its "grandiose ambitions" but would insist on recognition as a great power; he considered it unlikely that China would undertake any "wild military measures." "Wars of liberation" could not be successfully fed from outside the country in which they were being waged, and "the notion that the Chinese model of revolution is a kind of magic formula that will work everywhere in the 'underdeveloped world' once certain buttons are pressed in Peking is a notion based on the same fear of the diabolical cleverness of Communists which we used to direct to Moscow"; "I don't believe they are more clever than we are."

Further testimony that the U.S. should drop its opposition to diplomatic recognition and UN entry for Communist China was presented Mar. 18 by Dr. Morton M. Halperin of Harvard, Dr. Alexander Eckstein of the University of Michigan and retired Marine Brig. Gen. Samuel B. Griffith 2d, considered a leading expert on China's military power.

Griffith said: Communist China was "a paper tiger" and likely to remain one "for a decade or 2." China "cannot yet project conventional power beyond immediately peripheral areas." China's policy was "to remove our presence from Asia," and "her strategy . . . will be focused for the foreseeable future to attainment of this objective."

Eckstein said: Communist China was "expansionist at the verbal level but cautious at the action level." China's economic difficulties forced it "to pursue a relatively cautious foreign and domestic policy." The U.S. should change its "policy posture" and accept China "as a body politic, a society and an economy that seems to be here to stay. . . ."

Halperin said Mao Tse-tung's "image of what is going on in the '3d world' seems to be wildly out of touch with reality." "The 3d generation of Chinese leaders," he predicted, "may come to abandon their faith in this [Mao's] path to revolutionary power as it becomes clearer and clearer that it is doomed to failure."

Dr. Harold C. Hinton of George Washington University said Mar. 21 that Communist China was probably undertaking a "major rethinking of its foreign policy." He predicted "a long-term mellowing" of China's foreign policy "unless the United States gives China reason to act differently by relaxing its containment policy, which has already contributed substantially to moderating that foreign policy." He opposed U.S. recognition of Communist China or UN membership for China.

Dr. Donald S. Zagoria of Columbia University testified Mar. 21 that he favored U.S. recognition of Communist China and Chinese entry into the UN. He said "the effective containment of Communist China has been accomplished primarily by the Peking leadership itself." Zagoria asserted that North Vietnam had its own "hawks" and "doves" and that the U.S.' best hope for ending the Vietnamese war was to try to strengthen the "dove" group by sticking to the U.S. policy that the U.S. could not be forced out of Vietnam and that a military victory for the Viet Cong "is in fact impossible." Communist China "has consistently sought to strengthen Hanoi's hawks," he said, "and the Chinese Communists have recently expressed considerable apprehension that the Hanoi dove faction is, with Soviet backing, on the rise."

Testimony that the U.S. should not change its policy of isolation against Communist China was presented Mar. 28 by Prof. George E. Taylor of the University of Washington, Prof. David Nelson Rowe of Yale University and ex-Rep. Walter H. Judd (R., Minn.).

Taylor said: "At the present time there is no advantage to the United States in talking about [Communist China's] recognition or admission to the UN and there are a great many disadvantages." "Why help the Peking regime when it is in trouble?"

Rowe said Communist China should be barred from UN membership on "moral, legal and constitutional grounds."

Judd said the Communist regime "does not represent the Chinese people any more than the Quisling regime in Norway represented the Norwegian people." He opposed U.S. recognition of Communist China on the ground that it would undermine the Nationalist Chinese government and possibly open the door for communism in the Philippines.

Prof. Robert A. Scalapino of the University of California, editor of the monthly journal *Asian Survey,* asserted Mar. 30 that the U.S. should provide Communist China with "incentives for moderation" while maintaining "firm explicit deterrents" to aggression. He said: The U.S. "must find a way of making peaceful coexistence the only conceivable path for the next generation of Chinese leaders." Communist China should be confronted with "an elaborate structure of opportunities"— UN membership, recognition, commerce, cultural exchanges, etc.—to subject the Chinese leaders to pressures toward "moderation." On the other hand, the U.S. should emphasize that any external attempt to change the status of Taiwan or South Korea would be met with U.S. force. As for Vietnam, "nothing could be more calculated to pump life into the extremist movement within China and within the Communist world than a Maoist victory in Vietnam—and nothing would lead us more quickly into the awful choice between precipitous retreat everywhere and World War III." "It is highly unlikely China will intervene in the Vietnam war unless the obliteration of North Vietnam is threatened."

Prof. Hans J. Morgenthau, director of the Center for the Study of American Foreign Policy at the University of Chicago, favored ending the policy of isolation against Communist China but held Mar. 30 that this would have little effect on China. He said: China's isolation was largely "self-inflicted," and "our policy of isolation has nothing to do with it." The U.S. policy of military containment of Communist China was a "fundamental mistake" that could eventually lead to war. Instead, the U.S. should strengthen countries neighboring on China "politically, socially and economically" without asking in return "political and military alignments directed against China." The U.S.' retaliatory nuclear weapon capability, the ultimate instrument of containment as used in the containment policy against the Soviet Union, could be held in readiness against the "unlikely event" that China would undertake Asian or world conquest.

Policy Proposal: *'Containment Without Necessarily Isolation'*

While the Senate hearings on China were in progress, Vice Pres. Hubert H.Humphrey urged Mar. 13, 1966 that the U.S. policy toward Communist China be one of "containment without necessarily isolation." Interviewed on NBC-TV's "Meet the Press," Humphrey compared U.S. policy toward the Soviet Union in the 1950s with its current policy toward China. He said: The "program of responsible containment, the building of collective security in the West, but at the same time a probing and trying to find ways of communication, has been relatively successful, and I think it is in our interest and in the interest of humanity that the same kind of approach be exercised in Asia." Improved relations with China would require the retirement of the "Mao generation" from "positions of leadership. . . . In the meantime we ought to maintain . . . a spirit of friendship toward the Chinese people, but recognizing what the regime is, and making that regime understand they can not achieve their purpose by military power."

Humphrey stressed, however, that his remarks should not be interpreted to mean a change in the Administration's Vietnam policy. "It is in the interests of international peace," he declared, "that China be brought to understand that aggression is not a policy that can be pursued, that it is a dangerous policy in this nuclear age." He described the Senate Foreign

Relations Committee hearings on China as one of the "most fruitful procedures under way in this government." (His phrase "containment without necessarily isolation" was similar to words used by Columbia Prof. A. Doak Barnett Mar. 8 in testimony before the Senate committee.) Regarding UN membership for China, Humphrey said Western nations seemed more worried about it than Peking, which "doesn't worry about it at all."

Humphrey commended the current Administration decision (disclosed Mar. 9) to let scholars and writers visit Communist China and 4 other previously barred Communist nations. "It could be the beginning of a much better relationship," he predicted.

State Secy. Dean Rusk said at a Washington news conference Mar. 25 that the U.S. had been trying to improve relations with Peking by proposing exchanges of "newsmen, doctors and scholars and weather information." But, he declared, "we do not find at the present time a serious interest in Peking in improvement of relations." Replying to a question about Humphrey's "containment without necessarily isolation" statement, Rusk said: U.S. "commitments in the Pacific add up to the word 'containment.' . . . But on the question of isolation . . . we have made a number of efforts . . . with little or no response from the other side. A good deal of this isolation is self-imposed. . . ."

Rusk said Peking continued to insist on the "surrender [of] Formosa" as a condition of improved relations with the U.S. He pointed out that Communist China had also "indicated" that the "expulsion of the Republic of [Nationalist] China [from the UN] is essential if Peking is to consider" becoming a UN member. Rusk said that recognition of Mongolia was thought about by the Johnson Administration "from time to time, and we do have that in mind as one of the questions on our agenda." Rusk denied the Chinese Communist charge that the U.S. and the USSR had joined in a "plot" to encircle China; he said, however, that both the U.S. and the USSR "take a rather gloomy view of war, because we understand what it could mean."

Jenmin Jih Pao Mar. 29 rejected U.S. proposals for an exchange of scholars and newsmen. The paper said the U.S. was "feigning eagerness to improve relations to detract . . . attention" from plans to wage war with China. Improved relations with the U.S. were "out of the question," it said, until the U.S. pulled out of Formosa and removed the 7th Fleet from its defense of the island.

The newspaper charged editorially Apr. 6 that the U.S. was "planning a war in Asia." The editorial noted that the Chinese Foreign Ministry Apr. 5 had issued its "400th serious warning" about U.S. "crimes of aggression . . . [involving violations] of China's territorial waters and air space." (A spokesman for the Foreign Ministry had charged Apr. 5 that a U.S. ship had "intruded" in territorial waters off Fukien Province opposite Taiwan.) The editorial said that since Sept. 1958, "361 intrusions into China's territorial waters by 443 United States warships have been recorded, and 487 United States airplanes have intruded into China's air space on 314 occasions." These "provocations have been growing in intensity, frequency and scope every year," the editorial charged. The U.S. "is . . . constantly threatening China with war." The editorial said: The U.S. had "recently" hinted that it "wants to 'improve' . . . relations and adopt a 'flexible policy' toward China." These "hints of 'goodwill' . . . are very obviously . . . an attempt to undermine the Chinese people's fighting determination and their combat readiness." The U.S. had "built a 'new crescent cordon' in the Asian and Pacific regions extending from South Korea, through Japan, Taiwan, the Philippines, South Vietnam, Thailand, Malaysia and all the way to India." U.S. efforts to destroy China through either "military intimidation" or "peaceful evolution" were "useless" or a "pipedream." "The evidence is increasingly clear that the United States imperialists are preparing to impose war on the Chinese people." "Therefore, we must be prepared for a war they [the U.S.] may start at some later date, and be even more prepared for a smallscale war. An early war means one that will have to be fought this year or next. A largescale war means one in which the United States imperialists will use all their strength, sending a few million or even 10 million troops to China." China had grown "stronger in the last 10 years," and the U.S. "had grown weaker." China was prepared for a "possible sudden attack by United States imperialism."

Chinese Premier Chou En-lai, when interviewed by Ejaz Husain of the Pakistan newspaper *Dawn* Apr. 10, made a 4-point statement on Communist China's policy toward the U.S. The text of the 4 points, as published in the May 13 edition of Communist China's English-language *Peking Review:*

(1) China will not take the initiative to provoke a war with the United States. China has not sent any troops to Hawaii; it is the United States that has occupied China's territory of Taiwan Province. Nevertheless, China has been making efforts in demanding, through negotiations, that the United States withdraw all its armed forces from Taiwan Province and the Taiwan Straits, and she has held talks with the United States for more than ten years, first in Geneva and then in Warsaw, on this question of principle, which admits of no concession whatsoever. All this serves as a very good proof.

(2) The Chinese mean what they say. In other words, if any country in Asia, Africa or elsewhere meets with aggression by the imperialists headed by the United States, the Chinese government and people definitely will give it support and help. Should such just action bring on U.S. aggression against China, we will unhesitatingly rise in resistance and fight to the end.

(3) China is prepared. Should the United States impose a war on China, it can be said with certainty that, once in China, the United States will not be able to pull out, however many men it may send over and whatever weapons it may use, nuclear weapons included. Since the 14 million people of southern Vietnam can cope with over 200,000 U.S. troops, the 650 million people of China can undoubtedly cope with 10 million of them. No matter how many U.S. aggressor troops may come, they will certainly be annihilated in China.

(4) Once the war breaks out, it will have no boundaries. Some U.S. strategists want to bombard China by relying on their air and naval superiority and avoid a ground war. This is wishful thinking. Once the war gets started with air or sea action, it will not be for the United States alone to decide how the war will continue. If you can come from the sky, why can't we fight back on the ground? That is why we say the war will have no boundaries once it breaks out.

The U.S. took a unilateral step toward opening contacts with the Chinese on the mainland. The State Department disclosed Apr. 14 that U.S. universities that had requested permission to invite Communist Chinese scholars and scientists to the U.S. had been given permission to do so. Earlier State Department steps towards easing travel restrictions applied only to American citizens desiring to travel to China. A State Department spokesman said that "implicit" in the earlier decisions relaxing travel bans on Americans was the possibility that Chinese scholars and scientists would be able to come to the U.S. The spokesman said that Peking had been told directly of the U.S.' decision: "They have been advised that the United States government has discussed this principle with universities and is agreeable that American universities can invite Chinese scholars and scientists." (The Chinese reportedly had been informed at the last meeting [in Warsaw Mar.16] of U.S. Amb.-to-Poland John A. Gronouski and Chinese Amb. Wang Kuo-chuang.) The spokesman said the U.S. hoped that the visits would be on a reciprocal basis but that the U.S. would not insist.

The Chinese Communist Hsinhua news agency announced Apr. 17 that a Chinese Foreign Ministry spokesman had rejected the U.S. offer to permit Chinese scholars and scientists to visit the U.S. He called it "a fraud." He said: "It is obvious" that the U.S. government's goal was "to deceive the American people and world opinion and and exploit the American people's friendly sentiments for China." "The Chinese people are friendly towards the American people, and, like the American people, they want to see friendly contacts between the 2 peoples realized at an early date." But the U.S. government followed a "policy of hostility towards China" in Taiwan and Vietnam.

State Secy. Rusk indicated in remarks made public Apr. 16 that the Johnson Administration was seeking ways of lessening the antagonism between the U.S. and Communist China. His views were made known in testimony presented Mar. 16 at a closed session of the Far East Subcommittee of the House Foreign Affairs Committee and released by the subcommittee

Apr. 16. In his testimony, Rusk reviewed U.S. relations with Communist China since 1949, assessed Communist China's current foreign policy aims and submitted a 10-point statement of U.S. policy towards Peking. *Among Rusk's remarks:*

• "We look forward hopefully—and confidently—to a time in the future when the government of mainland China will permit the restoration of historic ties of friendship between the people of mainland China and ourselves." But "today we and Peiping are as far apart on matters of fundamental policy as we were 17 years ago."

• China's 3 major foreign objectives appeared to be (1) "to bring China on the world stage as a great power," (2) to achieve "dominance within Asia" and (3) to win the "leadership of the world Communist revolution."

• China's development of "nuclear weapons and missile development systems" could be used to "intimidate" Asian nations into "breaking defense alliances with the United States or . . . [could be used] in an attempt to create a nuclear 'balance' in Asia in which Peiping's potentially almost unlimited conventional forces might be used with increased effect."

• Since the Korean war, "Peiping has moved only against weaker foes . . . carefully avoid[ing] situations which might bring it face to face with the United States." "It is true that they [the Chinese leaders] have been more cautious in what they do themselves than in what they have urged the Soviet Union to do." "But it does not follow that we should disregard the intentions and plans for the future which they have proclaimed."

• "The Sino-Soviet dispute [had] a flavor and an intensity which rival even the current Chinese antagonism for the United States itself."

Rusk listed these "10 elements" of U.S. policy toward Communist China:

(1) "We must remain firm in our determination to help those allied nations which seek our help to resist the direct

or indirect use of threat or force against their territory by Peiping."

(2) "We must continue to assist the countries of Asia in building broadly based effective governments, devoted to progressive economic and social policies, which can better withstand Asian Communist pressures. . . ."

(3) "We must honor our commitments to . . . [Nationalist China]."

(4) "We will continue our efforts to prevent the expulsion of . . . [Nationalist China] from the United Nations or its agencies."

(5) "We should continue our efforts to reassure Peiping that the United States does not intend to attack mainland China. There are, of course, risks of war with China. It was true in 1950. It was true in the Taiwan Straits crisis of 1955 and 1956. It was true in the Chinese Communist drive into Indian territory in 1962. It is true today in Vietnam. But we do not want war. There is no fatal inevitability of war with Communist China. The Chinese Communists have . . . acted with caution when they foresaw a collision with the United States. We have acted with restraint and care in the past, and we are doing so today. I hope that they will realize this and guide their actions accordingly."

(6) "There is nothing eternal about the policies and attitudes of Communist China. We must avoid assuming the existence of an unending and inevitable state of hostility between ourselves and the rulers of mainland China."

(7) "Without jeopardizing other U.S. interests, we should continue to enlarge the possibilities for unofficial contacts between Communist China and ourselves. American libraries may freely purchase Chinese Communist publications. American citizens may send and receive mail from the mainland. We have in the past indicated that if the Chinese themselves were interested in purchasing grain we would consider such sales. We have indicated our willingness to allow Chinese Communist newspapermen to come to the United States. We are prepared

to permit American universities to invite Chinese Communist scientists to visit their institutions. . . . [Despite these efforts,] all the evidence suggests Peiping wishes to remain isolated from the United States. But we believe it is in our interests that such channels be opened and kept open. We believe contact and communications are not incompatible with a firm policy of containment."

(8) "We should keep open our direct diplomatic contacts with Peiping in Warsaw."

(9) "We are prepared to . . . [discuss] disarmament and nonproliferation of nuclear weapons [with China]. Peiping has rejected all suggestions and invitations to join in such talks."

(10) "We must continue to explore and analyze all available information on Communist China and keep our own policies up to date."

The Hsinhua news agency Apr. 18 described Rusk's "10 elements" as "a mixture of hostility to China and deception." It said: "The real [U.S.] aim is to be hostile to and launch aggression against China and to contain and encircle it. All talk of 'improving' relations and 'avoidance' of a state of hostility are a sham."

Rusk's statement was also criticized Apr. 18 by Tao Hsisheng, adviser to Nationalist Chinese Pres. Chiang Kai-shek. Tao said in Taipei that the U.S. hope for a change in Peking's policy "is perhaps an illusion born out of the tremendous pressure put on the Johnson Administration by appeasement-minded elements in the United States." It was a "mistake," declared Tao, to believe that the "Chinese Communist leaders after Mao Tse-tung will be more moderate."

CHINA'S GROWING ISOLATION (1966)

The Rise of Lin Piao

The war in Vietnam, added to the Sino-Soviet dispute, compounded Communist China's strategic and diplomatic problems. China confronted at once the super-powers as its adversaries with more will than power. Dissent from the Maoist foreign policy was voiced in a veiled form by Army Chief of Staff Lo Jui-ching. In an article published in *Hung Chi* (Red Flag) May 10, 1965, commemorating the 20th anniversary of VE Day, Lo praised Soviet contributions to World War II and asserted that the Soviet strategy in fighting Nazi Germany was applicable to the current situation in Vietnam. Lo excoriated the pre-World War II European statesmen Chamberlain and Daladier because they had refused to cooperate with the Soviet Union when the latter proposed to send troops across Poland. The implication of this criticism was that Chairman Mao Tse-tung and his followers who opposed cooperation with the Soviet Union were making a similar mistake.

Not long after this article had been published, Lo was quietly removed from his position. The Maoist faction headed by Defense Min. Lin Piao prevailed over the pragmatically-minded professionals in the high echelons of the People's Liberation Army. Lin's ascendancy was marked by his Sept. 3, 1965 speech: "Long Live the Victory of People's War."

Lin's speech stressed the importance of self-reliance: "The liberation of the masses is accomplished by the masses themselves—this is a basic principle of Marxism-Leninism. Revolution or people's war in any country is the business of the masses in that country and should be carried out primarily by their own efforts; there is no other way." External assistance, Lin asserted, was not needed in defense of China. The U.S. nuclear threat could be met by a Chinese "spiritual atom bomb." If the

U.S. should invade China, its invading forces would find themselves submerged in "the vast ocean of several hundred million Chinese people in arms."

A report published Jan. 19, 1966 in the Chinese Communist Party newspaper *Jenmin Jih Pao* indicated that a conflict had developed between army professionals and Communist Party members over control of the Chinese army. The report, reaffirming party control, had been adopted at a 20-day conference of the general political department of the Chinese Liberation Army. (The conference, on the political work of the army, concluded Jan. 18.) The report had been prepared by Hsiao Hua, chief of the department. It was republished Jan. 25 in all Peking newspapers and broadcast on radio the same day. (Hsiao Hua had been a general in the Chinese army until May 25, 1965, when the Chinese National Assembly abolished all ranks in a move "to create equality between the officers and men.")

The Hsiao report said: The basic problem was "whether the gun will direct the party or the party will direct the gun." It was a mistake to believe that the army and the party were of equal importance and to conclude that each "should be given first place in turn." The army had become "vain" and "self-satisfied" after 12 years of peace since the Korean War. It was therefore necessary to "keep politics in the fore, strengthen our political and ideological work, arm all our commanders and fighters with Mao Tse-tung's thinking, insure absolute leadership by the party over the army, make our army the party's most responsive instrument, which most faithfully carries out its line, its principles and its policies, thus insuring that the guns are always in the hands of the most reliable people." It was essential to eliminate "all kinds of bourgeois thinking in military matters."

According to Hsiao: China could expect the U.S. to attack. "Modern revisionists" were "shamelessly" aiding the U.S., thereby increasing the chances of war. China would have to "make full preparations against the war of aggression which

U.S. imperialism may launch at an early date, on a large scale, with nuclear or other weapons, and on several fronts." "We will also resolutely support and help the people of other countries in their struggle against U.S. imperialism." To say that "weapons decide everything" would be to admit that victory was unattainable. China's population and ideological superiority constituted a "moral atom bomb" giving China "absolute supremacy." If the U.S. were to attack China, "we can definitely drown the U.S. aggressors in an ocean of people's war."

Lin Piao's growing importance within the Chinese leadership was highlighted in the June 19 issue of *Jenmin Jih Pao*. The paper published a letter, signed by Lin and dated Mar. 11, 1966, in which Lin called for increased study and application of Mao Tse-tung's thought. The letter, given a banner headline, was republished in the June 24 issue of *Peking Review*. Lin's leadership of the People's Liberation Army had been hailed by *Hung Chi* in an editorial published June 13. The editorial said: Lin had "initiated a movement in the People's Liberation Army for the creative study and application of Chairman Mao's works. . . . Energetic emulation of the Liberation Army has become a universal call to action for all the people and all endeavors. In this emulation, the fundamental point is to learn from the Liberation Army how they persistently place Mao Tse-tung's thought in the forefront in all works and to learn from Comrade Lin Piao's extremely important instructions on the creative study and application of Chairman Mao's works."

Monitored radio broadcasts from China June 10 had urged the Chinese people to "follow the instruction of the Military Commission and Comrade Lin Piao." (Lin headed the Military Affairs Commission of the armed forces.) *Jenmin Jih Pao* July 1, in an editorial commemorating the 45th anniversary of the founding of the Chinese Communist Party, again hailed the "People's Liberation Army" for "launch[ing] the movement to creatively study and apply . . . Mao's works, in response to the call issued by the Military Commission of the Central Committee of the Party and Comrade Lin Piao."

External Complications for China

The ascendancy of the Maoist faction boded ill for China's external relations. This became apparent at the first Tri-Continental Conference of Asian, African and Latin American Revolutionary Solidarity which met in Havana Jan. 3-15, 1966.

The Communist-dominated Havana conference was sponsored by the Afro-Asian Peoples Solidarity Organization (AAPSO). At its 4th meeting, in Accra in Apr. 1965, AAPSO had decided to call its next meeting for Havana to consider inviting Latin America into a proposed Afro-Asian & Latin American Peoples Solidarity Organization (AALAPSO). Delegates to the Havana conference represented governments, opposition parties and revolutionary guerrilla movements. The meeting was highlighted by Sino-Soviet rivalry for control of revolutionary movements throughout the world. The Soviet delegation, headed by Sharaf R. Rashidov, first secretary of the Uzbek Communist Party, backed the creation of the proposed AALAPSO, reportedly because most Latin American Communist parties followed the Moscow line in the Sino-Soviet dispute. (The *N.Y. Times* had reported Dec. 31, 1965 that the USSR was paying for airline passage for many African and Asian delegates—some of whom departed for Havana from Moscow or Prague following consultations with Soviet officials.)

Decision on a permanent AALAPSO was deferred until the 2d Tri-Continental Conference of Asian, African & Latin American Revolutionary Solidarity, which was tentatively scheduled for Cairo in 1968. (AAPSO's 1967 meeting was scheduled to take place in Peking.) Reuters reported Jan. 15 that the postponement, a compromise proposed by Arab delegations, was adopted because China had threatened to walk out of the proposed AALAPSO. But the conferees Jan. 13 approved Havana as the temporary headquarters of a tricontinental secretariat to promote world revolution. The 13-nation secretariat would include 4 nations each from Asia, Africa and Latin America;

Cuba would be the 13th member, and a Cuban was to be secretary general.

The major issues debated at the conference were the Vietnam war, U.S. policy in the Dominican Republic and colonialism and neo-colonialism throughout the world. Chinese delegate Wu Hsueh-tsien charged Jan. 5 that the Soviet Union collaborated with the U.S. He called for more liberation wars and warned that U.S. "imperialism will not fall until it is felled."

Peking claimed a major victory in this conference over the Soviet Union. *Jenmin Jih Pao* said in an editorial Jan. 18 that "the true colors of the Khrushchev revisionists, with their maneuvers of sham anti-imperialism, sham support and sham unity, were further exposed, and their capitulationist and divisive line met with ignominious failure."

But in fact Peking's perception of its success contrasted starkly with its strained relations with other nations. China's relations with Cuba were a case in point. The day before the Havana conference opened, Cuban Premier Fidel Castro had revealed that Communist China had decided to reduce sharply its rice exports to Cuba and its sugar imports from Cuba in 1966. As a result, Castro said, it would be necessary to cut Cuban rice rations. Castro made his announcement Jan. 2 at a rally on Revolution Plaza celebrating the 7th anniversary of his revolution. This was Castro's first disclosure to Cubans of the 2-year deterioration in relations between his regime and Communist China. Castro said that the Chinese had cited these reasons for reducing their trade with Cuba: (1) Domestic sugar production had increased. (2) A 1961 USSR loan of 500,000 tons of sugar had been repaid; therefore, imports of Cuban sugar for reshipment to the USSR were unnecessary. (3) China had to stockpile rice "reserves in case of an imperialist attack," and the rice would also be needed in Vietnam.

Castro declared: "I thought this was a long-term proposition, but the other party did not understand it thus. . . ." "We have no resources to buy rice in other countries." "We now find we have only half the rice we had in 1964."

China replied to Castro Jan. 9 in a broadcast by Hsinhua. Quoting a "responsible official" in the Chinese Foreign Trade Ministry, Hsinhua denied that a long-term agreement had been signed to supply rice to Cuba in return for sugar. According to Hsinhua: Castro Oct. 1, 1964, had suggested a yearly exchange of 370,000 tons of sugar for 250,000 tons of rice. China "agreed to supply Cuba with 250,000 tons of rice . . . [in] 1965 but did not promise to supply the same amount each year or accept his [Castro's] proposed rate of exchange between sugar and rice." "Obviously, Premier Castro's idea that China was going to supply Cuba with 250,000 tons of rice yearly on a long-term basis was groundless." Cuba had demanded 285,000 tons of rice in 1966, and China had offered 135,000 tons, the amount shipped in 1964. A Cuban trade delegation was "still in Peking," and "preliminary negotiations" for the "annual protocol" were in process. Castro had "unilaterally and untruthfully made public contents of preliminary trade negotiations now going on between the governmental departments of the 2 countries."

It was reported from Moscow Feb. 1 that an anti-Chinese "memorandum" was being circulated to Communist Party cells throughout the USSR in preparation for the 23d Congress of the Soviet Communist Party, scheduled for Mar. 29. The memo contained speeches by top members of the Central Committee Presidium of the party— First Secy. Leonid I. Brezhnev, Premier Aleksei N. Kosygin, Pres. Nikolai V. Podgorny, Aleksandr N. Shelepin and Anastas I. Mikoyan—at party district meetings held in Moscow Jan. 25. The memo reportedly charged that China had provoked 150 Sino-Soviet border incidents in 1965, had conducted subversion along the Sinkiang-Soviet border, had directed a propaganda campaign by mail at Soviet citizens and was trying to persuade the USSR to open a 2d front or conduct some diversion to aid the Viet Cong. It was said that Podgorny had complained that the Vietnam conflict was the only hindrance to improved U.S.-Soviet relations.

Peking's first public reference to the scheduled 23d Congress of the Soviet Communist Party was made Feb. 6 by

Hsinhua. Hsinhua charged that the purpose of the 23d Congress was "to impose the revisionist line defended by the 5th column of American imperialism into the heart of the international Communist movement." "It is inconceivable," Hsinhua said, "to have any international conference with traitors. To participate at such a meeting would aid the traitors and permit them to save face."

Communist China Feb. 22 disclosed to its own people—for the first time—its growing rift with Cuba. Chinese news media charged that Castro had "added his voice to the anti-China chorus."

Elsewhere Communist China experienced more serious setbacks. In Indonesia, where Peking had had a staunch ally in the government of Pres. Sukarno, an army coup Oct. 1965 ousted the Indonesian Communist Party (PKI) from power. As Communist China was believed to have aided the Communist-dominated rebel forces, mob violence turned on Peking's embassy, consulates and information centers.

In Africa, pro-Peking regimes fell in succession. There was a coup in Dahomey Dec. 22, 1965, followed by the breaking off of Dahomey's diplomatic relations with Peking Jan. 3, 1966. Another coup unseated the pro-Peking regime of the Central African Republic Jan. 1, 1966. The new government Jan. 6 closed the Chinese embassy and ordered the embassy staff to leave the country within 2 days. Still another coup overthrew Dr. Kwame Nkrumah, the president of Ghana, Feb. 24, 1966, during Nkrumah's state visit to Peking.

Admitting these setbacks, *Jenmin Jih Pao* declared Mar. 1: "Under certain circumstances a counterattack mounted by imperialists and reactionaries may gain the upperhand for the time being, but this will raise still higher the political consciousness of the people and mobilize still greater numbers, thereby helping the revolutionary movement to grow in depth and scope on its onward march."

The Great Proletarian Cultural Revolution

A new revolutionary movement surfaced in China and engulfed China in turmoil for the next 2 years. Officially

designated "the Great Proletarian Cultural Revolution," it
seems to have been touched off with the publication of an article
Apr. 3, 1966 in *Liberation Daily* and *Wen Hui Pao,* both based
in Shanghai. The article was critical of Wu Han, the author
of "Dismissal of Hai Jui" and a deputy mayor of Peking. With
Jenmin Jih Pao joining in the attack on Wu Apr. 7, the campaign spread to Peking. The paper ran 3 editorials Apr. 6, 14
and 22 against "political degenerates" who claimed to be
"scholars" and "specialists."

For the first time since Nov. 1965 Chairman Mao Tse-tung
appeared in public May 10 when he greeted the visiting Albanian
leader Mehmet Shehu. The picture of the greeting carried in
Jenmin Jih Pao did not show Liu Shao-chi, the head of state.
An anticipated purge came to light with the announcement June
3 of the dismissal of Peng Chen, mayor of Peking and a member of the Politburo. A Hsinhua broadcast June 5 said that a
group of students at Peking University "sounded the first vol-
ley of guns in the great cultural revolution" May 25 by mounting wall posters against university officials.

Other dismissals announced June 3 by Peking radio included those of Lu Ping, president of Peking University, and
Peng Pei-yung, a member of the higher education department
of the Peking Municipal Committee. Both were charged with
shielding intellectuals at the university who had allegedly been
involved in the "anti-party" activities of Teng To, Wu Han
and Liao Mo-sha. Replacing Teng on the Peking committee was
Wu Teh, a member of the Communist Party Central Committee. The new leadership of the Peking Municipal Committee
announced June 6 the dismissal of Mrs. Fan Chin, director of
Peking Jih Pao and *Peking Wan Pao,* and the temporary suspension of publication of *Chienhsien.* Chai Hsiang-tung was appointed director, with Wu Hsiang and Lin Ching as his deputies.
The Peking committee also announced June 6 that a work team
headed by Chang Cheng-hsien would be "sent to Peking University to lead the great Socialist cultural revolution." It said
that "the work team will function as the Peking University

Party Committee during its reorganization. *Peking Jih Pao* June 6 denounced Yang Shu, then head of the political section of the Philosophy & Social Science Department of the Chinese Academy of Sciences, as a member of the "gangster inn" that included Teng To.

The announcements of the purge of the Peking Municipal Committee of the party and of Peking University were accompanied by massive street demonstrations in Peking June 3-7. Students, many of whom reportedly came from other Chinese cities for the demonstrations, massed outside Peking University June 5 shouting "Long Live Mao Tse-tung," clashing cymbals and beating drums. The university buildings were covered with large posters denouncing ex-Pres. Lu Ping. Demonstrations June 7 centered on the editorial offices of *Peking Jih Pao*.

The Central Committee and the State Council decided jointly June 13 to revise the procedure for admission to Chinese universities. The text of the decision, reprinted in the June 24 issue of *Peking Review,* said the change would be made to "ensure the successful carying out of the cultural revolution to the end." The announcement said: "A decision had been made to change the old system of entrance examination in higher educational institutions and to postpone this year's enrollment of new students for colleges and universities for half a year." The old method of examinations and enrollment "has failed . . . to free itself from the set pattern of the bourgeois system of examination" and was "harmful" to policy "formulated by the Central Committee of the Party and Chairman Mao and to absorption into the higher educational institutions of a still greater number of revolutionary young people from among workers, peasants and soldiers."

Hsinhua said June 24 that the former system of examination had been used by "anti-party bourgeois authorities" to keep students with proletarian or peasant backgrounds out of the universities.

Peking radio reported June 16 that Kuang Ya-ming, director of Nanking University, had been dismissed for conspiring to "suppress the revolutionary movement." *Jenmin Jih Pao* reported June 21 that Chang Wen-sung, head of the education department in the Peking Municipal Committee, had been dismissed for supporting the "educational line of modern revisionism." Sian city radio announced June 24 that a party secretary in the Sian Communications University had been ousted for attempting to keep demonstrators supporting the "cultural revolution" off the campus. It was reported from Hong Kong July 10 that Ko Lin, president of Canton's Sun Yat-sen Medical College, and his deputy, Liu Chih-ming, had been dismissed and that Li Ta, president of Wuhan University, was under attack.

Hung Chi, the party theoretical journal, warned June 13 in an article titled "Long Live the Great Proletariat Revolution" that a "reactionary bourgeoisie" threatened the "dictatorship of the proletariat" in China. The proletarian dictatorship, said the article, could not be safely established "unless a proletarian cultural revolution is carried out . . . to eradicate bourgeois ideology." The article cited the example of the Soviet Union, after Stalin's death, as a case in which the proletarian dictatorship had been "subverted" in a "palace coup" by "the Khrushchev revisionist group." In China, the article stated, the Communist Party "may change color and hundreds of people may lose their lieves" unless precautions were taken to prevent a "spontaneous outburst of burgeois strength."

Foreign Min. Chen Yi said at a conference of African and Asian writers in Peking June 27 that foreign enemies of China were mistaken if they believed they could benefit from the "cultural revolution" going on in China. He challenged the USSR and the U.S. to start "cultural revolutions" of their own.

Hsinhua reported July 10 that Lu Ting-yi, head of the propaganda department of the party's Central Committee, had been replaced by another Central Committee member, Tao Chu. The disclosure, similar to that of Peng Chen's dismissal, did not mention Lu. It merely listed the officials attending a conference of African and Asian writers; among them the name of Tao Chu appeared as head of the propaganda department.

Lu, 59, who had been an alternate member of the Politburo of the Central Committee and deputy premier in the State Council (*i.e.,* the government), ranked among the top 20 leaders of China. He became the 2d highest official ousted in the purge. Tao Chu, 60, first secretary of the CCP Central-South China Bureau, had been director of the Political Department of the 4th Field Army in 1949 when it was commanded by Lin Piao, currently defense minister. When Lin assumed command of the Central-South military region in 1950, Tao became political director of the army in the region. The *N.Y. Times* reported July 11 that during the last year Tao had been spearheading a cultural program that stressed "contemporary revolutionary themes" in opposition to operas and plays based on traditional themes from pre-revolutionary China.

U.S. Response: Call for a More Open China

The internal developments in China were watched carefully by puzzled officials in Washington. Answering a reporter's question as to whether "winds of change" were blowing in Peking, State Secy. Dean Rusk said at his press conference July 12, 1966: "Well we know that there are changes occuring in mainland China. The exact character and significance of those changes are not entirely clear. But we do not see those changes resulting in hands extended to other nations in the direction of peace."

Pres. Johnson made what White House officials called his first major statement on Communist China July 12. In an address at a meeting of the American Alumni Council in White Sulphur Springs, W. V., televised from the White House as Johnson delivered it by phone, the President assured Peking that the U.S. sought a "peace of conciliation," not of "conquest" in Asia. He asserted that "Asia is now a crucial arena of man's striving for independence and order—and for life itself." Although the U.S. had "a very big stake" in every region of the world, "nowhere are the [U.S.] stakes higher than in Asia," he said. "If peace fails there, nowhere else will our achievements be really secure."

"By peace in Asia," Johnson said, "I do not mean simply the absence of armed hostilities, for wherever men hunger and hate there can really be no peace. I do not mean the peace of conquest, for humiliation can be the seed-bed of war. I do not mean simply the peace of the conference table, for peace is not really written merely in the words of treaties. . . . The peace that we seek in Asia is a peace of conciliation between Communist states and their non-Communist neighbors; . . . between men whose skins are brown and black and yellow and white; between Hindus and Moslems and Buddhists and Christians." "The foundations for such a peace in Asia are being laid tonight as never before," the President, said, but "they must be built on these essentials: First is the determination of the United States to meet our obligations in Asia as a Pacific power. . . . The 2d . . . [is] to prove to aggressive nations that the use of force to conquer others is really a losing game. . . . The 3d essential is the building of political and economic strength among the nations of free Asia. . . . And there is a 4th essential for peace in Asia which may seem the most difficult of all: reconciliation between nations that now call themselves enemies. A peaceful mainland China is central to a peaceful Asia. A hostile China must be discouraged from aggression. A misguided China must be encouraged toward understanding of the outside world and toward policies of peaceful cooperation. For lasting peace can never come to Asia as long as the 700 million people of mainland China are isolated by their rulers from the outside world."

"For many years now," Johnson declared, "the United States has attemped in vain to persuade the Chinese Communists to agree to an exchange of newsmen as one of the first steps to increased understanding between our people. . . . We have taken steps to permit American scholars, experts in medicine and public health and other specialists to travel to Communist China. And only today we . . . cleared a passport for a leading American businessman to exchange knowledge with Chinese mainland leaders in Red China. All of these initiatives except the actions today have been rejected by Communist China. And we persist. . . . We persist because we believe that even the most rigid societies will some day . . . awaken to the rich possibilities of a diverse world. And we continue because we believe that cooperation, not hostility, is really the way of the future in the 20th century."

Johnson reiterated his explanation of why the U.S. was fighting in Vietnam: "We're there because we are trying to make the Communists of North Vietnam stop shooting at their neighbors; because we are trying to make this Communist aggression unprofitable; because we are trying to demonstrate that guerrilla warfare, inspired by one nation against another nation, just can never succeed. . . . I want the Communists in Hanoi to know where we stand: 'First, victory for your armies is impossible. You cannot drive us from South Vietnam. . . . 2d, the minute that you realize that a military victory is out of the question and you turn from the use of force, you will find us ready and willing to reciprocate.' . . ."

The State Department disclosed July 12 that the businessman Johnson had cited as receiving a passport for China was G. William Miller, president of Textron, Inc. of Providence, R. I. Communist China so far had not indicated whether it would give him a visa. In the 3d relaxation since Dec. 1965 of restrictions on travel by Americans, the State Department had announced July 11 that it would let Americans in "cultural, athletic, commercial, educational, public affairs and other fields" go to mainland China, Albania, Cuba, North Korea and North Vietnam if their trips "would be of benefit to the United States." The China Travel Service in Hong Kong, a Communist Chinese agency, confirmed July 11 that China had temporarily stopped admitting most types of foreign visitors. It was reported in Hong Kong that the step apparently was decided on in June during the political purge on the mainland. Hundreds of tentatively approved visas were reported suspended by the Chinese, and only foreigners whose presence was considered essential to China were being admitted.

The U.S. government came to view the Cultural Revolution essentially as a struggle for power within the Chinese Communist Party. Defense Secy. Robert McNamara, in an interview with Japanese journalist Kei Wakaizumi July 15, said: "We see Red China as now undergoing great change. Her leaders are currently involved in what appears to be a leadership struggle whose outcome is uncertain." Pres. Johnson voiced a similar view July 23 in an address at the Soldiers & Sailors Monument at Indianapolis, Ind. He said: "Inside Communist China there is a struggle for power. There is a great debate going on today on the future policy. It is obvious that their past policies have failed. In time, we hope and we believe, the mainland Chinese will come to terms with their neighbors and the rest of the world."

China Continues Atomic Tests

Notwithstanding the political ferment, Communist China moved ahead with its nuclear arms program. It detonated its 3d nuclear device May 9, 1966 at its Sinkiang Province test site near Lob Nor. Hsinhua reported that at "4 p.m. [Peking time] . . . China successfully conducted over its western areas a nuclear explosion which contained thermonuclear material." This was the first Chinese claim of the use of "thermonuclear material" in a test. The May 9 test, like China's 2 earlier tests, was conducted in the atmosphere.

The Hsinhua announcement, similar to the statements issued after China's earlier tests, hailed the "explosion" as a "new important achievement scored by the Chinese people in their efforts to further strengthen their national defense and safeguard the security of their country and the peace of the world." The success of the test was called a tribute to China's "People's Liberation Army," to its "scientists, technicians . . . workers, functionaries, who, under the correct leadership of the Communist Party of China and holding still higher the great red banner of Mao Tse-tung's thought, gave prominence to politics . . . and adhered to the '4 firsts.'"

In a footnote, Hsinhua explained the "4 firsts": "First place must be given to man in handling the relationship between man and weapons; to political work in handling the relationship between political and other work; to ideological work in relation to other aspects of political work; and, in ideological work, to the ideas currently in a person's mind as distinguished from ideas in books."

Hsinhua said: "China's purpose in conducting necessary and limited nuclear tests and in developing nuclear weapons is to oppose the nuclear blackmail and threats of U.S. imperialism . . . and to oppose the U.S.-Soviet collusion for maintaining nuclear monopoly and sabotaging the revolutionary struggles of all oppressed peoples and nations." China's "possession of nuclear weapons is a great encouragement to the peoples who are fighting . . . for their own liberation as well as a new contribution to the defense of world peace."

China repeated its proposal, made following its first and 2d tests, for "a summit conference of all countries of the world to discuss the complete prohibition and thorough destruction of nuclear weapons." The announcement said: The U.S., "in disregard of the statements of . . . [China,] continued to develop and mass produce nuclear weapons . . . , further expanded its nuclear bases all over the world and stepped up its nuclear blackmail and threats against China and the whole world." China's "sole purpose in developing nuclear weapons is defense, and her ultimate aim is to eliminate nuclear weapons. . . . [At] no time and in no circumstances will China be the first to use nuclear weapons." China was "convinced that a nuclear war can be prevented" if "all peace-loving . . . countries work together and persevere in the struggle."

Technical estimates of the nature of the Chinese test, aside from the Chinese announcement that the test "contained thermonuclear material," came principally from U.S. agencies. A State Department spokesman May 9 said the yield from the test was "in the same general range" as China's earlier 2 tests. (The first 2 had been in the low-yield range, *i.e.,* producing a blast force equivalent to less thon 20,000 tons of TNT, or 20 kilotons.) But the State Department May 11 increased its estimate of the yield to about 130 kilotons, thereby placing it in the low-intermediate range (20-200 kilotons).

The Atomic Energy Commission May 13 released a statement that did not estimate the size of the Chinese test but did say that Communist China had not produced a hydrogen bomb explosion. The AEC statement said: "Preliminary debris analysis indicated the 3d Chinese nuclear test on May 9 was not a thermonuclear weapon. The test was probably an experimental device, either attempting to increase the yield of the previous low-yield fission device [*i.e.,* an atomic bomb with a blast force of less than 20 kilotons] or looking toward an eventual theremonuclear capability. Specifically, the device employed enriched uranium, the same fissionable material that was used in the previous Chinese tests. It did not contain plutonium. The thermonuclear material, lithium-6, was present, although its specific function in the device is not yet clear."

Another AEC statement declared May 20: "Information now available . . . indicates that the yield [of the May 9 test] was in the lower end of the intermediate range." (The intermediate range was 200,000 to 1 million tons of TNT, or 200 kilotons to one megaton.) The AEC's May 20 statement, by re-estimating the force produced by the Chinese test to about 10 times the force originally estimated by the State Department, led to renewed speculation that the Chinese had achieved some form of thermonuclear reaction.

The *N.Y. Times* reported May 21 that the presence of the thermonuclear material lithium-6 in the test, in addition to the yield of the explosion, indicated that a thermonuclear reaction had occurred because a yield of more than 200 kilotons was greater than that usually obtained from just a fission bomb. According to the *Times:* The largest fission bomb ever tested by the U.S. at its Nevada test site had a yield of 74 kilotons. It was conceivable that the Chinese had achieved the 200-kiloton explosion using a fission device alone. But such an explosion would require the use of large amounts of fissionable material, which was thought to be in short supply in China. U.S. "experts" had therefore concluded that China's large yield had been accomplished by the combination of a fission and a fusion (thermonuclear) reaction.

The U.S. Public Health Service (PHS) reported May 20 that radioactive air samples from the Chinese test had been collected May 14-17 over Colorado, Idaho, California, North Carolina, Florida, Illinois and Utah. The PHS said the radioactive levels were lower than those following the earlier Chinese tests and presented no health hazard.

The State Department, which had announced Apr. 28 that a Chinese nuclear test would be conducted in the near future, described the Chinese test May 9 as "part of . . . [a] deliberate and costly . . . program to acquire nuclear weapons" that disregarded the "desires . . . of people throughout the world who may suffer from the ill effects of atmospheric nuclear testing, which most of the world has banned by adherence to the limited test ban treaty." The statement reiterated Pres. Johnson's 1964 pledge, issued 2 days after the first Chinese test Oct. 16, 1964, that the U.S. would defend non-nuclear nations against nuclear blackmail. State Secy. Rusk said in testimony before the Senate Foreign Relations Committee May 9 that he did not believe the Chinese test would "have any serious effect on the situation in Southeast Asia."

Indian Foreign Min. Swaran Singh told the Indian Parliament May 10 that the Chinese nuclear test was in "arrogant defiance" of world wishes.

The North Vietnamese News Agency reported May 10 that Pres. Ho Chi Minh had sent a message of congratulation to the Chinese leaders. Ho said that Chinese possession of nuclear weapons was "a great stimulus to the peoples now endeavoring to fight against the U.S. imperialist aggression."

Premier Eisaku Sato of Japan called a cabinet meeting May 12 to discuss the test. Japan's leading newspapers said the Chinese test heightened the urgency of a national debate on

Japan's defenses. Takao Kosaka, a scientist at Niigata University in Tokyo, said the fallout from the May 9 test was 33 times more radioactive than that from China's earlier tests.

U.S. Rejects Pledge Against A-Weapon Use

Premier Chou En-lai, at a Peking reception for visiting Albanian leader Mehmet Shehu, said May 9, 1966, that his government had proposed that the U.S. and China "undertake the obligation of not being the first to use nuclear weapons against each other, but U.S. imperialism rejected the idea. . . ." This rejection had forced China to continue developing nuclear weapons, Chou declared. Shehu described the 3d Chinese test as a "very great victory." Nuclear weapons "in the hands of revolutionaries educated in Marxism-Leninism and Mao Tse-tung's thought are in the service of peace and socialism and throw our enemy into panic," he declared. A joint communique on Chou's talks with Shehu, signed May 11, announced Albania's "full support of the Chinese government for a summit conference of all the countries of the world to discuss the question of complete prohibition and thorough destruction of nuclear weapons."

Washington was not interested in making the declaration suggested by Chou. State Department Press Officer Robert J. McCloskey confirmed May 11 that the U.S. had turned down a Chinese suggestion—made about a year previously—that the 2 nations formally pledge not to use nuclear weapons against each other. McCloskey said the offer had been rejected because the Chinese "profess to believe that such a public declaration without controls would constitute a sufficient guarantee" whereas "we do not [believe so], and we have given our views to the Chinese." McCloskey said the Chinese had not demonstrated a "constructive interest" in U.S. disarmament proposals; he cited China's refusal to sign the 1963 test ban treaty. He said that the U.S. had proposed a mutual ending of the production of fissionable materials and a freeze in the number of strategic (*i.e.*, long-range) delivery systems but that the Chinese had not responded.

State Secy. Rusk said at a May 17 news conference that the U.S. had rejected the Chinese proposal because "mere declarations on such matters would not be adequate." He said: The U.S. had "put forward . . . far-reaching proposals about limiting nuclear weapons and freezing and possibly reducing nuclear weapons delivery vehicles." In addition, the U.S. had "suggested they [China] ought to be associated with the preparatory committee . . . [that] might try to work out arrangements for a world disarmament conference, but we've had no indication from the Chinese that they are willing to do that."

Peking followed up its successful testing of a nuclear device with a guided missile test Oct. 27. Hsinhua reported: "On Oct. 27, 1966, China successfully conducted over its own territory a guided missile-nuclear weapon test. The guided missile flew normally and the nuclear warhead accurately hit the target at the appointed distance, effecting a nuclear explosion." The test was China's 4th nuclear explosion but the first involving a missile delivery. The Chinese communique continued:

> This successful test marks the fact that China's science, technology and defense capabilities are advancing at even greater speed under the brilliant illumination of Mao Tse-tung's thought. . . . [Its] complete success . . . was ensured by the Chinese People's Liberation Army and China's scientists, technicians . . . workers and functionaries, who, enthusiastically responding to the call of . . . [Defense Min.] Lin Piao and holding high the great red banner of Mao Tse-tung's thought, put politics in the forefront . . . and, propelled by the great proletarian cultural revolution, . . . displayed the spirit of self-reliance, hard work, collective wisdom and efforts and wholehearted cooperation. . . . Warm congratulations to all the commanders and fighters of the People's Liberation Army who took part in this test. . . . China's purpose in developing nuclear weapons is precisely to oppose the nuclear monopoly and nuclear blackmail by the United States and the Soviet Union acting in collusion. . . . The conducting of necessary and limited nuclear tests and the development of nuclear weapons by China are entirely for the purpose of defense, with the ultimate aim of destroying nuclear weapons. We solemnly declare once again that at no time and in no circumstances will China be the first to use nuclear weapons. . . .

The communique gave no details of the force of the explosion or the distance traveled by the missile. The U.S. Atomic

Energy Commission said Oct. 27 that preliminary estimates indicated that the yield from the test had been in the "low to low-intermediate range, similar to the first Chinese test." (Low-yield tests produced less energy than would result from the explosion of 20 kilotons [20,000 tons] of TNT; low-intermediate-yield tests produced force in the 20-200-kiloton range. The first Chinese explosion had been described by the AEC as a low-yield test, "roughly equivalent" to the U.S.' 20-kiloton bomb used against Hiroshima in World War II.) It was reported Nov. 1 that preliminary analysis of the radioactive debris from the test indicated that China had used enriched uranium as the material for the warhead.

Although there was no immediate confirmation of the Chinese claim that the warhead had been carried by a guided missile, it was reported Oct. 28 that preliminary data seemed to indicate that the missile had been fired 400 miles to its target —China's Sinkiang Province test site near Lob Nor.

The U.S. State Department said in a statement Oct. 28: "We have been aware of the Chinese efforts to develop missiles as well as nuclear weapons. A test of the type reported by Peking falls within the time period we have foreseen. We see no reason to alter our estimate of when they might have an operational capability. It can be expected that there will be further tests of this kind." (Defense Secy. Robert S. McNamara had estimated in Dec. 1965 that China might have an operational medium-range ballistic missile by 1967.)

Peking Sees U.S.-USSR Collusion

As the Cultural Revolution continued, Peking's foreign policy came to reflect to an increasing extent a concern with the attainment of ideological purity. It was cast rigidly in the Maoist mold. The deeper the nation sank into its own ideological sphere, the more isolated it became from the rest of the world. Press reports and official pronouncements from Peking in the latter part of 1966 portrayed a China encircled by hostile nations. They claimed that the U.S. and USSR were colluding against China.

A violent denunciation of the Soviet Union was issued by Peking's Foreign Ministry May 3, 1966. Intended as a reply to a Hungarian report in which Soviet Defense Min. Rodion Y. Malinovsky charged Chinese obstruction in aid to Vietnam, the Chinese statement said: "Malinovsky is a liar. China has never hampered the transit of Soviet aid materials to Vietnam. All military aid materials which Vietnam asked for and which the Soviet Union delivered to China have been transported to Vietnam by China with priority at high speed and free of charge. From Feb. 1965 when the Soviet Union asked for the sending of its aid materials to Vietnam through China up to the end of 1965, China transported a total of 43,000-odd tons of Soviet military aid supplies to Vietnam. The Vietnamese government is well aware of this. And so is the Soviet government. The facts are all there and nobody can succeed in distorting them."

Continuing opposition to the Soviet Union was underscored by an Albanian-Chinese communique issued May 11 by Chou En-lai and Mehmet Shehu at the conclusion of the latter's visit to China. The communique called on "Marxist-Leninists of the whole world" to wage "uncompromising and principled struggles" against modern revisionism, "whose center is the leading group of the CPSU."

The following month Premier Chou En-lai returned a state visit to Albania and included in his trip a week's visit to Rumania June 16-24. On arrival at Bucharest, Chou conferred with Rumanian Communist Party Gen. Secy. Nicolae Ceausescu, Premier Ion G. Maurer and First Deputy Premier Emil Bodnares. The highest ranking Chinese official accompanying Chou, Chao Yim-in, candidate member of the Party Central Committee, praised Rumania's independent policy in a speech delivered June 20 in Craiova. The Rumanian people, he declared, had been successful "in their fight against external control." In what was reported to have been the most significant development of Chou's visit, he and Ceausescu appeared 2 hours late at a June 23 Chinese-Rumanian friendship rally in Bucharest. Both leaders had been scheduled to make lengthy speeches, but instead made brief impromptu statements devoid of political content. It was reported that Chou had planned to make a strong anti-Soviet speech at the rally and that Ceausescu had objected because it would have compromised Rumania's neutrality in the Sino-Soviet dispute. No joint communique was issued at the end of Chou's visit. The Chinese news agency Hsinhua praised the Rumanian people June 24 for giving Chou a "grand and enthusiastic welcome" but made no mention of the Rumanian party leaders of government.

Chou arrived June 24 in Tirana, Albania, where he was greeted by Premier Mehmet Shehu with a speech assailing Rumania's "neutrality." Albania, Shehu declared, would not be misled by "acrobatic politicians" who were attempting to work with "the Khrushchev revisionists." Chou conferred June 25 with Communist Party First Secy. Enver Hoxha and left June 28 for Pakistan. He returned to Peking July 1.

It had been reported from Hong Kong May 8 that Chinese Communist Party Gen. Secy. Teng Hsiao-ping had said at a Shanghai rally that "in no circumstances" would China take united action with the USSR "or give them any help—not even a straw."

Soviet Pres. Nikolai V. Podgorny, in an address delivered June 1 in Khabarovsk, a city on the Amur river near the Chinese border, had declared: "The Khaborovsk territory is a border zone. The soldiers of the Far Eastern Military District . . . are faithfully guarding this . . . region. . . ." The people of the district, he added, should cooperate with the armed forces "to guard and, if necessary, to fight heroically and skillfully for the Far Eastern shores of our motherland."

Communist Chinese Foreign Min. Chen Yi, in a speech at a Peking rally July 10, said that the Soviet Union was "making military deployment along the Chinese borders in coordination with United States encirclement of China."

Peking's verbal attacks on the Soviet Union were matched by its outspoken hostility to the U.S. *Jenmin Jih Pao*

Aug. 30, 1966 called editorially for worldwide uprisings against the U.S. so that "imperialism can be nibbled up bit by bit." The editorial said: The U.S.' sending of armed forces to Southeast Asia "creates a favorable condition for the further growth of the anti-United States struggle of the people in other parts of the world." "To be quite frank, if the United States imperialism kept its forces in Europe and America, the Asian people would have no way of wiping them out. Now, as it is so obliging as to deliver its goods to the customers' door, the Asian people cannot but express welcome."

According to the editorial, U.S. "ground forces in Asia and the Pacific have increased . . . to 7 divisions and 4 brigades at present. This represents about 34% of the total United States ground forces of 21 divisions and 10 brigades. Of the [U.S. Navy's] 939 vessels . . . , more than 500 now have been assigned to the Pacific Fleet. The United States Air Force and Navy have a total of more than 5,000 planes in Asia and the Pacific compared with 3,000 or more in Europe, Africa, the Middle East and the Atlantic."

Describing the U.S. as a "paper tiger," the editorial charged that the U.S., the USSR, India and Japan were cooperating to encircle China. It held that the Soviet Union "follows a policy of appeasement in Europe, betrays the interests of the German Democratic Republic and the other Socialist countries in Eastern Europe, works energetically for a *detente* with Washington to freeze the situation in Europe." As a result, the editorial said, the U.S. was able to "concentrate its strength to deal with the peoples of Asia."

The official attitude was not entirely one of unremitting hostility, however. Communist Chinese Foreign Min. Chen Yi was quoted as having said to a visiting Japanese Diet delegation Sept. 6 that China did not want a "clash" with the U.S. and was not "necessarily dismissing" the possibility of talks with the U.S. on the subject of Vietnam. Chen, whose remarks were reported by the Japanese news agency Kyodo, was said to have stressed that Peking did not intend to force its political system on other nations. He was quoted as saying that "it is up to a given nation to choose whichever it likes, socialism, capitalism or revision."

State Department press officer Robert J. McCloskey said in Washington Sept. 7 that "if Chen Yi did in fact say that neither the United States nor Communist China wants a clash, we would welcome that statement. Certainly, we have no desire for a clash with China and would want to avoid one."

A revised version of Chen Yi's interview was reported by Kyodo from Peking Sept. 8. According to Kyodo, a spokesman for the Japanese delegation had called a press conference to give newsmen a "supplementary" briefing on Chen's remarks. The spokesman said that Chen and Chinese officials did not want to give the impression that China was "vacillating" on the issue of talks with the U.S. "Under the circumstances," said the spokesman, "Peking has no intention whatever to talk with the United States for peace in Vietnam." The UPI reported from Tokyo that the Japanese delegation had decided to present a revised report of Chen's interview following optimistic reactions in the West to the original reports of Chen's statements. The UPI suggested that Chinese officials had asked the Japanese delegation to give the "supplementary" briefing.

U.S. Amb.-to-Poland John A. Gronouski and Chinese Amb. Wang Kou-chuan met in Warsaw the same day to continue the periodic U.S.-Communist Chinese consultations (dating from 1958), the only official diplomatic contact between the U.S. and Red China. Following the meeting, Wang broke a long-standing rule of secrecy by issuing to the press the statement he had read at the meeting. Wang's statement, a sharp criticism of U.S. policy in Asia, said that the Chinese people would not be "hoodwinked" by U.S. declarations about "entering into 'peaceful' cooperation with China." Wang charged that since the last previous meeting of the ambassadors (in March), U.S. aircraft and warships had "again intruded into China's airspace and territorial waters on many occasions" and China had "served the 403d to 411th serious warnings on the United States government." Reiterating China's claim to Taiwan, Wang charged that the U.S. was "tightening its military encirclement of China."

Peking Sept. 16 and 18 again charged that U.S. planes had attacked points in Chinese territory at least twice during 3 intrusions Sept. 5, 9 and 17. The U.S. conceded Sept. 19 that its planes might have strayed over China. The Chinese Defense Ministry said Sept. 16 that U.S. planes had bombed Chinese territory Sept. 5 near Munankwan Pass, a main border-crossing point on the North Vietnamese frontier. In the 2d incident, the Peking statement said that U.S. F-105 jets had "intruded into China's territorial airspace over the Tunghing multinational county of the Kwangsi-Chuang autonomous region [bordering northeastern North Vietnam]" Sept. 9 and had "strafed Chinese villages and commune members," wounding 3 persons. The statement claimed Chinese planes had intercepted the U.S. aircraft, damaging one and driving off the others.

Pres. Johnson commented on Peking's militancy in an address to the American Legion convention in Washington Aug. 30. The U.S., Johnson warned, could not safely assume that China's militant words were "only rhetoric." The war in Vietnam was "meant to be the [Chinese Communists'] opening salvo in a series of bombardments," Johnson said, and "if it succeeds in South Vietnam, then, as Marshal Lin Piao [Communist China's defense minister] says, . . . 'the people in other parts of the world will see that what the Vietnamese people can do they can do too.'" Johnson quoted the London *Economist* as warning that "until and unless there is solid evidence that China does not intend to do what Lin Piao says it wants to do, or cannot do it, the only safe assumption for the Americans or anybody else to make is that the Chinese mean every word they say."

Against the backdrop of continuing war of words in Sino-American relations, Johnson, in a speech before the National Writers Conference Oct. 7, called for reconciliation with the East (the Soviet Union and Eastern Europe)—"a shift from the narrow concept of coexistence to the broader vision of a peaceful engagement." Johnson suggested the possibility of reciprocal troop reductions in Europe by the Soviet Union and the Western nations. He declared: "The Atlantic allies will of course continue together to study what strength NATO needs in light of the changing technology and the current threat. Reduction of Soviet forces in Central Europe would of course effect the extent of that threat. If changing circumstances should lead to a gradual and a balanced revision in force levels on both sides, the revision could, together with the other steps that I have mentioned, help gradually to shape an entire new political environment." The President called for "measures to remove territorial and border disputes as a source of friction in Europe." "The Atlantic nations oppose the use of force to change existing frontiers," he asserted.

Johnson listed these new steps his Administration was taking in its effort to improve East-West relations:

● "We will reduce export controls on East-West trade with respect to hundreds of nonstrategic items."
● "I have just today signed a detemination that will allow the Export-Import Bank to guarantee commercial credits to 4 additional Eastern European countries—Poland and Hungary, Bulgaria and Czechoslovakia."
● The State Secretary was "reviewing the possibility of easing the burden of Polish debts to the United States through expenditures of our Polish currency holdings."
● "The Export-Import Bank is prepared to finance export for the Soviet-Italian Fiat auto plant."
● "We are negotiating a civil air agreement with the Soviet Union. . . . This will, we think, greatly facilitate tourism in both directions."

The President said his Aministration was pressing for "early Congressional action" on a U.S.-Soviet consular agreement and would "press for legislative authority to negotiate trade agreements which could extend most-favored-nation tariff treatment to European Communist states." Johnson noted with satisfaction recent U.S. actions in pursuit of the goal of improved East-West relations: a 2-year cultural exchange agreement signed with the USSR, steps taken to "liberalize travel to Communist countries in Europe and Asia" and an exchange of photos taken by U.S. and Soviet weather satellites.

Soviet Communist Party Gen. Secy. Leonid I. Brezhnev said in Moscow Oct. 15 that Johnson's appeal for improved East-West relations was a "strange and persistent delusion" in view of the U.S.' "aggression" and bombing of North Vietnam. Brezhnev said: "We have declared many times that if the United States wants to develop mutually beneficial relations with the Soviet Union—in principle, we also would like this—then it is necessary to clear the major obstacles from the path. The piratical bombing attacks against a socialist country, the Democratic Republic of Vietnam, must be halted and the aggression against the Vietnamese people stopped." "The sovereignty and territorial inviolability of other countries must be respected, not just in words but in deeds."

Brezhnev made these remarks at a Soviet-Polish friendship meeting attended by Polish Communist Party First Secy. Wladyslaw Gomulka and Premier Jozef Cyrankiewicz. Brezhnev said that Communist China's "policies, . . . actions can only discredit socialism in the eyes of the people and confuse them." He criticized China's alleged failure to join in united action to support North Vietnam.

Jenmin Jih Pao Oct. 16 denounced Johnson's Oct. 7 speech. It said that a Soviet-U.S. alliance was "already in existence" but that it was "simply inconvenient" for both countries to make it public. The editorial was signed Observer, a name reserved for high Chinese Communist Party officials.

CHINA IN TURMOIL (1967-9)

Cultural Revolution Enters 'New Stage'

What had begun in June 1966 as a protest by a small group of students at Peking University turned by the year's end into a nationwide youth rebellion. Chairman Mao Tse-tung seized the ferment and visited its fury on his opponents in the Chinese Communist Party and state bureaucracy. In the next 2 years, 1967-8, China presented the bizarre spectacle of a Communist nation in revolt against itself. Countless youths calling themselves "Red Guards" were seen moving from place to place in search of revolutionary experience. They formed the vanguard of the "Great Proletarian Cultural Revolution."

The central issue of the Cultural Revolution, as defined by the Chinese Communist Party newspaper *Jenmin Jih Pao* Jan. 1, 1967, was "whether or not the proletariat is able to maintain political power and prevent capitalist restoration after it has seized political power." The paper asserted that Chairman Mao had set "a new and great example for the whole world proletariat." "Intense class struggles" were reported in various parts of the country. Among the details—many of them contradictory—were the following:

> *Shanghai*—Peking Radio reported Jan. 9, 1967 that many workers in Shanghai had gone on strike and that there had been "plots" to disrupt the city's utilities and transportation. The broadcast was the first acknowledgement by an official Chinese Communist news agency of the disorder reported in the Red Guard posters.
>
> The broadcast quoted a letter that had been signed by 11 pro-Mao organizations in Shanghai and that had appeared Jan. 5 in the Shanghai daily *Wen Hui Pao*. The letter said: "Recently at very many factories some or the greater part of the 'Red Workers Corps' had stopped production or left their jobs. . . . Recently, furthermore, a handful of reactionary elements plotted to cut off water and electricity and paralyze transportation." A "handful" of opponents to the cultural revolution "have tried in every possible way to go against Mao's policy of taking hold of the revolution to stimulate production." These persons must be "severely punished." "All the revolutionary

147

students and cadres" should join the "revolutionary workers" to "smash the counterattack by bourgeois reactionaries and raise the cultural revolution to a new stage in the factories." "We hope you [workers] can follow Chairman Mao's teachings and distinguish between right and wrong . . . and go back to your production positions and back to the road of the cultural revolution." Workers who returned to their jobs "would not be scolded."

The broadcast said the disturbances in Shanghai were "not only the problem of Shanghai but also of the whole country." It quoted an editorial in *Jenmin Jih Pao* that referred to the Shanghai letter as "very important." The editorial called for a "general attack on the bourgeois reactionary line."

Hsinhua, the Chinese Communist news agency, reported Jan. 10 that a "large number" of workers at the No. 17 textile mill in Shanghai had "deserted their posts" but "are our class brothers so we are eager to welcome them back." It said the workers had been "taken in" by anti-Maoist elements.

Foochow—It was reported from Hong Kong Jan. 10 that Foochow Radio had disclosed "plots" in that city by persons opposed to the cultural revolution and strikes by workers who had "left their equipment." The broadcast said that the workers had apparently gone on strike over "wages, benefits and other economic demands." It said that production in some factories had been curtailed because of sabotage and the fact that many workers had left for Peking to "report on conditions."

Chusan Islands—The correspondent of the Japanese newspaper *Yomiuri* reported Jan. 8 that, according to wall posters he had seen in Peking that day, 5,000 to 6,000 peasants had clashed with Red Guard units Jan. 6 at the port of Tinghai in the Chusan Islands, southeast of Shanghai. 2 persons were reported killed in the incident and many others injured. The posters said the peasants had destroyed a broadcasting station in Tinghai and had attacked the Red Guards headquarters for the Chusan Fisheries School. The posters charged that Chusan Communist Party First Secy. Tsao Szu-ying had instigated the riots.

Canton—Travelers arriving in Hong Kong from Canton Jan. 10 reported that fighting between workers and Red Guards had broken out in that city Jan. 7-8. They said several persons had been killed and scores wounded. According to one traveler: "About 20, maybe more, were hurt when Red Guards fought with clubs. They were taken to the Canton hospital. When the hospital refused to turn over the injured workers, Red Guards smashed windows, broke down the door and wrecked the entrance room." A Chinese woman reported that she had seen several hundred workers attacking a group of Red Guards. The workers "were shouting that they were sick of Red Guards and sick of Mao's thought," she said. The travelers reported that they had seen anti-Mao posters in the city and that Canton Radio had appealed to Mao's supporters to "crush the enemies of our great leader."

Peking—Red Guard posters reported in Peking Jan. 6 a clash between rival groups of workers in the city's western district. Peking residents said they had heard gunfire for about 5 minutes the previous evening in the vicinity of the railway station. The Kyodo correspondent reported Jan. 8 that fighting had broken out between workers at an aircraft factory in Peking. (*The East is Red*, a Red Guard newspaper, had reported Nov. 23, 1966 that Red Guards and workers had battled for 15 hours Nov. 16-17 at the Machine Tool Factory 1.)

An official of the All-China Federation of Trade Unions said Jan. 3 that Red Guard forces had closed the federation's newspaper, the *Workers Daily*. They did so after Red Guard posters had attacked Liu Ning-yi, chairman of the federation and a member of the party's Central Committee. The closing of the paper reduced the number of dailies in Peking to 2—*Jenmin Jih Pao* and *Kwangming Jih Pao*—as compared to 7 a year previously. About 10 Red Guard papers appeared irregularly.

Nanking—Japanese and East European correspondents in Peking reported Jan. 8 that clashes between Red Guards and workers in Nanking, 530 miles southeast of Peking, had erupted into bloody fighting Jan. 3, 5 and 6. The dispatches, based on Red Guard posters displayed in Peking Jan. 7, said that 54 persons had been killed and 900 wounded in the fighting. A correspondent for Japan's Kyodo news service reported that 6,000 persons had been arrested by the rebel workers. A Czech dispatch said 60,000 persons had been arrested on both sides. *Yomiuri* reported that, according to the posters, some of those arrested had "their fingers and noses chopped off while girl students had their clothes ripped off." A correspondent for the Japanese newspaper *Asahi* reported a Jan. 6 poster announcement to the effect that rail service between Nanking and Shanghai had been suspended as an "emergency" measure "in view of bloody clashes between workers' groups."

The Kyodo correspondent, piecing together the wall poster announcements, gave this account of the fighting: 100,000 members of the "Workers Red Corps," an apparently anti-Maoist organization, attacked Nanking Red Guards headquarters Jan. 3; they killed 14 persons and seriously wounded 400. The Red Guards appealed to Nanking officials for assistance, but Nanking Mayor Yue Wei-fan sided with the "conservative faction." Fighting was renewed Jan. 5-6, and in these clashes 40 persons were killed, 500 wounded and 6,000 arrested. The posters charged that the workers were led by Li Shih-ying and Hsu Chia-tun, Communist Party secretaries in Kiangsu Province.

The *Yomiuri* correspondent reported that some of the posters had appealed for help from other parts of the country. The posters quoted a Red Guard official who had fled Nanking and phoned Peking as saying that "we revolutionaries were surrounded and our headquarters . . . destroyed." There were reports that 400,000 to 500,000 anti-Maoists were marching to Nanking from Shanghai, from other cities in Kiangsu Province and from neighboring Anhwei Province.

Some posters charged that Deputy Premier and Propaganda Min. Tao Chu had incited the workers to riot. Tao, who had been elevated from 95th to 4th position in the party hierarchy in Aug. 1966, had only recently come under attack. He was criticized for the first time Dec. 29, 1966. He was denounced in Red Guard posters for alleged counter-revolutionary activity. Some

Western observers suggested that the poster accounts had been exaggerated in order to discredit Tao.

Toward the end of January, with the entire nation seemingly given over to chaos, the People's Liberation Army (PLA) was ordered by Chairman Mao to intervene on the side of the Maoist revolutionaries. With the help of the army, the Maoists were reported to have seized power in Tsingtao (Jan. 23), Nanchang (Jan. 24), Kweichow (Jan. 25), Kiangsi (Jan. 26), Anhwei (Jan. 26), Shensi (Jan. 27), Taiyuan (Jan. 28), and Heilunkiang (Jan. 31). The PLA assumed direct control over such civilian services as airlines, airports and storehouses of grain.

Hung Chi (Red Flag), the Communist Party theoretical journal, in its editorial Jan. 31, discussed the problems of new revolutionary organizations. The model it suggested was the Paris commune. The editorial stated that the cultural revolution's "new stage"—the seizure of power—required the formation of new governing bodies. It disclosed that Mao had referred to the eventual formation of a "Peking People's Commune" as early as June 1, 1966—"predicting even then that our state organs would take on completely new forms." It continued:

The current seizure of power from the handful of persons within the party who are in authority and taking the capitalist road is not effected by dismissal and reorganization from above, but from below by the mass movement called for and supported by Chairman Mao himself. . . . Experience proves that in the course of the struggle for the seizure of power, it is necessary, through exchange of views and consultations among leading members of revolutionary mass organizations, leading members of local People's Liberation Army units and revolutionary leading cadres in party and government organizations, to establish provisional organs of power to take up the responsibility of leading this struggle. These provisional organs of power must 'take firm hold of the revolution and promote production,' put the system of production into normal operation, direct the existing set-ups in administrative and professional work (they should be readjusted where necessary) to carry on with their tasks, and organize the revolutionary masses to supervise these set-ups. These provisional organs of power must also shoulder the task of giving unified direction in suppressing counter-revolutionary organizations and counter-revolutionaries. . . . Through a period of transition, the wisdom of the broad masses will be brought into full play and a completely new organizational form of political power better suited to the socialist economic base will be created. . . .

It was reported Feb. 7 that a Peking preparatory committee had been formed to establish a "people's commune" in that
city. A resolution adopted by the committee enjoined pro-Mao
forces to "unite closely, seize power of the powerholders tread-
ing the capitalist road, firmly grasp in your own hands the party,
political and financial power in Peking and push the cultural
revolution in the capital to a new stage." Posters in Peking reported Feb. 11 that Public Security Min. Hsieh Fu-chih had
been appointed head of the committee. These reports contrasted with earlier ones Jan. 30 that a "Peking Revolutionary Cor-
poration" had taken over the city administration.

Maoist-controlled news media had repeatedly urged the
establishment of "a completely new proletarian order" to replace state organs that had fallen prey to the "bourgeois-reac-
tionary line." The "people's commune" appeared to be the new
form of government devised by the Maoist faction to supplant
the established ruling organs—specifically (for the moment, at
least) the municipal party committees—in order to consolidate
its power in areas said to have been "seized."

The party Central Committee and the State Council (cabinet)
Feb. 7 ordered the Red Guards to "return to the places and
schools from which they came and take part there in the great,
historical, decisive battle." The order, posted by the secretariat
of the Peking "Revolutionary Rebel Group," said the cessation
of Red Guard marches marked a "new stage" in the cultural
revolution. It stated that too many Red Guards had gathered
in Peking and in such "sacred revolutionary places" as Shaoshan
in Hunan Province (Mao's birthplace) and Yenan in Shensi
Province (Mao's headquarters before the Communist victory
in 1949). "These places are jammed," it said, "and the weather
is very cold and arrangements for food, lodging and transportation are very difficult to make." It added that local economies
had been disrupted and "in some places epidemics have spread"
as a result of the marches. The order stipulated that:

1. The exchange of experiences on foot over long distances shall be suspended all over the country. Those expeditionary units who have stayed more

than 5 days and have attained their objectives should return to the places from which they came. The exchange of experiences within county borders shall be suspended in the revolutionary sacred places to avoid congestion of transportation.

2. In returning to their hometowns, the Red Guards shall go on foot. Those Red Guards who have come from places that are more than 500 kilometers [310 miles] away may be given free tickets for trains and steamers within 15 days.

3. Chairman Mao Tse-tung told the people, 'Let us economize and carry out the revolution.' . . . During the exchange-of-experiences period and the period of returning to hometowns, the Red Guards should pay their own food and transportation expenses in the cities. The food ration can be increased appropriately. Necessary expenses for clothes should be held to a minimum.

4. Until now the Red Guards in Peking have been given free meals. However, begining Feb. 8, expenses for food will be charged and food will not be given free from now on.

Deepening Isolation

China's internal turmoil deepened its external isolation. In the early part of Jan. 1967, Communist Chinese diplomats stationed abroad were ordered home. Chinese students in Moscow clashed Jan. 25 with Russian police while trying to lay wreaths on Lenin's mausoleum and Stalin's tomb. The incident prompted the Chinese Foreign Ministry to lodge a protest Jan. 26 against the "fascist atrocities committed by the Soviet revisionist clique." Peking's relations with North Korea and the Japanese Communist Party (JCP) were also strained due to the Cultural Revolution. It was reported that a Red Guard poster in Peking in February portrayed Premier Kim Il Sung as "fat revisionist" and "Khrushchev's disciple." Akahata (Red Flag), the JCP newspaper, repudiated the Red Guards Jan. 24. At the same time, the JCP expelled from its membership 10 members who were living in Peking and who sympathized with the Cultural Revolution. By Sept. 1967, Peking had been involved in quarrels with 32 different nations.

Relations with the U.S. deteriorated further, growing even more distant, non-communicative and hostile. At the request of the Communist Chinese ambassador in Warsaw, the bi-lateral U.S.-Chinese ambassadorial talks, which had been scheduled for Jan. 11, were postponed for 2 weeks. Chinese Amb.-to-Poland Wang Kuo-chuan and U.S. Amb.-to-Poland John A. Gronouski met Jan. 25 for $3\frac{1}{2}$ hours in a closed session. At the end of the meeting Gronouski announced further suspension of the talks until June 7. Gronouski said: "I had proposed an earlier date but Amb. Wang said anything earlier than the June 7 which he proposed would be inconvenient." According to the U.S. embassy in Warsaw, the postponement would constitute the longest break in the talks since they began in Warsaw in 1958.

The Cultural Revolution was seen in Washington, however, as improving the prospect for ending the Vietnam War. State Secy. Dean Rusk said in a TV interview with 5 British journalists (made public Feb. 1): "It may be that the events in China may give Hanoi somewhat more freedom of action than they might have felt they had a little earlier." Therefore, Rusk said, "we're exploring the possibilities here to find out whether or not that is possibly the case, but we just don't know yet."

The U.S., Rusk said, had informed the Viet Cong that it was prepared to discuss the inclusion of the National Liberation Front as a "full negotiating party" in future peace talks; if the Viet Cong "were to lay down their arms, ways could be found to permit them" to participate in the South Vietnamese governmental processes; "the leadership of the Viet Cong in the South is made up of North Vietnamese generals . . ., so we're not very much impressed with this alleged difference between the Liberation Front and Hanoi."

Reported political contacts between U.S. and North Vietnamese officials were confirmed Feb. 4 by Presidential Asst. Walt W. Rostow. Rostow said officials of both countries were involved in "what is or might turn out to be a negotiating process" toward settling the war in Vietnam.

But events belied the U.S. officials' optimism. U.S. officials in Washington reported Apr. 11 that the Soviet Union and Communist China had reached agreement "in the last 6 weeks" on speeding the shipment of Soviet military supplies to North

Vietnam across Chinese territory. The accord was believed to have ended a long-standing dispute in which Moscow had accused Peking of harassing and impeding the flow of North Vietnam-bound Soviet supplies carried on Chinese railroads. The Washington report said one of the compromise solutions provided for North Vietnam to take title to Soviet military shipments as they reached the Sino-Soviet border.

Despite the reported Sino-Soviet agreement on aid to North Vietnam, Communist China declared Apr. 30 that "under no circumstances" would it align itself with Moscow to "take any united action" on the Vietnamese war.

Peking charged May 3 that 4 U.S. jets May 2 had bombed the southern Chinese town of Ningming, about 20 miles north of the North Vietnamese border. One house was said to have been destroyed. The Chinese Foreign Ministry said the planes, F-105 jets, had fled after Chinese air force planes attacked them. The U.S. Defense Department May 2 denied the incident.

However, the Defense Department spokesman May 26 made the first public acknowledgment that American air intrusions had occurred over Communist China during recently intensified air strikes against North Vietnam. The spokesman said the U.S. planes had not penetrated deeply into Chinese territory. China had accused the U.S. of 4 violations of its airspace since Apr. 24.

Peking radio reported May 23 that Foreign Min. Chen Yi May 22 had repeated Peking's warning that China would intervene in the war if such action was requested by North Vietnam. In a meeting in Peking with North Vietnamese Charge d'Affaires Le Chung Thuy, Chen was said to have stated that China was "paying serious attention" to the U.S.-South Vietnamese invasion of the southeastern sector of the Vietnamese demilitarized zone (DMZ). *Jenmin Jih Pao* May 23 called the allied move into the DMZ "a danger signal that United States imperialism wants to invade North Vietnam and extend the flames of the war of aggression to the whole of Indochina."

An unnamed State Department official warned May 23 that the U.S. would attack the Chinese mainland if Peking's forces intervened in the Vietnam war on a massive scale. The American official, briefing a group of newspaper editors and broadcasters, first said U.S. forces would respond with conventional weapons. He later said Chinese intervention would elicit retaliation by the U.S. with everything it had. Department officials explained that this did not mean that the U.S. would employ nuclear weapons in countering a Chinese military thrust.

In contrast, U.S. relations with the Soviet Union continued to show marked improvement. Pres. Lyndon B. Johnson and Soviet Premier Aleksei N. Kosygin met June 25 at Glassboro College in Glassboro, N.J. Communist China assailed the Johnson-Kosygin summit conference as a meeting of conspirators. The Chinese views were contained in 2 statements published by the news agency Hsinhua June 24 and 25.

Hsinhua charged June 24 that Johnson and Kosygin had met to plot "close collaboration" against Peking. China charged that Kosygin's principal reason for coming to the U.S. was not to lead the Soviet delegation to the UN General Assembly "but actually" "to meet Johnson face to face . . . and discuss with him ways and means of betraying the revolutionary interests of the Vietnamese people, the Arab people and other Asian, African and Latin-American people as is required by U.S. imperialism."

Speaking at a Peking dinner honoring Zambian Pres. Kenneth Kaunda, Chinese Premier Chou En-lai charged June 24 that Johnson and Kosygin were "engaging in a dirty bargain" that would "probably result in further damaging and selling out the interest of the Vietnamese people."

Hsinhua's June 25 statement asserted that in his Glassboro talks with the President, Kosygin was "actually getting near the conclusion of a vicious deal with Johnson" that was "first and foremost directed against China." Peking contended that although Kosygin's mission to the U.S. was "allegedly to support the Arab states," he would continue to support Washington's "line of forcing the Arab states to submit to the United States and Israeli aggression."

In the summer of 1967 the U.S. stepped up air raids against North Vietnam. Communist China complained of more incursions in its air space by U.S. planes. Hsinhua claimed June 12 that Chinese armed forces had shot down a pilotless U.S. reconnaissance plane over the southern part of the Kwangsi Chuang Autonomous Region. The U.S. Defense Department announced June 26 that an unarmed U.S. F-4 Phantom jet, being ferried from the Philippines to Danang, had strayed off course and was shot down that day by Chinese planes near or directly over China's Hainan Island. The 2 crewmen parachuted from the plane and were rescued unhurt from the China Sea by a U.S. Navy helicopter. Communist China claimed July 12 that its planes had forced 4 U.S. jets that day to flee after they had attacked a Chinese frontier post near Tunghing, in the Kwangsi Chuang Autonomous Region. The Peking report said the U.S. planes had fired 2 guided missiles, injuring 4 soldiers and damaging a house. China charged Aug. 6 that a U.S. plane that day had flown over the Hsi-sha Islands, in the South China Sea.

Pres. Johnson was reported Aug. 12 to have authorized the lifting of the air-raid restrictions in a directive issued Aug. 8 to Adm. Ulysses S. Grant Sharp, U.S. commander-in-chief in the Pacific. The new target list included transportation and industrial installations in the Hanoi-Haiphong area and rail lines linking Hanoi with Communist China. The lifting of these restrictions permitted American pilots to attack objectives within 10 miles of the Chinese border. Heretofore U.S. planes had been under orders to stay at least 25 miles away from the frontier.

The first air strikes carried out under the expanded bombing orders were directed Aug. 11 against the Paul Doumer (Longbien) Bridge, which spanned the Red River in the northeast part of Hanoi. The raids reportedly cut a span of the bridge, Hanoi's only rail and road connection with Haiphong and with the Chinese border.

U.S. pilots Aug. 12 bombed railroad and highway bridges crossing the Canal des Rapides, 5 miles northeast of Hanoi. Other targets hit during the day included fuel and ammunition depots of the Kienan MiG air base, 5 miles southwest of Haiphong, military barracks 33 miles south of Hanoi and 35 miles northwest of the capital, and surface-to-air missile sites 11 miles southeast of Hanoi.

U.S. planes Aug. 13 bombed the 360-foot Langson rail and highway bridge spanning the Kikung River, 10 miles from the Chinese border. It was the closest target to China ever hit by U.S. planes; the closest previous strike had been on the Caonung railroad yard, 30 miles from the Chinese frontier. Langson was at the northern end of the northeast rail connection between Hanoi and China. The bridge's entire span was reported to have caved into the river. American pilots also bombed rail yards at Langgai and at Langdang, 19 and 26 miles from the Chinese border. 151 locomotives and freight cars were said to have been destroyed or damaged.

U.S. Navy pilots returned to the Langson bridge Aug. 14 and claimed to have knocked out another span, described as "a by-pass bridge" a mile to the east of the center span.

During one of the air strikes of the new attacks, 2 U.S. Navy jets strayed off course Aug. 21 and were shot down over China.

Reporting on the Aug. 21 incident, the U.S. Defense Department said that day that the 2 Navy A-6 Intruder jets downed over China had strayed off course after encountering heavy anti-aircraft fire during the bombing of the Ducnoi rail yard, 7 miles north of Hanoi and about 75 miles from the Chinese border. Department officials said the jets were probably brought down by MiGs, but they were not certain whether the jets were Chinese or North Vietnamese. A pilot of one of the 4 Navy planes involved in the Ducnoi raid reported on returning to the aircraft carrier *Constellation* that the 2 missing jets had developed trouble in their navigational equipment.

Peking claimed its air force had shot down 2 American planes over the Kwangsi Chuang Autonomous Region bordering North Vietnam. One of the American pilots was said to have been captured. The Chinese news agency Hsinhua charged that the American aircraft had "flagrantly intruded" into Chinese air space in "an act of deliberate war provocation."

White House Press Secy. George Christian said Aug. 21 that "with all precautions, you are going to have incidents like this one." He added, however, that "we are confident Peking is aware that the United States does not seek involvement of Red China" in the war.

China Explodes Thermonuclear Device

Communist China detonated its first hydrogen bomb June 17, 1967. An official communique broadcast by Hsinhua June 17 said: "Today, on June 17, 1967, after the 5 nuclear tests in 2 years and 8 months, China successfully exploded its first hydrogen bomb, over the western region of the country." The communique continued:

The success of this hydrogen bomb test represents another leap in the development of China's nuclear weapons. It marks the entry of the development of China's nuclear weapons into an entirely new stage. . . . With happiness and elation, we hail this fresh great victory of Mao Tse-tung's thought, this fresh splendid achievement of the great proletarian cultural revolution. . . . Warmest congratulations to all the commanders of the Chinese People's Liberation Army, the workers, engineers, technicians and scientists and other personnel who have been engaged in the research, manufacture and testing of the nuclear weapons. . . . It is hoped that . . . [these persons], following the teachings of Chairman Mao and the call of Comrade [Defense Min.] Lin Piao, . . . will guard against conceit and impetuosity, continue to exert themselves and win new and still greater merit in accelerating the development of our country's national defense, science and technology. . . . China has got atom bombs and guided missiles, and she now has the hydrogen bomb. . . . The success of . . . [the] test has further broken the nuclear monopoly of U.S. imperialism and Soviet revisionism and dealt a telling blow at their policy of nuclear blackmail. It is a very great encouragement and support to the Vietnamese people in their heroic war against U.S. aggression and for national salvation, to the Arab people in their resistance to aggression by the U.S. and British imperialists and their tool, Israel, and to the revolutionary people of the whole world. . . . The conducting of necessary and limited nuclear tests and the development of nuclear weapons by China are entirely for the purpose of defense, with the ultimate aim of abolishing nuclear weapons. We solemnly declare once again that at no time and in no circumstances will China be the first to use nuclear weapons. We always mean what we say. . . .

The explosion of the Chinese hydrogen bomb lent support to advocates of the deployment of an anti-ballistic missile system in the U.S. In an Aug. 2 report, the U.S. Congress' Joint Atomic Energy Committee had warned that China "could possibly" be capable of launching an intercontinental nuclear missile attack "by the early 1970s." At a news conference May 18, however, Defense Secy. Robert S. McNamara had estimated that China would have no "significant ICBM [intercontinental ballistic missile] capability until the mid-1970s." In a statement in response to the Joint Atomic Energy Committee report, a Defense Department spokesman said Aug. 2 that the committee's and McNamara's estimates were "generally consistent" but that any missile defense system could not be equivalent to what McNamara called the "assured destruction capability" of U.S. missiles.

The Senate Appropriations Committee Aug. 4 reported a bill in which was earmarked $269 million for procurement of a Nike-X missile defense system. The House version included the same amount, but it was not earmarked. In its report June 9, the House Appropriations Committee had recommended deployment as soon as possible of a "thin" antimissile system for protection against a "light" attack, such as it was felt China would be capable of mounting within the next decade, or from an accidental Soviet firing.

The U.S. Atomic Energy Commission (AEC) announced Dec. 24 that it had "detected the 7th Chinese Communist atmospheric nuclear test in the Lob Nor area [Sinkiang Province] on Dec. 24, Chinese time." The AEC said the detonation was in the "low-yield range [less than 20 kilotons]." Contrary to its policy in the past, China did not confirm the test. In a Japanese-language broadcast Dec. 25, Peking radio said simply that China had conducted 6 successful tests "from 1964 through

1967." The broadcast declared that "the Chinese people certainly have the chance and the capability to catch up with and surpass the world's advanced standards in nuclear-bomb development in the not-distant future." Noting that Chinese Communist Party Chairman Mao Tse-tung had predicted in 1958 that China would have atomic and hydrogen bombs in about 10 years, the broadcast asserted that Mao's prediction had become a "complete reality."

The AEC reported Jan. 3, 1968 that "preliminary analysis [of the fallout] of the 7th Chinese Communist nuclear test indicates that it contained uranium-235, uranium-238 and lithium-6 and did not employ plutonium." The AEC reaffirmed its previous assessment that the test had been in the "low-yield range." Atomic energy specialists speculated that China had attempted to detonate a fission-fusion-fission thermonuclear weapon but that the test had been a failure in light of the reported low yield. That the Chinese had attempted to test such a triple-stage weapon was indicated by these facts: (1) the presence of uranium-235 (enriched uranium), used as the fission triggering device for a thermonuclear explosion; (2) the presence of lithium-6, which provided the fusionable material for a thermonuclear explosion; (3) the presence of normally stable uranium-238 (natural uranium), which was placed around the lithium-6 and in which fission was induced by the bombardment of high-energy neutrons emitted in the hydrogen explosion. The low yield of the explosion suggested, however, that only the first-stage fission triggering device had detonated properly. An AEC spokesman said Jan. 3 that "it was possible that the test was a dud."

Mao Tse-tung, commenting (apparently in July 1967) on the significance of China's achievements in nuclear weapons, suggested that these developments were important in ultimately making China "the military and technical center of the world revolution." His remarks were circularized in Peking wall posters and, by September 1967, as handbills. They were headed "China Must Become the Arsenal for the World Revolution." The text of his remarks:

Modern weapons, guided missiles and atom bombs were made very quickly [in China], and we produced a hydrogen bomb in only 2 years and 8 months. Our development has been faster than that of America, Britain and France. We are now in 4th place in the world. Guided missiles and atom bombs are great achievements. This is the result of Khrushchev's "help." By withdrawing the [Soviet nuclear and missile] experts, he forced us to take our own road. We should give him a big medal.

U.S. imperialism is even more isolated. All the peoples of the world know that U.S. imperialism is the chief cause of war. The peoples of the whole world, even the American people, are against it. Soviet revisionism has been further exposed, particularly in this Middle East affair. The Soviet revisionists used Khrushchev's tricks again. They sent over 2,000 military experts to the UAR. First they went in for adventurism and sent warships in. Then they persuaded the UAR not to be the first to attack, and at the same time told Johnson on the hot line—there was no hot line in Khrushchev's day. Johnson lost no time in telling Israel to launch a surprise attack. 60% of the UAR's aircraft was destroyed on the ground. Soviet aid to the UAR amounted to $2.3 billion, but in the end the UAR surrendered and stopped fighting. This is another big exposure of how the nationalist states are betrayed.

A lot of places are anti-China at the moment, which makes it look as though we are isolated. In fact they are anti-China because they are afraid of the influence of China, of the thought of Mao Tse-tung, and of the Great Cultural Revolution. They oppose China to keep the people in their own countries down and to divert popular dissatisfaction with their rule. This opposition to China is jointly planned by U.S. imperialism and Soviet revisionism. This shows not that we are isolated, but that our influence throughout the world has greatly increased. The more they oppose China the more they spur on popular revolution; the people of these countries realize that the Chinese road is the road to liberation. China should not only be the political center of the world revolution. It must also become the military and technical center of the world revolution.

U.S. State Secy. Rusk was accused of raising a "yellow peril" issue as a result of comments he made during a press conference in Washington Oct. 12, 1967. Rusk had asserted that Communist China posed a threat to world peace. He said: "Within the next decade or 2 there will be a billion Chinese on the mainland armed with nuclear weapons. . . . The free nations of Asia will make up at least a billion people. They don't want China to overrun them on the basis of a doctrine of the world revolution." "From the strategic point of view it is not very attractive to think of the world cut in 2 by Asian communism, reaching out through Southeast Asia and Indonesia . . . and that these . . . people in the free nations . . . should be under the deadly and constant pressure of the anthorities in

Peking, so that their future is circumscribed by fear." The
Administration was "not picking out Peking as some sort of
special enemy. Peking has nominated itself by proclaiming a
militant doctrine of the world revolution, and doing something
about it."

Sen. Eugene J. McCarthy (D., Minn.) charged in the
Senate Oct. 16 that Rusk had raised the "specter" of the
"yellow peril." McCarthy said: This could only "obscure the
issue upon which judgment should be made and cause further
frustration and division within the country as well as between
the Congress and the Executive Branch"; "if this is the specter
that is haunting Asia, it is difficult to see how we will rid Asia
of it even though we achieve an unpredictable and total victory
in South Vietnam."

A State Department statement later Oct. 16 said Rusk
"wholly repudiates the effort to put into his mouth or into his
mind the notion of a 'yellow peril.' " The concerns of the free
nations of Asia over the militancy of Red China, the statement
said, "have much to do with their security, with our security
and with the peace of the world. They have nothing to do
with race."

U.S. State Undersecy. Nicholas deB. Katzenbach suggested
in an address before the World Affairs Council in Philadelphia
Nov. 27, 1967 that the development of its nuclear capability
might have a "sobering" effect on China. He said:

   . . . Communist China is rushing to an advanced nuclear capability at
the same time that it is showing not the least inclination to adjust itself to the
realities of world affairs. Its military strength is maturing far more rapidly
than the political and social institutions which are the custodians of that
strength. We can only view with apprehension growing power controlled by
individuals who, at least at present, are devoted to a doctrine of extreme revolutionary militancy.
   But nuclear weapons have a sobering effect of their own. Once a nation
is a nuclear power among other nuclear powers, it has to begin thinking of
what Herman Kahn has called the unthinkable—nuclear strategy. And at that
juncture a country begins to think not only of the damage it can do but of its
own vulnerabilities. It may be that Peking will come to take a soberer second
look at its present policies and world view. We, of course have an important
interest in encouraging prudence on Peking's part. And we hope that, together

with our retaliatory strength, our planned sentinel ABM defense will make a contribution to that end. At the same time the struggle in Vietnam should drive home the point that neither outright aggression nor its twin brother, the forcible manipulation of change, will be permitted to succeed.

Beyond physical defense we have to look upon Asia today much as we did upon Europe in the days of the Marshall Plan. . . . [T]he basic concept of pursuing a policy which contains the aggressors, helps strengthen those who might otherwise fall victim and thus creates a situation in which time runs in favor of constructive change, is both sound and relevant.

It would not be visionary, I think, to hope for some change someday in the view of Communist China's leaders, too. In the meantime, the United States must be prepared to work toward ways of living with Peking, however difficult that job seems today. We have already suggested—and must keep suggesting—those steps which would increase contacts and communications. . . .

'Revolutionary Committees' Take Over

Meanwhile, political developments in China had been dominated by a campaign against "the handful of people in authority taking the capitalist road." As the campaign progressed, the list of villains included such erstwhile luminaries as Peng Chen, former Peking mayor; Lu Ting-yi, former deputy premier, culture minister and director of the party's propaganda department; ex-Deputy Premier Lo Jui-ching, former army chief of staff; Teng Hsiao-ping, the party general secretary, and Liu Shao-chi, chief of state.

Correspondents for the Japanese newspapers *Asahi Simbun* and *Yomiuri Shimbun* reported from Peking Feb. 6, 1967 that Liu Shao-chi and Teng Hsiao-ping had been dismissed from all their party and government positions. The correspondents cited "diplomatic sources" in Peking; there was no official corroboration. The *Yomiuri* correspondent said that the 2 officials had been "absolved of all duties." The *Asahi* correspondent said that it was "common knowledge" that they had not acted in an official capacity since Aug. 1966. *Hung Chi,* the party theoretical journal, stated in an editorial Feb. 7, 1967 that Liu and Teng "are no longer revolutionary higher-ups; on the contrary, they are counter-revolutionary revisionists." The editorial added: "During war, when a commander becomes a traitor and surrenders to the enemy, a revolutionary fighter should not obey his commands but instead should turn his gun against him. This is true during war and it should also be so in a political struggle."

A Japanese Kyodo correspondent in Peking reported June 1 that Chou En-lai was taking over Liu Shao-chi's position as chief of state. Liu himself was reported to have made July 9 a self-criticism of his role during the Cultural Revolution at Peking Civil Engineering College. Liu was reported to have made another self-criticism Aug. 1 in the form of answers to questions that had been posed Apr. 1 in *Jenmin Jih Pao* and *Hung Chi*.

The People's Liberation Army (PLA) played a key role in the destruction of the old regime. The task of building a new order devolved on it as well. *Liberation Army Daily* reported Aug. 12 that Defense Min. Lin Piao, "the closest comrade-in-arms and best pupil of Chairman Mao," had been confirmed as Mao's successor by the 11th plenary session of the CCP Central Committee. The CCP Central Committee Sept. 5 issued a decree empowering the PLA to maintain order.

In a joint 1968 New Year's editorial, the 2 official Chinese Communist publications, *Jenmin Jih Pao* and *Hung Chi*, declared that the PLA was "the main pillar of the dictatorship of the proletariat, the great steel wall defending the Socialist motherland, the powerful backing of the Great Proletarian Cultural Revolution." It said that the army's contribution to the successes of the Cultural Revolution had been "tremendous" and that it would "undertake still more tasks of still greater importance" in 1968.

In reference to political activity, the editorial said that "a number of outstanding, advanced proletarian elements who have come forward in the Great Cultural Revolution should be admitted into the party." On the other hand, "the renegades, the secret agents and the diehard capitalist-roaders should be purged from the party," while "the small number of party members who made serious mistakes should undertake serious self-criticism." In addition to efforts to rectify the party organization, "the Communist Youth League, the Red Guards and the various revolutionary mass organizations should be rectified ideologically and organizationally," the editorial asserted. Such organizations should "affirm their achievements, overcome their shortcomings, strengthen their proletarian party spirit and get rid of bourgeois and petty-bourgeois factionalism."

The editorial defined as the "fighting tasks": (a) development of mass movement for creative study and application of Mao's thought; (b) consolidation of the revolutionary alliance, the "3 in one" combination of the party, the army and revolutionary masses; (c) rebuilding of the party; (d) the unity of the army and people; and (e) promotion of production and preparation for war. Emphasis in the editorial was no longer on the liquidation of the "capitalist-roaders" in authority but instead on the "revolutionary great alliance" based on Chairman Mao's thought, referred to as a "spiritual atom bomb."

Organizationally, the new drive for consolidation was directed toward the establishment of provincial revolutionary committees. During 1967, 9 such committees had come into existence (in Shanghai, Heilungkiang, Shantung, Kweichow, Shansi, Peking, Chinghai, Tientsin and Inner Mongolia). In 1968, revolutionary committees were established in 20 other areas. The province of Kiangsi led the list.

It was reported Jan. 6, 1968 that a broadcast in Nanchang, capital of Kiangsi Province, had announced earlier in the week the establishment of a revolutionary committee to succeed the Kiangsi Provincial Committee as the ruling body in the province. The broadcast said the committee was headed by Yang Tung-liang, an army commander. According to the broadcast, those attending a rally celebrating the formation of the committee had denounced Fang Chih-chun, the provincial governor and secretary of the Kiangsi Provincial Committee.

The formation of other revolutionary committees during 1968 was reported in the following chronological sequence: Kansu (Jan. 24), Honan (Jan. 27), Hopei (Feb. 3), Hupeh (Feb. 5), Kwantung (Feb. 21), Kirin (Mar. 3), Kiangsu (Mar. 23),

Chekiang (Mar. 24), Hunan (Apr. 8), Ninghsia (Apr. 10), Anhwei (Apr. 18), Shensi (May 1), Liaoning (May 10), Szechwan (May 31), Yunnan (Aug. 13), Fukien (Aug. 19), Kwangsi (Aug. 26), Sinkiang (Sept. 5) and Tibet (Sept. 5).

In each instance the seizure of power by Maoists was attended by violent struggles. Clashes among rival groups were reported to have continued in widespread areas of China in the spring and early summer of 1968. Evidence of the disorders was found in the wall posters of Maoist and rival factions, in the official Chinese press and in the discovery of bodies in the sea off the Chinese coast. The areas of China believed most affected by the fighting included Kwangsi, Kwangtung, Liaoning, Peking, Shensi and Tibet. *Among the details reported:*

Kwangsi— A June issue of *Angry Waves of the West River*, a Canton newspaper, reported severe fighting in the city of Wuchow, 125 miles from Canton. The violence was said to have resulted in hundreds of deaths, more than 3,000 arrests and many executions. More than 2,000 buildings were destroyed, leaving more than 40,000 homeless. The opposing forces apparently were the Apr. 22 Wuchow Revolutionary Rebel Grand Army and the Kwangsi Alliance Command; according to the *N.Y. Times* July 16, the Kwangsi Alliance Command, supported by the provincial governor, Wei Kuo-ching, had the upper hand. Earlier reports from travelers to the mainland indicated that 400 people had been killed at Liuchow in March during a fierce clash between the rival groups.

Kwangtung—Accounts of intense fighting in Kwangtung reached Hong Kong almost daily during June and July according to the *Washington Post* July 17. *Time* magazine reported July 19 that decomposed bodies, thought to be those of victims of the fighting in Kwangtung, had been found in the sea off Hong Kong in June and July. Many of the bodies were bound and bore evidence of execution. Canton, capital of the province, was the scene of particularly bloody clashes in May, June and July between 2 local Red Guard factions, each calling itself Maoist—the Tung Feng (East Wind) and the Hung Chi (Red Flag). The Tung Feng, as reported by the *Washington Post* July 17, was believed to represent about 70% of Canton's workers and was considered more conservative than its opponent. The Hung Chi was described as an aggressively revolutionary student group.

A visitor to Kwangtung was quoted as reporting that 47 people had died in a fire June 14 at Dr. Sun Yat-sen University in Canton. Another visitor reported the shooting in June of 10 students who had tried to stop an armored vehicle. The Kwangtung Revolutionary Committee June 15 authorized the army to shoot at unruly factions, but reports indicated that most troops had acted with restraint, presumably to prevent splits within the army itself. The clashes continued during July, and Canton radio reported July 16 that the latest outbreaks were "very acute and complicated." A Kwangtung radio broadcast July 18 spoke of a "white terror" struggle raging in the province. The fighting was aggravated by severe floods, which caused food shortages, cut communications and caused an internal refugee problem.

Reports from Canton appearing in the *N. Y. Times* July 25 indicated that the army had actively intervened in clashes between the Red Flag and East Wind revolutionaries. Previous Maoist policy had permitted mass organizations to carry out revolutionary activities with little interference from the army.

Liaoning—According to Peking wall posters Apr. 16, more than 100 people were killed in clashes in early April in Dairen, a port in northeast Liaoning Province. Shenyang, an industrial center in the province, was reported to have been hit by violence Apr. 4. The street fighting reportedly involved tanks and machine guns.

Peking—Wall posters in Peking June 30 announced that 15 students had been killed in clashes between 2 rival organizations at Chinhua University in Peking. Earlier reports by Agence France-Presse referred to battles at Peking University Apr. 28 between the warring Ching Kang-shan and New Peking factions. In each case rival groups occupied buildings of the university and barricaded them. Students charged rival fortresses with stones, spears and iron bars, wearing home-made armor and helmets fashioned from buckets.

Shensi—Wall posters in Peking said that 70 people had been killed and more than 100 wounded in clashes Apr. 12 between the armed forces and "counter-revolutionaries" in Shensi Province. The fighting reportedly took place Apr. 5—Apr. 14.

Tibet—Reports indicated that strife had broken out in Tibet between 2 rival groups, each claiming to be the true adherents of Mao Tse-tung. According to the *Asian Recorder* of New Delhi Apr. 29, People's Liberation Army units in Tibet were split between the 2 warring factions—the Great Alliance Group and the Rebel Revolutionary Group—and both sides were armed. It was reported that at least 700 people, including about 250 Tibetans, had been killed.

A series of executions for opposition to the Cultural Revolution was reported from China in April. Moscow radio said Apr. 3 that about 900 opponents of Mao had been executed in Canton, capital of the southern Chinese province of Kwangtung. 2 "spies" were publicly executed in Canton Mar. 23 after a public trial attended by more than 50,000 people. The trial, reported by a provincial newspaper quoted by Agence France-Presse, condemned 2 other "spies" to death, but they were given a 2-year reprieve. Shanghai radio reported Apr. 28 that 7 "counter-revolutionaries" had been executed in Shanghai's Cultural Revolution Square Apr. 27. The executions followed a public trial, witnessed by more than 10,000 people who were said to have "jumped with joy" when the executions took place. The broadcast, monitored in Hong Kong, reported that the trial was held "to defend the proletarian headquarters headed by Chairman Mao Tse-tung."

Economic Setbacks

The internal turmoil took a toll in the nation's economy. The Nationalist Chinese *Free China Weekly* Jan. 7, 1968 quoted a Jan. 3 Moscow broadcast as saying that Communist China's coal output had been reduced by 50% in 1967 because of the turmoil associated with the Cultural Revolution and that the shortage of coal had cut into rail transportation and power supplies. According to the account, Moscow also reported that iron and steel production had decreased markedly in 1967 at the Anshan (Lioning Province), Paotow (Inner Mongolian Autonomous Region) and Wuhan (Hupeh Province) plants.

Soviet trade with Communist China reached an all-time low in 1967. Figures released by the Soviet Ministry of Foreign Trade and reported by the *Washington Post* July 6 and 10 showed that Sino-Soviet trade in 1967 totaled $107 million, compared with $318.4 million in 1966 and $2.2 billion in 1959. Soviet exports to China aggregated $49.2 million in 1967, compared with $173.5 million in 1966; imports from China fell to $56.2 million, compared with more than $141.6 million in 1966.

A decline in Chinese trade with Communist countries in 1967 had been matched by an increase in mainland China's trade with Western Europe and Japan, countries that supplied China with machinery, chemicals, iron and steel and other items previously provided by the Soviet Union and Eastern Europe. But figures for the first quarter of 1968 indicated a substantial drop in trade with the West and Japan. The *Washington Post* reported July 10 that Chinese trade with Japan during the first quarter of 1968 was 26% below that of the first quarter of 1967. For the same period, China's trade with Great Britain declined by 38%, with West Germany by 19%.

Speaking at a Peking conference of transport workers May 12, 1968, Premier Chou En-lai had confirmed reports that political turmoil had stopped or slowed rail, port and other communications facilities throughout China. The text of his speech became available in Hong Kong after publication in *Hung Chi Tung-hsin [Red Flag Bulletin]*, a Canton Red Guard publication.

Discussing armed clashes in Liuchow, an important rail junction in Kwangsi, Chou stated: "As a result, traffic is at a standstill. Material cannot be transported to Hankow or Vietnam. Goods brought from Szechwan, Kweichow and Yunnan are piled up there." Chou also mentioned problems in the port of Dairen, where "transport timetables were disrupted and the production plans of the state undermined."

The *N.Y. Times* reported July 14 that statistics from countries trading with Communist China placed its total 1967 trade at $4.2 billion, down 1.4% from 1966. Chinese imports increased in 1967 to approximately $2.2 billion, but exports dropped about 9% to $1.97 billion.

China's industrial production for the first part of 1968, though slightly above 1967's level, was still substantially below levels reached before the start of the cultural revolution, according to the *Times* July 14. The production of coal, the source of 90% of all energy utilized in China, was estimated to be 20% to 25% below the normal 1966 output of 240 million tons. Similar cutbacks were noted in railway mile-tonnages.

Drive for Unity

The Cultural Revolution entered the phase of consolidation in the latter part of 1968. Chinese Communist Party journals and newspapers stressed the need for order and unity. A 1969 New Year's editorial jointly published by *Jenmin Jin Pao (People's Daily)*, *Hung Chi (Red Flag)* and *Chieh-fang-chun Pao (Liberation Army Daily)* said: "All revolutionary comrades and revolutionary masses should pay close attention to considering the interests of the whole. The interests of the part. must be subordinated to the interests of the proletariat as a whole. Any tendency towards the mountain-stronghold mentality and sectarianism . . . runs counter to the fundamental interests of the masses." The editorial called on the Chinese people to establish "democratic centralism" and to "consciously use Mao Tse-tung's thought to achieve unified thinking, policies, plans, command and actions."

The emphasis on China's need for unity was taken as an attempt to counter the decentralization of power that apparently had occurred in the past year. The *N.Y. Times* reported Jan. 5 that monitored broadcasts showed that a number of provincial leaderships had taken divergent stands on major policy issues. The *Times* also reported that signs of conflict had appeared in some revolutionary committees.

Among other indications of Peking's new orientations was the return of former party Gen. Secy. Teng Hsiao-ping to Peking, as reported by the *Washington Post* Jan. 22, 1969. Teng had been assailed as a leading critic of Mao Tse-tung and had been denounced as, after former Chief-of-State Liu Shao-chi, the "other top party person taking the capitalist road." He had been purged from the party Politburo, Secretariat and State Council and had been publicly reviled. Although Teng's re-emergence was not officially confirmed, he reportedly was seen attending "self criticism" classes in Peking, a sign that he was being exonerated.

After 2 months of seclusion, Mao Tse-tung attended a massive, 40,000-person reception in Peking Jan. 25. Mao's appearance ended Western press speculation about his ill-health or death. Mao was described as in "excellent health and high spirits."

Tillman Durdin of the *N.Y. Times* reported Jan. 16 that a massive migration from urban areas to the countryside had taken place in China. The main reason behind the exodus, which reportedly involved 15 to 20 million persons, was believed to be the desire to clear the cities not only of intellectuals and undisciplined youths but also of persons who had been disruptive during the Cultural Revolution.

The draft of a new Chinese Communist Party constitution, which became available outside China early in January, formally designated Defense Min. Lin Piao as Mao's "close comrade-in-arms and successor." The proposed constitution, together with a report on the "crimes" of Liu Shao-chi, was circulating among Chinese provincial officials. The new draft appeared to be a nonlegalistic, flexible document that would be susceptible to manipulation by party factions and regional authorities. Compared with the 1956 constitution then in force, which consisted of 9 chapters and 60 articles, the new constitution contained only 6 chapters and 12 articles.

In addition to the unusual act of constitutionally designating a successor to Mao, the proposed charter declared the absolute leadership of the party under Mao and emphasized the party's goal "to overthrow the bourgeoisie completely, to replace the bourgeois dictatorship with the dictatorship of the proletariat and to defeat capitalism with socialism." It militantly confirmed the Communist Party fight "to overthrow imperialism headed by the United States, modern revisionism headed by the Soviet revisionist renegade clique, and reactionaries of all countries. . . . " The 1956 constitution had not mentioned Mao by name and had emphasized the principle of "collective leadership" and China's friendship for the Soviet Union as the leader of the Socialist world.

While the draft's emphasis centered on Mao's leadership and the party's aims, its provisions for changes in party organization were considered possibly more significant. The text proposed that new members be accepted on recommendation of 2 party members with approval by the party branch and a higher party committee, while the 1956 constitution required new members to be elected. Further, under the draft constitution, new members would no longer be required to serve a probationary period. In addition, the proposed draft provided that local and national party congresses, to be held at regularly scheduled intervals, could, if circumstances dictated, be convened early or not at all.

The long-awaited 9th Congress of the Chinese Communist Party opened in Peking Apr. 1, 1969. The congress, attended by 1,512 delegates, was the first one held since 1956, and it began without any advance announcement. The meeting, which lasted until Apr. 24, adopted the new party constitution naming Lin Piao as successor to Mao, approved a political report submitted by Lin and elected a new Central Committee.

For the first 2 weeks, the only official report on the meeting was contained in a press communique issued by the Secretariat of the congress's Presidium Apr. 1. The communique said that Mao had given an "extremely important speech," but it did not describe its contents. Mao had formally opened the congress, which then unanimously elected him chairman of the meeting's Presidium. Lin Piao was elected as vice chairman and Chou En-lai as secretary-general. A total of 176 persons were elected to the Presidium, including Mao's wife, Chiang Ching; Lin's wife, Yeh Chun; army chief of staff Huang Yung-sheng, Foreign Min. Chen Yi, and 5 army marshals. (The marshals, Liu Po-cheng, Chu Teh, Hsu Hsiang-chien, Nieh Jung-chen and Yeh Chien-ying, all had been denounced at one time or another during the Cultural Revolution.) Chien Hsueh-shen, former colonel in the U.S. Air Force during World War 11 and a leading missile expert, also was elected.

After the Apr. 1 communique, there was official silence until Apr. 14, when a communique of the Presidium's Secretariat announced that the congress that day had unanimously adopted the party constitution, which "clearly stipulated that comrade Lin Piao is the successor of Chairman Mao," and had approved Lin's political report. The communique gave no details of the documents, but Hsinhua publicized Lin's report Apr. 27.

The main thrust of Lin's 24,000-word report was a program for continued hard-line revolutionary action at home and abroad. Lin said that the Cultural Revolution, initiated by Mao, had won a "great victory"; it had purged revisionist leaders and influences "headed by the renegade, hidden traitor and scab Liu Shao-chi." Lin asserted, however, that the revolution's work was not finished: "All revolutionary comrades must be clearly aware that class struggle will by no means cease in the ideological and political spheres. The struggle between the proletariat and the bourgeoisie by no means dies out with the seizure of power. . . ." Lin underscored the importance of the armed forces as the "mighty pillar of the dictatorship of the proletariat." He declared: "From the Marxist point of view, the main component of the state is the army."

In the economic sphere, Lin did not appeal for rapid industrialization. Rather, he called for "new leaps forward" in construction and economic production and said that the emphasis would be on increasing agricultural production, not on industrial output. Lin warned that any opposition to Mao or his doctrines "would be condemned and punished by the whole party and the whole nation." But he advocated leniency for oppositionists who confessed. He said: "The policy of 'killing none and not arresting most' should be applied to all except the active counterrevolutionaries against whom there is conclusive evidence of crimes, such as murder, arson or poisoning and who should be dealt with in accordance with the law."

Lin sharply attacked "U.S. imperialism" and Soviet "revisionism." Claiming that the U.S. and USSR had colluded and attempted to divide and control the world, Lin said that China had to make preparations for the possibility that either the U.S. or the USSR might "at an early date" launch a conventional or nuclear war. Quoting a hitherto unpublicized statement of Mao, Lin said: "With regard to the question of world war, there are but 2 possibilities: One is that the war will give rise to revolution and the other is that revolution will prevent war." Lin assailed the U.S. "occupation" of Taiwan and added that the Chinese army was "determined to liberate the sacred territory of Taiwan."

Terming the USSR's leadership a "revisionist, renegade clique," Lin attacked the Soviet doctrines of "limited sovereignty," "international dictatorship" and "Socialist community." He said: "What does all this [the doctrines] mean? It means that your sovereignty is 'limited' while his is unlimited. You won't obey him? He will exercise 'international dictatorship' over you—dictatorship over the people of other countries to form the 'Socialist Communist' rule by the new czar. . . ."

Lin pledged Peking's support for national revolutionary movements everywhere, but in particular he cited Albania's "struggle against imperialism and revisionism," the Vietnamese people's "war of resistance against U.S. aggression," and "the people of Czechoslovakia and other countries in their just struggle against Soviet revisionist social imperialism." In stressing Chinese support of wars of national liberation, Lin said: "Our proletarian foreign policy is not based on expediency; it is a policy in which we have long persisted. This is what we did in the past, and we will persist in doing the same in the future."

The 3d item on the agenda, the election of Central Committee members, took place Apr. 24, the final day of the congress. The size of the committee was expanded considerably: 170 members and 109 alternates were elected, compared with a total membership of 198 persons elected at the 8th Party Congress in 1956. Mao was elected chairman and Lin vice chairman. Other prominent members of the Central Committee included Chou En-lai; Chen Po-ta, director of the Cultural Revolution; Yeh Chun; Chiang Ching; Wu Fa-hsien; Chang Chun-chiao, political commissar of the Nanking region; Wang Tung-hsing, deputy minister of Public Security; Yao Wen-yuan, vice chairman of the Shanghai Revolutionary Committee; Kang Sheng, adviser to Chen; Huang Yung-sheng, chief of the General Staff; Wen Yu-cheng; and Hsieh Fu-chih, chairman of the Peking Revolutionary Committee. Gen. Wang En-mao, leader of Sinkiang Province, who had come under attack by the Peking government, was elected an alternate member. Liu Shao-chi was removed from the Central Committee.

Of the 99 members of the Central Committee elected in 1956, only 32 were reelected to the new committee, and 2 others were elected as alternates. Of the 99 alternates elected in 1956, only one remained as candidate member, 13 were promoted to full membership, and 85 were dropped entirely. The N.Y. Times commented Apr. 26 that the list of committee members revealed that the army, "pragmatists" and "moderates" had emerged from the congress slightly strengthened. But it noted that confirmed Maoists associated with the purported excesses of the Cultural Revolution remained numerous.

The final communique of the congress Apr. 24 indicated that the party would continue the programs and policies begun during the Cultural Revolution. It called on the people to implement Mao's policies and carry "struggle-criticism-transformation" "through to the end." The communique also said:

... The 9th National Congress of the Communist Party of China extends a warm and militant salute to the heroic Albanian Party of Labor and the genuine fraternal Marxist-Leninist parties and organizations all over the world, to the revolutionary people of the 5 continents who are waging valiant struggles against imperialism headed by the United States, modern revisionism with the Soviet revisionist renegade clique as its center and the reactionaries of various countries, and to the heroic Vietnamese people who persist in carrying through to the end the war of resistance against U.S. aggression and for national salvation. The Congress solemnly declares: The Communist Party of China, nurtured by the great leader Chairman Mao, always upholds proletarian internationalism and firmly supports the revolutionary struggles of the proletariat and the oppressed peoples and nations of the whole world. We are determined to unite with the genuine Marxist-Leninists all over the world and the broad masses of the proletariat and of the revolutionary people in all countries, thoroughly smash the plot of U.S.-Soviet collusion to redivide the world and carry through to the end the great struggle against imperialism, revisionism and all reaction.

U.S. imperialism, Soviet revisionism and the reactionaries in the world are all paper tigers. They cannot escape their doom. Their difficulties are insurmountable. The revolutionary cause of the people the world over will definitely triumph. We are fully aware: There will still be difficulties and twists and turns on our way forward, and the reactionaries at home and abroad will still put up a last-ditch struggle. But all this cannot stop the victorious advance of our great cause of socialism. Armed with Mao Tsetung Thought, the Chinese people and the Chinese people's Liberation Army are invincible. We are determined to liberate Taiwan! We are determined to defend the sacred territory and sovereignty of our great motherland! All the schemes, sabotage and shameless aggression by U.S. imperialism, Soviet revisionism and the reactionaries abroad and all the schemes and sabotage by the domestic reactionaries are bound to be smashed to smithereens by the iron fist of the Chinese people and the Chinese people's Liberation Army who are fully prepared! Ours is an era in which imperialism is heading for total collapse and socialism is advancing to worldwide victory, a great era in which Marxism-Leninism-Mao Tsetung Thought triumphs all over the world. Let us closely follow the great leader Chairman Mao and advance valiantly to win new and greater victories! ...

The Central Committee elected a 21-man Politburo with 4 alternates and a 5-man Politburo Standing Committee Apr. 28. According to Hsinhua, the members of the standing committee —which made all decisions when the Central Committee and Politburo were not in session—were Mao (chairman), Lin (vice chairman), Chen Po-ta, Chou En-lai and Kang Sheng. (The announcement said that after Mao and Lin, the names of the other members were listed in the Chinese equivalent of alphabetical order, indicating that Chou had lost his position as 3d man in the Chinese hierarchy after Mao and Lin.) The size of the new standing committee was smaller than the old one, which originally had 7 members and which had been enlarged by at least 3 during the Cultural Revolution. Prominent members dropped from the new Politburo were Chen Yi, foreign minister; Li Fu-chun, chairman of the State Planning Commission; Chen Yun, one-time economic planner of the Peking regime; Nieh Jung-chien, leader of China's nuclear weapons development, and Hsu Hsiang-chen, a military officer. The new Politburo contained 9 military men.

Revolution Runs Full Cycle

A new campaign to strengthen control over China's youth emerged May 4, 1969. In a joint editorial published by *Jenmin Jih Pao (People's Daily)*, the Communist Party ideological journal *Hung Chi (Red Flag)* and *Chiehfang Chun Pao (Liberation Army Daily)*, the Peking government emphasized that "young intellectuals" must "integrate themselves with the masses of workers and peasants." The editorial, timed to coincide with the 50th anniversary of the May 4th Movement—a campaign begun in 1919 by Chinese students protesting sections of the Versailles Treaty that deprived China of parts of its territory—said that while "young intellectuals and Red Guards" had made great contributions to the Cultural Revolution, they also "must take the road of integrating themselves with the workers, peasants and soldiers." The editorial warned that "many intellectuals often vacillate and lack a thoroughly revolutionary spirit." To overcome this condition, the editorial said, intellectuals "must make up their minds to take the workers, peasants and soldiers as their teachers for a long period of time and honestly accept their re-education and unswervingly keep to this correct road." The editorial quoted an article written 30 years ago by Mao Tse-tung: " . . . the dividing line between revolutionary intellectuals and non-revolutionary or counterrevolutionary intellectuals is whether or not they are willing to integrate themselves with the workers and peasants and actually do so."

An editorial in *Jenmin Jih Pao* May 5, entitled "The Proletariat Must Unite the Overwhelming Majority of People Around Itself," declared that the proletariat had "the resolution, strength and daring to unite with, educate and remold the intellectuals." The editorial quoted Mao's dictum that the children of intellectuals who had commited crimes or mistakes "can be educated."

In a joint editorial published by *Jenmin Jih Pao, Hung Chi* and *Chiehfang Chun Pao* June 8, the Peking government announced a new drive to unite the Chinese people. The editorial, reported in English June 9 by the official New China News Agency, was circulated by the provincial press and radio. According to the editorial, the unity drive was begun on instructions given by Mao Tse-tung during the 9th Party Congress. Mao was reported to have said: "Unite for the single purpose of consolidating the dictatorship of the proletariat. This must be realized in every factory, village, office and school." In offering a reprieve for those who had committed mistakes during the Cultural Revolution, the editorial quoted another teaching of Mao: "We have come together from every corner of the country and should be good at uniting in our work not only with comrades who hold the same view as we but also with those who hold different views. There are some among us who have made very serious mistakes; we should not be prejudiced against them but should be ready to work with them."

The 3 Chinese Communist papers July 1 called for the rebuilding of the party's structure and leadership. In a joint editorial entitled "Long Live the Communist Party," they called for total obedience to the party's policies and leadership. The editorial said: The party Central Committee "is the only center of leadership for the whole party, the whole army and the people throughout the country. The whole party must observe unified discipline and be subordinate to the Central Committee." It asserted that no organization was free of the committee's leadership—not the Red Guards, the army or the Communist Youth League.

Nearly 2 months later the Peking government, through a joint editorial in the 3 papers Aug. 24, again announced a campaign against factionalism and opposition to the Cultural Revolution. Entitled "Firmly Grasp Revolutionary Mass Criticism," the editorial said that the view that mass criticism had ended "was completely out of keeping with the actual situation on the ideological front." Stating that "the bourgeoisie has never ceased its ideological struggle against the proletariat," the editorial listed three targets:

(1) Revisionism and the "pernicious influence of Liu Shao-chi's counterrevolutionary revisionist line in the political and economic spheres and in all spheres of culture." The editorial singled out the areas of art and literature, where, it said, "there are still a number of poisonous weeds, and we must choose the typical ones and subject them to more deep-going criticism." In this category, the editorial included the "Soviet revisionist renegade clique."

(2) Mistaken ideas and erroneous tendencies in the revolutionary ranks and party. The factions in this category were sectarianism, mountain-stronghold mentality, small-group mentality, anarchism, liberalism and individualism. The editorial then quoted a teaching of Mao Tse-tung: "We stand for active ideological struggle because it is the weapon for ensuring unity within the party and the revolutionary organizations in the interest of our fight. Every Communist and revolutionary should take up this weapon."

(3) "Capitalist tendencies in general." People in this category—unreformed landlords, counterrevolutionaries, rich peasants and "bad elements and rightists"—had attempted to "sabotage the Socialist ownership, use various methods to corrupt our old and new cadres and the youth, whip up the evil wind of counterrevolutionary economism to disrupt the Socialist production and the tasks of struggle—criticism—transformation."

The editorial concluded: "We should also organize small groups of people who will collect abundant material . . . and produce convincing analytical articles of comparitively high quality, strike home, so as to promote the development of mass criticism."

Western observers regarded the editorial as an indirect admission that factionalism and ideological deviations still remained serious problems in China.

ELUSIVE PEACE (1969-70)

New Beginning

Richard Milhous Nixon became the 37th President of the U.S. Jan. 20, 1969. His inaugural address, cast for the most part in general terms, was solemn and restrained. It stressed the importance of international peace and America's need for reconciliation of black and white. It made no specific references to the war in Vietnam, nor did it chart the new Administration's policy on such issues as the nuclear nonproliferation treaty or U.S.-Soviet talks on arms limitation.

But the new President declared: "As we learn to go forward together at home, let us also seek to go forward together with all mankind. Let us take as our goal: where peace is unknown, make it welcome; where peace is fragile, make it strong; where peace is temporary, make it permanent. After a period of confrontation, we are entering an era of negotiation. Let all nations know that during this Administration our lines of communication will be open. We seek an open world—open to ideas, open to the exchange of goods and people, a world in which no people, great or small, will live in angry isolation. We cannot expect to make everyone our friend, but we can try to make no one our enemy. Those who would be our adversaries, we invite to a peaceful competition—not in conquering territory or extending dominion, but in enriching the life of man."

At his first press conference as President, held Jan. 27, Nixon expressed his views on China and Vietnam—again in general terms:

China—"The policy of this country and this Administration at this time will be to continue to oppose Communist China's admission to the United Nations." But the Nixon Administration looked forward to the scheduled Feb. 20 meeting with Peking's negotiators in Warsaw, and "we will be interested to see what the Chinese Communist representatives may have

181

to say at that meeting, whether any changes of attitude on their part on major substantive issues may have occurred. Until some changes occur on their side, however, I see no immediate prospect of any change in our policy."

Vietnam—The talks in Paris were "going to take time," and "overly optimistic statements" were not "helpful." "Rather than submitting a laundry list of various proposals, we have laid down those things which we believe the other side should agree to and can agree to. . . , matters that we think can be precisely considered and on which progress can be made." There was "a new team" in Paris with "new direction" and "a new sense of urgency." "There will be new tactics. We believe that those tactics may be more successful than the tactics of the past."

Direct communication between Red China and the U.S. appeared to have lapsed in Nov. 1968 due to another postponement of the Warsaw meetings between the 2 governments and the closing of a telephone-radio link across the Pacific. However, Peking Nov. 26 proposed that its representatives meet with those of the Nixon Administration Feb. 20, 1969 in Warsaw. The statement, issued by the Foreign Ministry, called on the U.S. to join "an agreement on the 5 principles of peaceful coexistence" and "to immediately withdraw all its armed forces from China's Taiwan Province and the Taiwan Straits and dismantle all its military installations in Taiwan Province." According to the *N.Y. Times* Nov. 27, there was no previous record of a "public" call by China for a peaceful co-existence agreement with the U.S. The "5 principles of peaceful coexistence," one of the public tenets of Chinese foreign policy in the mid-1950s, were: mutual respect for territorial integrity and sovereignty, mutual nonagression, mutual noninterference in internal policy, equality and mutual benefit and peaceful coexistence.

The Chinese Foreign Ministry statement of Nov. 26, 1968 indicated some of the problems involved in the acrimonious U.S.-Chinese ambassadorial talks. The text of the Chinese statement:

On Nov. 18, the U.S. State Department press officer and the U.S. embassy in Poland issued statements in which they did their utmost to distort the fact and divulged the discussions between China and the United States about the date of the 135th meeting of the Sino-U.S. ambassadorial talks, falsely accusing the Chinese side of having no intention of holding the meeting as scheduled and failing over a long period of time to respond to the U.S. proposal. In this connection, the spokesman of the Information Department of the Ministry of Foreign Affairs of the People's Republic of China has been instructed to refute as follows:

1. The position of the Chinese side on the date of the 135th meeting of the Sino-U.S. ambassadorial talks has been consistent and explicit and is in conformity with the principle of reaching agreement through consultation between the 2 sides. The 135th meeting of the Sino-U.S. ambassadorial talks was originally scheduled for May 29. On May 18, the Chinese side suggested that the meeting be postponed till the middle of November or late November, and the U.S. side later agreed to this suggestion. Since then, the Chinese side has not changed its view. It is utterly groundless and most absurd for the U.S. side to assert that the Chinese side has no intention of acting upon its own proposal.

2. The U.S. side has played a host of tricks on the date of this meeting. In its letter of Sept. 12, it wanted to fix the date of the meeting rigidly for Nov. 20. On Nov. 8, it gave an oral notice demanding that the Chinese side reply to its suggestion of Sept. 12 within a time limit of 5 days. This is a typical imperialist attitude. Furthermore, on Nov. 15, it sent over a written notice, in which it groundlessly "assumed" that China has no intention of acting upon its original proposal and suggested that the meeting be postponed till Feb. 5 or 11 next year. Without waiting for a reply from the Chinese side, the U.S. government unilaterally announced on Nov. 18 a postponement of the meeting in violation of the principle of reaching agreement through consultation. It must be pointed out that the days when U.S. imperialism can ride roughshod over the world and order others about are long gone, never to return. It is a sheer pipe dream to expect that the Chinese government will accept such insolence from U.S. imperialism!

3. What is the aim of the U.S. side in putting up such a singular performance within a short space of 10 days? Evidently, the U.S. government has no intention whatsoever to hold the Sino-U.S. ambassadorial talks within this year but is trying hard to postpone the 135th meeting of the Sino-U.S. ambassadorial talks till February next year while shifting the responsibility for the postponement onto the Chinese side. To put it bluntly, this is because the United States is going to change its president, and the U.S. government is now in a stage wherein the incoming is superseding the outgoing; hence it must try to drag on until the present period is over.

4. Actually why should the U.S. side have taken the trouble of doing all this? Since you find it necessary to postpone the meeting, say it outright! The Chinese side can give consideration to it. Chen Tung, charge d'affaires a. i. of the embassy of the People's Republic of China in Poland, already wrote to the U.S. ambassador to Poland, Mr. Walter J. Stoessel Jr., on Nov. 25, making a concrete suggestion that the 2 sides might as well meet on Feb. 20 next year. By that time, the new U.S. president

will have been in office for a month, and the U.S. side will probably be able to make up its mind.

5. Over the past 13 years the Chinese government has consistently adhered to the following 2 principles in the Sino-U.S. ambassadorial talks: first, the U.S. government undertakes to immediately withdraw all its armed forces from China's territory Taiwan Province and the Taiwan Straits area and dismantle all its military installations in Taiwan Province; 2d, the U.S. government agrees that China and the United States conclude an agreement on the 5 principles of peaceful coexistence. But in the past 13 years, while refusing all along to reach an agreement with the Chinese government on these 2 principles, the U.S. government, putting the cart before the horse, has kept on haggling over side issues. The Chinese government has repeatedly told the U.S. side in explicit terms that the Chinese government will never barter away principles. If the U.S. side continues its current practice, no result whatsoever will come of the Sino-U.S. ambassadorial talks no matter which administration assumes office in the United States.

U.S. Amb.-to-Poland John A. Gronouski conferred with Communist Chinese Charge d'Affaires Chen Tung in Warsaw for 2½ hours Jan. 8, 1968. According to custom, neither side divulged what had been discussed. Gronouski said simply that the conferees had "frank and serious discussions on a number of problems which face the United States and the Chinese People's Republic." Although the talks were normally held at the ambassadorial level for both sides, the U.S. agreed to meet with the Chinese charge in view of the absence of Chinese Amb.-to-Poland Wang Kuo-chuan, who was still in Peking after having been called home in the summer of 1967.

The U.S. State Department announced Feb. 4 that the U.S. and Communist China had agreed to continue bilateral talks in Warsaw Feb. 20, one month after the resumption of formal talks Jan. 20 following a 2-year suspension. The U.S. again would be represented by Amb.-to-Poland Walter J. Stoessel Jr., and the Chinese by Charge D'Affaires Lei Yang. According to the *New York Times* Feb. 5, 2 sets of proposals were said to have been presented at the January meeting. The U.S. had offered exchanges of travelers in order to broaden contacts prior to any political agreements. Financial and trade arrangements also were reported to have been included in the U.S. proposal. Peking was said to have proposed political negotiations in an effort to achieve formal agreement on principles of peaceful coexistence.

At that time, Peking was engaged in negotiations with Italy and Canada for the establishment of diplomatic relations. This seemed to indicate that Communist China was moving toward resumption of the normal relations with the West that had been disrupted by the Cultural Revolution.

Then an unexpected event occurred. Liao Ho-shu, acting Communist Chinese charge d'affaires to the Netherlands, resigned his post Jan. 24 and asked permission to remain in the Netherlands. Sources in The Hague said that Liao feared he would be punished for his role in the 1966 death in Holland of a Chinese technician. Liao, 46, who did not ask for asylum, was granted permission to remain in the Netherlands for a period of time. The London *Times* reported Feb. 3 that Liao had been transferred to the Central Intelligence Agency in Bonn for interrogation before coming to the U.S. It also said that the Rumanian embassy had played a role in the defection and that Liao's final decision had been made after he received confirmation that his family had been smuggled to Hong Kong. The *Washington Post* reported Feb. 5 that The Hague was the center for Communist China's espionage system in Europe and that Liao, who was in charge of the mission, was expected to have intimate knowledge of its workings.

Liao arrived in Washington Feb. 4 and requested political asylum in the U.S.

Peking had protested Liao's defection and had demanded that the U.S. return him. A Chinese broadcast had said that the affair showed that Presidents Nixon and Johnson "are jackals of the same lair" and that the defection was "another towering crime committed by the U.S. government."

Liao's defection prompted Peking to cancell the ambassadorial meeting scheduled for Feb. 20. In a note delivered to U.S.-Amb. Stoessel, Peking charged that Liao "was incited to betray his country and [was] carried off to the United states by the Central Intelligence Agency," and it asserted that the Nixon Administration had "inherited the mantle of the preceding U.S. government in flagrantly making itself the enemy of the 700 million Chinese people."

In a statement distributed Feb. 18 by the State Department, Secretary of State William P. Rogers asserted that China's "charges . . . that the U.S. had engineered the defection of Liao Ho-shu are untrue." Rogers implied that the U.S. was prepared to accept a Chinese recommendation that the 2 countries agree to principles of peaceful coexistence. He indicated that the Nixon Administration intended to extend previous offers for cultural and scientific exchanges. Rogers also said that Stoessel had been directed to propose the reestablishment of telecommunications links severed Nov. 18, 1968.

Officials in Washington said that Peking had used the defection of Liao as a pretext for its action and that the 2 countries were still too far apart in their attitudes for meaningful talks.

Domestic Pressure on Nixon Administration

From the beginning, the Nixon Administration was under considerable domestic pressure to seek an accommodation with mainland China. Many of the arguments in favor of such a course—and the history of U.S.-Communist China relations—were summed up by Sen. Edward M. Kennedy (D., Mass.) in New York Mar. 20, 1969 in an address before the National Committee on United States-China Relations. Among Kennedy's remarks:

. . . For 20 years, our China policy has been a war policy. For far too long, we have carried out hostile measures of political, diplomatic and economic antagonism toward one of the world's most important nations. Now we must turn away from our policy of war and pursue a policy of peace. We must seek a new policy, not because of any supposed weakness in our present position or because we are soft on China, but because it is in our own national interest and the interest of all nations. By its sheer size and population, China deserves a major place in the world. As a nuclear power and a nation of 750 million citizens—likely to exceed one billion by the 1980's—China demands a voice in world efforts to deal with arms control and population control, with Asian security and international economic development, with all the great issues of our time.

Yet 16 years after the end of the Korean War, we do not trade with China. We have no scientific or cultural exchanges. We oppose the representation of China in the United Nations. We refuse to give any sort of diplomatic recognition to the Communist regime on the mainland and continue to recognize the Nationalist regime of Chiang Kai-shek on Taiwan as the government of all China. Instead of developing ways to coexist with China in peace, we assume China will attack us as soon as she can, and we prepare to spend billions to meet that threat. . . .

The division between us goes back to American support of the Chinese Nationalist regime during World War II and to the immediate post-war struggle between the Communists and the Nationalists. In the beginning, our policy was uncertain. The Communists gained power over the mainland in 1949. Between then and the outbreak of the Korean War in 1950, the United States seemed to be preparing to accept the fact of the Chinese Revolution. After the retreat of the Nationalists to Taiwan, our government refused to go to their aid and refused to place the American 7th Fleet in the Taiwan Straits to prevent a Communist takeover of the island. To do so, we said, would be to intervene in the domestic civil war between the Communists and the Nationalists.

This policy was fully debated by the Congress and the public. Although we deplored the Communist rise to power, we recognized we could do nothing to change it. We anticipated that we would soon adjust to the new Asian reality by establishing relations with the Communist regime.

This situation changed overnight on June 25, 1950, when North Korea attacked South Korea. Fearing that the attack foreshadowed a Communist offensive throughout Asia, the United States ordered the 7th Fleet into the Taiwan Strait and sent large amounts of military aid to the weak Nationalist government on the island. . . .

Shortly thereafter, in response to the attempt of our forces to bring down the North Korean government by driving toward the Chinese border, China entered the Korean War. With hindsight, most experts agree that China's action in Korea was an essentially defensive response, launched to prevent the establishment of a hostile government on her border. At the time, however, the issue was far less clear. At the request of the United States, the United Nations formally branded China as an aggressor, a stigma that rankles Peking's leaders even today.

While we fought the Chinese in Korea, we carried out a series of political and economic actions against their country. We imposed a total embargo on all American trade with the mainland. We froze Peking's assets in the United States. We demanded that our allies limit their trade with China. We conducted espionage and sabotage operations against the mainland, and supported similar efforts by the Nationalists. We began to construct a chain of bases, encircling China with American military power, including nuclear weapons. . . .

Let us look at our policy from the viewpoint of Peking: China's leaders see the United States supporting the Nationalists' pretense to be the government of the mainland. They see thousands of American military personnel on Taiwan. American warships guard the waters between the mainland and Taiwan. American nuclear bases and submarines ring the periphery of China. The United States supports Nationalist U-2 flights over the mainland, as well as Nationalist guerrilla raids and espionage. Hundreds of thousands of American soldiers are fighting in Vietnam to contain China. America applies constant diplomatic and political pressure to deny Peking a seat in the United Nations, to deny it diplomatic recognition by the nations of the world, and to deny it freedom of trade. We turn our nuclear warheads toward China. And now we prepare to build a vast ABM system to protect ourselves against China. In light of all these facts, what Chinese leader would dare to propose anything but the deepest hostility toward the United States? . . .

In large part, our continuing hostility toward China after the Korean War has rested on a hope that is now obviously forlorn, a hope that under a policy of military containment and political insolation the Communist regime on the mainland would be a passing phenomenon and would eventually be repudiated by the Chinese people. Few of us today have any serious doubt that communism is permanent for the foreseeable future on the mainland. There is no believable prospect that Chiang Kai-shek and the Nationalists will return to power there, however regrettable we may regard that fact. . . .

Almost âll other nations have adjusted to the reality of China. For years, Peking has had extensive diplomatic, commercial and cultural relations with a number of the nations in the world, including many of our closest allies. Outside the United Nations, our policy of quarantine toward China has failed. To the extent that the Communist regime is isolated at all, it is isolated largely at China's own choosing, and not as a consequence of any effective American policy.

Our actions toward China have rested on the premise that the People's Republic is an illegitimate, evil and expansionist regime that must be contained until it collapses or at least begins to behave in conformity with American interests. . . .

The Communist regime was said to be illegitimate because, we claimed, it had been imposed on the supposedly unreceptive Chinese people by agents of the Soviet Union. Communist China, according to this view, was a mere Soviet satellite. . . . This evaluation grossly exaggerated the extent to which Soviet aid was responsible for the Communist takeover of China, and the events of the past decade—amply confirmed by the intense hostility of the current border clashes—have shattered the myth of Soviet domination of China.

The Communist regime was said to be evil because of the great violence and deprivation of freedom that it inflicted on millions of people who opposed its rise to power. Obviously, we cannot condone the appalling cost, in human life and suffering, of the Chinese Revolution. Yet, in many other cases, we have recognized revolutionary regimes, especially when the period of revolutionary excess has passed. Even in the case of the Soviet Union the United States waited only 16 years to normalize relations with the revolutionary government.

Unfortunately, we have tended to focus exclusively on the costs of the Chinese revolution. We have ignored the historical conditions that evoked it and the social and economic gains it produced. We have ignored the fact that the Nationalists also engaged in repressive measures and deprivations of freedom, not only during their tenure on the mainland, but also on Taiwan. We have created a false image of a struggle between "Free China" and "Red China," between good and evil. . . .

Finally, there is the charge that the Communist regime is an expansionist power. At the bottom, it is this view that has given rise to our containment policy in Asia, with the enormous sacrifices it has entailed. The charge that the Communist regime is expansionist has meant different things at different times. On occasion, American spokesmen have conjured up the image of a "Golden Horde" or "Yellow Peril" that would swoop down over Asia. Today, most leaders in Washington employ more responsible rhetoric, and it is the Russians who perpetuate this image of China.

Virtually no experts on China expect Peking to commit aggression, in the conventional sense of forcibly occupying the territory of another country—as the Soviet Union recently occupied Czechoslovakia. Such action is in accord with neither past Chinese actions nor present Chinese capabilities. Despite their ideological bombast, the Chinese Communists have in fact been extremely cautious about risking military involvement since the Korean War. . . . [China's] navy and air force are small. She can neither transport her troops nor supply them across the long distances and difficult terrain of a prolonged war of aggression.

Obviously, our concern today is not so much the danger of direct Chinese aggression as the danger of indirect aggression, based on Chinese efforts to subvert existing governments and replace them with governments friendly to Peking. Yet, until Vietnam led to our massive involvement in Southeast Asia, Peking enjoyed only very limited success in its attempts to foster "wars of national liberation." Although China of course will claim to play a role wherever political instability occurs in Asia, Africa and even Latin America, its record of subversion is unimpressive. On the basis of the past, it is very likely that nations whose governments work for equality and social justice for their people will be able to overcome any threat of Chinese subversion.

Furthermore, we can expect that time will moderate China's revolutionary zeal. Experience with the Soviet Union and the Eastern European Communist nations suggests that the more fully China is brought into the world community, the greater will be the pressure to behave like a nation-state, rather than a revolutionary power.

Ironically, it is Communist China's former teacher, the Soviet Union, that it now determined to prevent any moderation of Chinese-American hostility. We cannot accept at face value the current Soviet image of China, for the Soviets have far different interests in Asia than we do. Although we must persist in our efforts to achieve wider agreement with Moscow, we must not allow the Russians to make continuing hostility toward Peking the price of future Soviet-American cooperation. Rather than retard our relations with Moscow, a Washington-Peking thaw might well provide the Soviet Union with a badly needed incentive to improve relations with us. . . .

Both of us—Chinese and Americans alike—are prisoners of the passions of the past. What we need now, and in the decades ahead, is liberation from those passions. Given the history of our past relations with China, it is unrealistic to expect Peking to take the initiative. It is our obligation. We are the great and powerful nation, and we should not condition our approach on any favorable action or change of attitude by Peking. For us to begin a policy of peace would be a credit to our history and our place in the world today. To continue on our present path will lead only to further hostility, and the real possibility of mutual destruction.

Of course, we must not delude ourselves. Even if the United States moves toward an enlighted China policy, the foreseeable prospects for moderating Chinese-American tensions are not bright. It is said that there is no basis for hope so long as the current generation of Communist Chinese leader's remains in power. This may well be true. Yet, Peking's invitation last November to resume the Warsaw talks, although now withdrawn, suggests the possibility that China's policy may change more rapidly than outside observers can now anticipate.

We must remember, too, that the regime in Peking is not a monolith. As the upheavals of the Great Leap Forward and the Cultural Revolution have shown, China's leaders are divided by conflicting views and pressures for change. We must seek to influence such change in a favorable direction. We can do so by insuring that reasonable options for improved relations with the United States are always available to Peking's moderate or less extreme leaders.

The steps that we take should be taken soon. Even now, the deterioration of Chinese-Soviet relations in the wake of the recent border clashes may be stimulating at least some of the leaders in Peking to re-evaluate their posture toward the United States and provide us with an extraordinary opportunity to break the bonds of distrust.

What can we do to hasten the next opportunity? . . . We must actively encourage China to adopt the change in attitude for which we now simply wait. We must act now to make clear to the Chinese and to the world that the responsibility for the present impasse no longer lies with us.

First, and most important, we should proclaim our willingness to adopt a new policy toward China—a policy of peace, not war, a policy that abandons the old slogans, embraces today's reality, and encourages tomorrow's possibility. We should make clear that we regard China as a legitimate power in control of the mainland, entitled to full participation as an equal member of the world community and to a decent regard for its own security. . . .

2d, we should attempt to reconvene the Warsaw talks. . . . If the talks are resumed, we should attempt to transform them into a more confidential and perhaps more significant dialogue. The parties might meet on an alternating basis in their respective embassies, or even in their respective countries, rather than in a palace of the Polish government. Whether or not the talks are resumed, more informal official and semi-official conversations with China's leaders should be offered.

3d, we should unilaterally do away with restrictions on travel and non-strategic trade. We should do all we can to promote exchanges of people and ideas, through scientific and cultural programs and access by news media representatives. In trade, we should place China on the same footing as the Soviet Union and the Communist nations of Eastern Europe. We should offer to send trade delegations and even a resident trade mission to China, and to receive Chinese trade delegations and a Chinese trade mission in this country. Finally, we should welcome closer contacts between China and the rest of the world, rather than continue to exert pressure on our friends to isolate the Peking regime.

4th, we should announce our willingness to re-establish the consular offices we maintained in the People's Republic during the earlist period of Communist rule, and we should welcome Chinese consular officials in the United States. . . .

5th, we should strive to involve the Chinese in serious arms controls talks. We should actively encourage them to begin to participate in international conferences, and we should seek out new opportunities to discuss Asian security and other problems.

6th, we should seek, at the earlist opportunity, to discuss with China's leaders the complex question of the establishment of full diplomatic relations. For the present, we should continue our diplomatic relations with the Nationalist regime on Taiwan and guarantee the people of that island against any forcible takeover by the mainland. . . .

To help elicit Peking's interest in negotiations, we should withdraw our token American military presence from Taiwan. This demilitarization of Taiwan could take place at no cost to our treaty commitments, or to the security of the island. Yet, it would help to make clear to Peking our desire for the Communists, the Nationalists, and the Taiwanese to reach a negotiated solution on the status of the island.

A dramatic step like unilateral recognition of Peking would probably be an empty gesture at this time. . . .

7th, without waiting for resolution of the complex question of Taiwan, we should withdraw our opposition to Peking's entry into the United Nations as the representative of China, not only in the General Assembly, but also in the Security Council and other organs. . . .

In addition, we should work, within the United Nations, to attempt to assure representation for the people on Taiwan that will reflect the island's governmental status. It may be that the Chinese Nationalists can continue to enjoy a seat in the General Assembly. Or, if an independent republic of Taiwan emerges, it might be admitted into the United Nations as a new state. Possibly, if a political accommodation is reached between the Communist regime on the mainland and the government on Taiwan, the people of Taiwan might be represented in the United Nations as an autonomous unit of China. . . .

There are many possible solutions to the China problem in the United Nations. Without insisting on any one, we should move now to free the United Nations to undertake the long-delayed process of adjusting to the reality of the People's Republic of China, and we should clearly indicate to Peking our willingness to discuss these questions.

In dealing with the problems of diplomatic recognition and United Nations representation, I have placed primary emphasis on the need to initiate discussions with Peking in these areas. Since it is impossible to predict when or how the Chinese will respond to a change in American policy, we cannot maintain a hard and fast position on these questions. We cannot afford to close any options by endorsing detailed schemes at this time. What we can do, however, is act now on the broad range of initiatives I have mentioned and make clear to Peking that our views are not rigid on even the most difficult issues that have divided us so bitterly in recent years.

We will have to be patient. Peking's initial reaction to serious initiatives on our part will probably be a blunt refusal. But, by laying the groundwork now for an improved relationship in the '70s and beyond, we will be offering the present and future leaders in Peking a clear and attractive alternative to the existing impasse in our relations.

. . . According to Chinese tradition, the model Confucian gentleman was taught that, whenever involved in a dispute, he should first examine his own behavior, ask himself whether he bears some responsibility for the dispute, and take the initiative to try to arrive at a harmonious settlement. It may prove futile for us to follow this advice when dealing with Chinese who claim to reject many of China's great traditions. But we will never know unless we try. If nothing changes, we Americans will have to live with the consequences of arms and fear and war. We owe ourselves, we owe the future, a heavy obligation to try.

Russian-Chinese Border Clashes

Soviet and Chinese border forces fought 2 skirmishes Mar. 2 and 15, 1969 on the Manchurian border 250 miles north of Vladivostok. The fighting, over a disputed island in the frozen Ussuri River, involved thousands of men, tanks and artillery;

its severity was indicated by the fact that 31 Soviet border guards were reported killed in the first clash. Unlike earlier border clashes between the 2 countries, the latest were immediately publicized by both governments. The incidents were regarded as the most dramatic development in Sino-Soviet relations since the rift between the 2 countries became public 10 years previously.

The first account of the fighting came from the Soviet Union, which announced Mar. 2 that its border guards had been fired on earlier that day by a Chinese military unit that crossed the border between Chinese Manchuria and the USSR's Maritime Territory. The Soviet government said that it had immediately protested to the Foreign Ministry in Peking. The note warned Peking: "The Soviet government reserves to itself the right to take resolute measures to stop provocations on the Soviet-Chinese border and warns the government of the Chinese People's Republic that responsibility for possible consequences of its adventurist policy, directed at exacerbating the situation on the borders between China and the Soviet Union, rests with the government of the Chinese People's Republic."

Peking rejected the Soviet protest the same day, charging the USSR with responsibility for the incident. In a note to the Soviet embassy in Peking, the Foreign Affairs Ministry asserted that "Soviet frontier guards intruded into the area of Chenpao [Damansky] Island, Heilungkiang Province, China, and killed and wounded many Chinese frontier guards by opening fire on them, thus creating an extremely grave border armed conflict. . . . This grave incident of bloodshed was entirely and solely created by the Soviet authorities." Peking warned Moscow to "immediately stop its encroachment upon China's territory" and further admonished: "China's sacred territory brooks no violation; if you should willfully cling to your reckless course and continue to provoke armed conflicts along the Sino-Soviet border, you will certainly receive resolute counter-blows from the Chinese people; and it is the Soviet government that must bear full responsibility for all the grave consequences arising therefrom."

Sovereignty over the islands in the Ussuri River had long been disputed by China and the USSR. Peking had contended that the 1860 Sino-Russian (Peking) treaty, which established the frontier, in effect had been imposed on China to enable Russia to seize vast tracts of its territory. Under the treaty, China had ceded to Russia all of its territory east of the Ussuri River. The New China News Agency claimed Mar. 3 that "Chenpao Island is indisputable Chinese territory and it always has been under Chinese jurisdiction and patrolled by Chinese frontier guards since long ago." The NCNA also reported that "between Nov. 1967 and Jan. 5, 1968, the Soviet revisionist renegade clique sent Soviet frontier guards on 18 occasions to intrude into the area of Chibiching Island, north of Chenpao Island . . . disrupting Chinese people's production and on many occasions killing and wounding Chinese people who were engaged in productive labor." Moscow, on the other hand, had argued that Peking was attempting to regain roughly 500,000 square miles of Far Eastern territory from the Soviet Union.

The *Washington Post* reported March 4 that about 800,000 Chinese troops—about 1/3 of China's armed forces—were believed to be positioned along the 6,000-mile Soviet-Chinese border, from Manchuria to Central Asia. Western intelligence analysts, according to the *N.Y. Times* Mar. 3, would not reveal their estimates of the number of Soviet troops along the border; however, they did say that the USSR had gradually built up its Far East defenses under a "large-scale program" under way for some time. The analysts also said that the build-up had continued even at the expense of Soviet troop commitments in Central Europe.

The Soviet embassy in Peking was besieged Mar. 3 by an estimated 10,000 demonstrators protesting the border incident. 2 Soviet correspondents were manhandled by the crowd but managed to enter the embassy compound. Posters throughout the city denounced "Soviet aggression" and "imperialism." A 2d protest note was delivered to Soviet officials by Deputy Foreign Min. Chi **Peng-fei,** who warned that decisive measures" would be taken if Moscow continued to "provoke incidents." The note was rejected by Moscow.

A joint editorial published March 4 by *Jenmin Jih Pao* and *Chiehfang Chun Pao,* the Communist Party and army newspapers, attacked Soviet leaders as "imperialists and prototype tsars." The editorial accused the Soviet Union of having collaborated with the U.S. "in the hope of rigging up an anti-China encirclement." It asserted that by their occupation of Czechoslovakia and their conversion of the "Mongolian People's Republic into their colony," Soviet leaders had shown that "they are more greedy than the tsar."

Thousands of demonstrators continued their protest against the USSR in the streets of Peking March 4. Carrying posters with the new slogan "Down with the Tsars!", the marchers denounced Soviet Premier Aleksei N. Kosygin and Communist Party Gen. Secy. Leonid I. Brezhnev. Soldiers and police protected the entrances to the Soviet embassy compound. Other massive anti-Soviet rallies were held throughout China's provinces.

In Moscow, the Soviet government Mar. 4 rejected Peking's version of the clash as "without foundation." The official news agency Tass charged the Peking regime with having taken "the road of dangerous provocative action." The Tass report also accused Peking of creating "nationalistic hysteria in the country. . . . The Mao Tse-tung group needed the latest anti-Soviet campaign to rally its supporters on a platform of adventurism and extreme chauvinism."

A new aspect was added to the conflict Mar. 5 and 6 when China accused the Soviet Union of collusion against it with the Nationalist Chinese regime on Taiwan, the U.S. and Japan. A reported 50,000 demonstrators in Wenchow, Chekiang Province, denounced Moscow Mar. 5 for "currying favor with the Nixon Administration and collaborating with bandit Chiang [Kai-shek] to wage anti-China activities and conduct acts of social imperialism and social fascism." The accusation of Soviet-Nationalist Chinese "collaboration" was based on a visit by the Soviet journalist Victor Louis to Taiwan in Oct. 1968.

In Moscow, a reported 100,000 Russians demonstrated outside the Chinese embassy Mar. 7. Shouting "Down with the Maoist clique" and "Hands off our Soviet borders," the rock-throwing protestors broke about 100 windows in the embassy. (The demonstrations were regarded as the largest government-organized protest in the Soviet capital in 50 years.) At a press conference held in Moscow that evening, Leonid M. Zamyatin, Foreign Ministry press chief, again warned China that "reckless provocations" would be met "with a proper rebuff." Zamyatin confirmed that 31 Soviet border guards had been killed in the Mar. 2 incident and another 14 had been injured; he also identified the commander of the Soviet border unit as a Senior Lt. (Ivan I.) Strelnikov. Zamyatin declared that China had provoked the incident to cover up its political and economic failures. He said that it was no accident that the "provocation" had come during preparations for the 9th Chinese Communist Party Congress. With a background of "anti-Soviet hysteria," Zamyatin said, it would be "easier to impose on the congress a platform hostile to the Soviet Union and the Communist Party and to give anti-Sovietism the status of state policy."

Another massive demonstration was held in Moscow Mar. 8 outside the Chinese embassy; the demonstrators burned and hanged effigies of Mao Tse-tung. In contrast to the demonstrations of the day before, strict discipline was kept.

In Peking, radio broadcasts Mar. 8 urged the Soviet people to begin "the 2d revolution" and set "the red star over the Kremlin shining again." The broadcasts said that over 260 million Chinese had participated in anti-Soviet demonstrations since Mar. 3.

The Peking government asserted Mar. 10 that the USSR had acknowledged in 1964 that Chenpao Island belonged to China. A Foreign Ministry statement said that "during the Chinese-Soviet boundary negotiations in 1964, the Soviet side could not but admit that these islands [Chenpao, Kapotze and Chilichin] are Chinese territory." Peking charged that Moscow had been unwilling to recognize the Sino-Soviet boundary treaties of 1858 and 1860 as "unequal"—imposed on China—and also had "refused to take these treaties as the basis for settling the boundary question . . . in its vain attempt to force China to accept a new unequal treaty and thus to perpetuate in legal form its occupation of Chinese territory that it seized by crossing the boundary line defined by the unequal treaties." Because of this situation, the statement said, "the Chinese side will have to reconsider its position as regards the Chinese-Soviet boundary as a whole."

In a note delivered to the Soviet embassy in Peking, the Chinese Foreign Ministry charged Mar. 13 that the USSR had made "repeated grave encroachments on Chinese territory" between Mar. 4 and 12 and had carried out "a series of military provocations in an attempt to provoke fresh armed conflicts." The Chinese listed 6 "intrusions" during the period.

Sources in Moscow said Mar. 14 that China had halted all Soviet shipments across its territory to North Vietnam. Trade Ministry officials said the blockage had come into effect after Mar. 2. *Le Monde,* quoting Communist diplomats at the UN, confirmed the Moscow report.

Peking Radio reported Mar. 16 that Chinese forces had held a victory celebration on Chenpao Island after the latest clash. The broadcast said that the Chinese troops had evicted the "intruders."

The Soviet newspaper *Izvestia* disclosed Mar. 17 that a Soviet colonel, D.V. Leonov, had been killed during the fighting Mar. 15. (The presence of a colonel, a regimental command rank, added to the speculation on the intensity and scale of the battle.)

The Communist Party newspaper *Pravda* reported March 18 that Chinese forces had initiated another attack on Damansky Island during the previous night.

Paris Peace Talks Deadlocked

The new U.S. Administration was preoccupied with mounting domestic dissent over the Vietnam War.

Prior to his inauguration, Pres. Nixon had appointed his former running mate in the 1960 presidential campaign, Henry Cabot Lodge Jr., as chief U.S. negotiator at the Paris negotiations on Vietnam. An expanded conference including the representatives of South Vietnam and the National Liberation Front (NLF) in addition to North Vietnam and the U.S. met Jan. 25, 1969 and promptly reached an impasse. Lodge proposed immediate restoration of the neutrality of the Demilitarized Zone (DMZ) along the border of South and North Vietnam as the first step toward peace. Xuan Thuy, chief North Vietnamese delegate, charged Jan. 30 that the U.S. proposal was a scheme to conceal "American aggressive design." He suggested instead that political questions be discussed first.

Allied and Communist negotiators failed to make progress at the 3d and 4th plenary sessions of the Paris peace talks Feb. 6 and 13. After the Feb. 13 meeting, Lodge said: "I don't expect much to come out of these public meetings."

The Paris talks still had made no headway by Feb. 23, when the Communist forces in Vietnam launched a major offensive. In a coordinated series of shellings and ground assaults, Viet Cong and North Vietnamese troops struck simultaneously at Saigon and at about 115 other towns and military targets. The attackers pounded at least 18 provincial capitals, 28 district towns and 60 military bases. In the first 15 hours of fighting, about 100 U.S. soldiers and 1,000 Communist troops were reported killed. South Vietnamese military casualties were reported light. But government officials reported Feb. 25 that in 3 days of mortar and rocket attacks the Communist forces had killed 52 civilians, wounded 263 and destroyed 123 buildings. 12 civilians were said to have been kidnapped.

U.S. and South Vietnamese forces launched 2 separate major drives in South Vietnam—in the Ashau Valley Mar. 1 (not disclosed until Mar. 23 for security reasons) and around Saigon Mar. 18—to counteract the Communist offensive. Viet Cong and North Vietnamese troops, however, continued to press their drive with widespread ground and rocket attacks against military and civilian centers throughout South Vietnam. U.S. military bases were the most frequently hit targets as the Communists exerted particularly strong pressure around Saigon and Danang.

Fighting continued until mid-June. Tran Buu Kiem, the NLF representative to the Paris talks, presented at the talks May 8 a 10-point peace proposal that called for the unconditional withdrawal of U.S. and allied troops from South Vietnam under "international supervision," the holding of free elections and the ultimate establishment of a coalition government, the restoration of the DMZ between North and South Vietnam, the exchange of war prisoners, the eventual reunification of North and South Vietnam and the application of the 1962 agreements on Laos. Text of the NLF's 10-point peace proposal:

Principles and main content of an over-all solution to the South Vietnam problem to help restore peace in Vietnam.

Proceeding from a desire to reach a political solution with a view to ending the United States imperialists' war of aggression in South Vietnam and helping restore peace in Vietnam,

On the basis of the guarantee of the fundamental national rights of the Vietnamese people,

Proceeding from the fundamental principles of the 1954 Geneva agreements on Vietnam and the actual situation in Vietnam,

On the basis of the political program and the 5-point position of the South Vietnam National Liberation Front, which keeps with the 4-point stand of the government of the Democratic Republic of North Vietnam,

The South Vietnam National Liberation Front sets forth the principles and main content of an overall solution to the South Vietnam problem to help restore peace in Vietnam as follows:

1. To respect the Vietnamese people's fundamental national rights, *i.e.*, independence, sovereignty, unity and territorial integrity, as recognized by the 1954 Geneva agreements on Vietnam.

2. The United States government must withdraw from South Vietnam all United States troops, military personnel, arms and war materiel of the other foreign countries of the United States camp without posing any condition whatsoever; liquidate all United States military bases in South Vietnam; renounce all encroachments on the sovereignty, territory and security of South Vietnam and the Democratic Republic of Vietnam.

3. The Vietnamese people's right to fight for the defense of their fatherland is the sacred, inalienable right to self-defense of all peoples. The question of the Vietnamese armed forces in South Vietnam shall be resolved by the Vietnamese parties among themselves.

4. The people of South Vietnam shall settle themselves their own affairs without foreign interference. They shall decide themselves the political regime

of South Vietnam through free and democratic general elections; a constituent assembly will be set up, a constitution worked out and a coalition government of South Vietnam installed, reflecting national concord and the broad union of all social strata.

5. During the period intervening between the restoration of peace and the holding of general elections, neither party shall impose its political regime on the people of South Vietnam.

The political forces representing the various social strata and political tendencies in South Vietnam that stand for peace, independence and neutrality —including those persons who, for political reasons, have to live abroad— will enter into talks to set up a provisional coalition government based on the principle of equality, democracy and mutual respect with a view to achieving a peaceful, independent, democratic and neutral South Vietnam.

The provisional coalition government is to have the following tasks:

A. To implement the agreement to be concluded on the withdrawal of the troops of the United States and the other foreign countries of the American camp.

B. To achieve national concord, and a broad union of all social strata, political forces, nationalities, religious communities and all persons, no matter what their political beliefs and their past may be, provided they stand for peace, independence and neutrality.

C. To achieve broad democratic freedoms—freedom of speech, freedom of the press, freedom of assembly, freedom of belief, freedom to form political parties and organizations, freedom to demonstrate, etc.; to set free those persons jailed on political grounds; to prohibit all acts of terror, reprisal and discrimination against people having collaborated with either side, and who are now in the country or abroad, as provided for by the 1954 Geneva agreements on Vietnam.

D. To heal the war wounds, restore and develop the economy, to restore the normal life of the people and to improve the living conditions of the laboring people.

E. To hold free and democratic general elections in the whole of South Vietnam with a view to achieving the South Vietnam people's right to self-determination, in accordance with the content of point 4 mentioned above.

6. South Vietnam will carry out a foreign policy of peace and neutrality:

To carry out a policy of good neighborly relations with the Kingdom of Cambodia on the basis of respect for her independence, sovereignty, neutrality and territorial integrity within her present borders: to carry out a policy of good neighborly relations with the Kingdom of Laos on the basis of respect for the 1962 Geneva agreements on Laos.

To establish diplomatic, economic and cultural relations with all countries, irrespective of political and social regime, including the United States, in accordance with the 5 principles of peaceful coexistence: mutual respect for independence, sovereignty and territorial integrity, nonaggression, noninterference in internal affairs, equality and mutual benefit, peaceful coexistence, to accept economic and technical aid with no political conditions attached from any country.

7. The reunification of Vietnam will be achieved step by step, by peaceful means, through discussions and agreement between the 2 zones, without foreign interference.

Pending the peaceful reunification of Vietnam, the 2 zones shall re-establish normal relations in all fields on the basis of mutual respect.

The military demarcation line between the 2 zones at the 17th Parallel, as provided for by the 1954 Geneva agreements, is only of a provisional character and does not constitute in any way a political or territorial boundary. The 2 zones shall reach agreement on the status of the demilitarized zone, and work out modalities for movements across the provisional military demarcation line.

8. As provided for in the 1954 Geneva agreements on Vietnam, the 2 zones, North and South Vietnam, shall undertake to refrain from joining any military alliance with foreign countries, not allow any foreign country to maintain military bases, troops and military personnel on their respective soil, and not recognize the protection of any country or military alliance or bloc.

9. To resolve the aftermath of the war:

A. The parties will negotiate the release of soldiers captured in war.

B. The United States government must bear full responsibility for the losses and devastations it has caused to the Vietnamese people in both zones.

10. The parties shall reach agreement on an international supervision about the withdrawal from South Vietnam of the troops, military personnel, arms and war materiel of the United States and the other foreign countries of the American camp.

Pres. Nixon proposed May 14 an 8-point peace plan for Vietnam that included provisions for mutual withdrawal of "the major portions" of U.S., allied and North Vietnamese troops from South Vietnam and internationally supervised elections to insure "each significant group in South Vietnam a real opportunity to participate in the political life of the nation."

The President's plan was advanced in a nationally televised speech, his first full-length report to the American people on the war in Vietnam. It was in direct response to the 10-point peace plan offered by the NLF. The text of Nixon's 8 "specific measures" for a Vietnam settlement, proposed "on the basis of full consultation" with South Vietnamese President Nguyen Van Thieu:

As soon as agreement can be reached, all non-South Vietnamese forces would begin withdrawals from South Vietnam. Over a period of 12 months, by agreed-upon stages, the major portions of all U.S., allied and other non-South Vietnamese forces would be withdrawn.

At the end of this 12-month period the remaining United States, allied and other non-South Vietnamese forces would move into designated base areas and would not engage in combat operations.

The remaining U.S. and allied forces would complete their withdrawal as the remaining North Vietnamese forces were withdrawn and returned to North Vietnam.

An international supervisory body, acceptable to both sides, would be created for the purpose of verifying withdrawl, and for any other purpose agreed upon between the 2 sides.

This international body would begin operating in accordance with an agreed timetable and would participate in arranging supervised cease-fire in Vietnam.

As soon as possible after the international body was functioning, elections would be held under agreed procedures and under the supervision of the international body.

Arrangements would be made for the release of prisoners of war on both sides at the earliest possible time.

All parties would agree to observe the Geneva accords of 1954 regarding South Vietnam and Cambodia and the Laos accords of 1962.

The NLF and the North Vietnamese government May 15 objected to Nixon's call for mutual troop withdrawals from South Vietnam. An NLF statement said: "Faced by the just and reasonable character of the National Liberation Front's 10-point over-all solution and by a favorable response of world opinion to this solution, Pres. Nixon seeks to give an appearance of goodwill in his speech of May 14. In fact, the United States still clings to its old unjust and unreasonable formula for a mutual withdrawal of troops, now submitted in a new form that places the aggressor and the resisting victims of aggression on the same footing—a proposal that we have repeatedly rejected." A North Vietnam broadcast called it "completely unrealistic to talk of mutual withdrawal of aggressor troops and defender troops. The plan of the Nixon Administration is not to end the war but to replace the war of aggression fought by U.S. troops into a war of aggression fought by the puppet army of the United States."

'Vietnamization'

The peace talks showing no sign of progress, the Nixon Administration sought to extricate the U.S. from Vietnam through unilateral withdrawal of American troops preceded by the strengthening of South Vietnamese forces. This policy was dubbed "Vietnamization." Indications of this policy came during a fact-finding tour of Vietnam by Defense Secy. Melvin Laird Mar. 6-10, 1969.

Laird undertook the tour at the request of Pres. Nixon. On arriving in Saigon Mar. 6, Laird charged that the recent Communist attacks on South Vietnamese cities was an "ominous" violation of the U.S.-North Vietnamese "understanding" that had led to the halt in the U.S. bombing of North Vietnam and to the Paris peace talks. "I want to state unequivocally that if these attacks continue unabated, an appropriate response will be made," Laird warned.

Laird conferred Mar. 8 with U.S. Amb. Ellsworth Bunker and Gen. Creighton W. Abrams, commander of the U.S. forces in Vietnam. The 3 men then met with South Vietnamese Premier Tran Van Huong and President Nguyen Van Thieu.

In a news conference at the U.S. base at Danang Mar. 9, Laird said he would ask Congress to increase the budget for the Vietnam War by $70 million in the next fiscal year. The additional funds, he said, would finance a build-up of South Vietnamese forces. "If we are going to be in a position where, through the building up of the South Vietnamese forces, we can relieve American service personnel from combat here, we must fully fund that effort," Laird said.

Laird toured the I Corps area comprising South Vietnam's 5 northernmost provinces Mar. 9. At a stopover in Hue, he conferred with Maj. Gen. Ngo Quang Truong, commander of the South Vietnamese First Infantry Division. Laird later said he had been "very impressed" with the improvement he saw in the effectiveness and training of South Vietnamese forces. Despite these improvements, Laird said, the time had not yet come to replace Americans with South Vietnamese soldiers. He explained: "This is not the time to discuss troop withdrawals. Not when there's an offensive being conducted by the enemy and while we are engaged in very important discussions in Paris where the No. 2 item on the agenda is mutual troop withdrawal." The No. 1 item on the Paris agenda, Laird pointed out, was the U.S. proposal for restoration of the neutrality of the demilitarized zone separating South and North Vietnam.

Laird made the remark to reporters before boarding a plane to return to Washington. He also made these points: "It would be desirable and possible" to replace some of the 540,000 U.S. troops in South Vietnam with South Vietnamese; the current Communist offensive had achieved no great military advantage despite the shelling of population centers; he had been "encouraged and impressed" in his meetings with government leaders "with their repeatedly stated desire to take on more of the responsibility for the fighting"; the U.S. had not intensified the fighting in the South following the halt in bombing of the North Nov. 1, 1968, as charged by the Communists; "the only escalation that has taken place so far as the war in Southeast Asia is concerned has been the escalation of the Viet Cong and North Vietnamese forces."

Nixon announced June 8 that 25,000 U.S. troops would be withdrawn from South Vietnam by Aug. 31. The pullout was to start in 30 days. The decision to reduce the 540,000-man American force in Vietnam had been agreed to by Nixon and South Vietnamese Pres. Nguyen Van Thieu at a conference on Midway Island during which they reviewed political, economic and military developments in Vietnam and the general situation in Southeast Asia. Nixon termed the troop withdrawal plan a "significant step forward" toward a lasting peace. He said he would announce plans for a further U.S. troop pullback "as decisions are made." He said the withdrawal had been recommended by Thieu and Gen. Abrams. Seeking to allay fears that the removal of American troops would harm the allied war effort, Nixon said: "I want to emphasize 2 fundamental principles: No actions will be taken which threaten the safety of our troops and the troops of our allies, and 2d, no action will be taken which endangers the attainment of our objective, the right of self-determination for the people of South Vietnam."

On returning to Washington from Midway June 9, Defense Secy. Laird expressed the hope that if the South Vietnamese continued to assume more of the burden of fighting, further American troop withdrawals could be made in August and at "regular intervals thereafter." Laird said that the 25,000 U.S. soldiers to be taken out of South Vietnam would be largely combat units of the Army and Marine Corps. No Air Force or Navy elements were involved in the initial cutback, Laird explained, because, as support forces, they were required to supply and support the South Vietnamese units that were to replace the American forces in the combat zones. Laird said that as a result of the Midway conference, "we return closer to peace, and we have a program moving forward to change the role of the United States in Vietnam and Southeast Asia." The decisions reached at Midway, he said, "should be a signal to North Vietnam that the United States is going to maintain its objective, the right of self-determination for the people of South Vietnam."

The Nixon Administration planned to withdraw 45,000 to 75,000 more U.S. troops from South Vietnam in two stages, in August and in October, the *N.Y. Times* reported June 17. The additional pullout would depend on whether the South Vietnamese forces operated more aggressively and whether Communist forces attempted successfully to launch new military drives, the *Times* reported. The *Times* said that if North Vietnam refused to agree to a mutual foreign troop withdrawal from South Vietnam, the U.S. would remove 340,000 American soldiers from the country over the next 3 years, while "indefinitely" retaining a force of 200,000 men to bolster South Vietnamese troops against any Communist attack.

Nixon June 19 expressed hope that his Administration could "beat" a proposed timetable for withdrawal of 100,000 combat troops from Vietnam in 1969 and an additional 100,000 to 150,000 troops by the end of 1970. The President's views were made known at a televised news conference.

The withdrawal timetable had been proposed by former Defense Secy. Clark M. Clifford June 18 in an article in the quarterly *Foreign Affairs*. Clifford had called for a total pullout of U.S. ground combat forces, coupled with continued U.S. logistic and air support for South Vietnamese armed forces. He said this would pose "a painful dilemma" for the enemy— that of either accepting "a prolonged and substantial presence of American air and logistical personnel" or agreeing to a mutual withdrawal of all external forces.

Clifford suggested that U.S. field commanders be given new orders "to discontinue efforts to apply maximum military pressure on the enemy and to seek instead to reduce the level of combat." As for the South Vietnamese government, Clifford said the Administration should make it clear that (1) the proposed initial withdrawal of 100,000 troops would be "the beginning of a process" leading to the withdrawal of all U.S. ground combat forces, and (2) "American objectives do not demand the perpetuation in power of any one group of South Vietnamese." If the latter were made clear to Saigon, Clifford said, it would put pressure on the South Vietnamese regime to open itself to "individuals representative of other nationalist elements in South Vietnamese society."

Nixon, commenting on the Clifford proposal at his news conference, said: "I would hope that we could beat Mr. Clifford's timetable, just as I think we've done a little better than he did when he was in charge of our national defense." He expressed his belief that "we're on the right road in Vietnam" and his hope "that we will not be in Vietnam as long as" Clifford had suggested "we will have to be there." Referring to Clifford's call for new orders to field commanders, Nixon said his orders were "to conduct this war with a minimum of American casualties." American casualties, he said, were in direct ratio to the level of enemy attacks.

As for the Paris negotiations, Nixon said "there is no substantial evidence . . . to report," but "we hope within the next 2 to 3 months to see some progress in substantive discussions." Pres. Nguyen Van Thieu, he said, "will be making an offer of his own with regard to a political settlement," and "under those circumstances there is no question about our standing with Pres. Thieu. . . . We are not going to accede to the demands of the enemy that we have to dispose of Pres. Thieu before they will talk." Nixon denied that the U.S. was "wedded" to the Thieu regime, but he pointed out that Thieu was "the elected president of Vietnam" and was working with the U.S. "to bring this war to a conclusion."

Presidential aides stressed June 20 that Nixon's statements were expressions of "hope" rather than firm commitment. The

President's remarks had quickly been applauded by some Senate "doves" opposed to the Vietnam War. Sen. Edward M. Kennedy (D., Mass.) June 20 interpreted the remarks as "a definite commitment that ought to be carried out." Sen. J. W. Fulbright (D., Ark.) said June 20: "I certainly hope he can do it. If he means it, I will certainly applaud him." Senate Democratic leader Mike Mansfield (Mont.) said June 20 he hoped "this schedule can be met." But Mansfield June 21 characterized the President's remarks as "overreaction" to Clifford's article.

The first contingent of U.S. troops to withdraw from Vietnam under Nixon's pullout plan left Vietnam July 8. The returning soldiers, 814 men from the 3d Battalion of the 60th Regiment, 9th Infantry Division, were the first of 25,000 troops scheduled to leave Vietnam by Aug. 31.

The Guam Doctrine

July 1969 saw a continuing lull in the Vietnam War. The White House announced July 14 that Pres. Nixon would go on a global tour that would include visits to the Philipines, Indonesia, Thailand, India, Pakistan, Rumania and Britain.

Nixon, accompanied by his wife, began his tour after flying to the carrier *Hornet* in the Pacific to witness the successfull splashdown and recovery July 24 of the Apollo 11 astronauts. *En route,* the Presidential party stopped at Guam. It was during this stop that the President outlined July 25 his new Asian policy in an informal news conference (no direct quotation permitted).

According to the new policy, to be known as the Guam Doctrine (subsequently changed to the Nixon Doctrine), the U.S. would not become involved in more wars like that in Vietnam; it would reduce its military commitments throughout Asia; it would keep its treaty commitments and watch Asian developments. The President opposed military involvements (such as the Vietnam War) that tended to generate emotional and economic discord at home. As for the problem of military defense, the U.S. would provide a nuclear shield for nations with which it is allied or those whose survival is considered vital to American security but would look to the Asian nations themselves to carry the primary responsibility in dealing with internal subversion or external aggression of conventional types.

The President said on his arrival in Manila July 26 that "if peace is to come from Asia—and I emphasize this point—the United States will play its part and provide its fair share." "But," he continued, "peace in Asia cannot come from the United States. It must come from Asia. The people of Asia, the governments of Asia, they are the ones who must lead the way to peace in Asia." The crux of Nixon's message to Philippine leaders, according to Presidential aides, was that the responsibility for Asian security must be borne primarily by Asians. While the U.S. realized the importance of Asia and was determined to honor its treaty commitments, it would shun future wars of the Vietnam type and reduce its Asian military commitments.

Senate Democratic leader Mike Mansfield (Mont.) expressed support July 28 for Nixon's Asian policy as outlined in his Guam news conference. "He is not advocating isolationism," Mansfield said in a Senate speech, "nor is he advocating the abandonment of Asia." He added: "His intent, I believe, is to avoid future Vietnams but, at the same time, to render what assistance is feasible and possible to the nations of Asia."

Opposition to War Intensifies

The lull in the Vietnam fighting ended Aug. 11 when Communist forces mounted a new offensive. Allied military authorities were reported Aug. 15 to have concluded that the new offensive would continue for weeks or possibly months.

Against this backdrop of renewed fighting, anti-war forces in the U.S. rallied against Nixon's war policy. Sen. Charles E. Goodell (R., N.Y.) added a new dimension to the renewed war protest movement Sept. 25 by proposing legislation to require withdrawal of all U.S. troops from Vietnam by the end of 1970. The proposal stirred immediate reaction from spokesmen of both parties. Goodell's legislation would bar the use of Congressionally appropriated funds after Dec. 1, 1970 for maintaining U.S. military personnel in Vietnam. The purpose of his proposal, Goodell told the Senate, was "to help the President and Congress develop a workable plan for ending American participation in the war—and the slaughter of American servicemen— in the very near future." "At present," he said, "there is no visible plan of this kind, and the assumptions under which the military is now operating will probably keep us fighting for years."

The Goodell proposal was attacked Sept. 25 by New York Gov. Nelson A. Rockefeller, who called it "ill advised," and by Defense Secy. Melvin R. Laird, who said it would be "a grave error" to "project figures and set dates that we might not be able to deliver on." Laird said he hoped that "all Americans" would support the President's program. "That is the thing that Hanoi will understand," he said.

Democratic National Chairman Fred R. Harris said after a secret caucus of Democrats Sept. 26, "it's time to take the gloves off on Vietnam." Sen. J. W. Fulbright (D., Ark.), one of the foremost Vietnam critics, had announced Sept. 25 he was "ready to speak out" once more on Vietnam. He had muted his criticism of the war during the early months of the new Administration. The secret Democratic caucus was attended by about 24 Congress members. It was reportedly called by Harris to discuss support for a planned nationwide student antiwar protest Oct. 15 and troop pullout legislation.

Republican Congressional leaders appealed Sept. 29 for a 60-day moratorium on criticism of the Administration's Vietnam policy to provide time and a "common front" for the negotiation of a peace settlement.

A number of prominent professors and liberal and moderate Congress members declared their support for an Oct. 15 nationwide campus boycott to protest the war in Vietnam. The idea for a nationwide protest was attributed to Jerome Grossman, a Boston businessman and president of the Political Action for Peace organization in Massachusetts. He had suggested organizing a "general strike" against the war. He consulted Sam-(uel Winfred) Brown (Jr.), 25, a former divinity student turned organizer (he was youth coordinator for Sen. Eugene J. McCarthy's Presidential campaign in 1968). Brown took the idea to 2 friends—David Hawk, a former staff member of the National Student Association, and David Mixner, a helper in the McCarthy campaign. They decided to change a "strike" call to a call for a "moratorium." An office was set up in Washington where the details were disseminated, originally through Brown's organizing lists, for Moratorium Day observance, not as a partisan political action but as an "educational experience"—a day for a pause in normal activity to express protest against the war.

The planning and organizing produced one of the most massive antiwar protests in the nation's history Oct. 15 as part of an effort to demonstrate to Nixon the broad public mandate to end the war. The event drew diverse support from thousands of students and other youths, professors and clerics and, surprisingly, many representatives of the middle class, who generally had remained aloof from public opposition to the war effort.

The activities on Moratorium Day were as diverse as the elements of support—rallies, speeches, church and synagogue services, memorial readings of the names of the Vietnam War dead, the tolling of bells, candlelight marches, teach-ins, seminars, folk-song concerts, vigils, leaflet distributions, petition-signings, wreath-layings and door-to-door canvassing. A nationwide symbol of sympathy with the Moratorium was the wearing of a black armband. Another was the flying of the flag at half-staff. Opposition to the Moratorium, which was also manifested, was signaled by proper display of the flag and the driving of vehicles during the day with headlights on. But the extent of the opposition, like the support for the Moratorium, was difficult to assess. Only a few incidents of confrontation between protesters and hecklers occurred.

The dominant tone of the Moratorium Day protests was illustrated by Mrs. Martin Luther King Jr., who led an estimated 45,000 persons from the Washington Monument to the White House, where she lit a candle for peace. "The only solution to the problem is to bring the boys home and to bring them home now," she told the demonstrators.

One of the largest antiwar gatherings was in Boston, where an estimated 100,000 persons gathered on Boston Common. 20,000 had marched there from Cambridge. A major speaker in Boston, Sen. Edward M. Kennedy (D., Mass.), announced his "hard compromise" to advocate a U.S. withdrawal of combat forces from Vietnam within a year and its air and support units by the end of 1972.

War Extends to Cambodia

While Pres. Nixon declined to comment directly on the Oct. 15 Vietnam Moratorium protests, moves by the Administration Oct. 15-21, 1969 indicated that Nixon was seeking to enlist ranking Democratic leaders in open support of his plans for ending the war and defusing the antiwar demonstrations. The White House circulated a 3-page "fact sheet" on Capitol Hill Oct. 21 outlining political and military steps taken by the Nixon Administration to de-escalate and end the war.

The document asserted that the Nixon Administration had succeeded in reducing the level of fighting and cutting the number of casualties by withdrawing U.S. troops and by altering battlefield strategy. The paper used figures from the Johnson Administration to illustrate "that for the first time" the Administration had made "concrete and comprehensive political proposals for settlement of the war."

Nevertheless, the prospect of reaching an accord for peace appeared as remote as ever. This fact was conceded by both the U.S. and North Vietnamese sides. State Secy. William P. Rogers, at his press conference Nov. 18, 1969 said that he saw "no immediate prospects" for peace. Le Duan, the first secretary of the Vietnamese Workers (Communist) Party, Feb. 1,

1970 issued a statement saying that the Vietnamese people "must be prepared to fight many years more" until the American "enemy gives up his aggressive design, brings home all his troops and respects the sovereignty of our people and the territorial integrity of our country."

The withdrawal of American troops proceeded on course. Nixon told the nation Apr. 20, 1970 that he planned to bring 150,000 more U.S. troops back from Vietnam by the spring of 1971. The reduction would lower the authorized force ceiling from 434,000 to 284,000, a continuation of the current pullout rate of about 12,000 men a month. Actual troop strength was somewhat below the authorized level, totaling 425,000 men the week before the President's speech.

10 days later, the White House announced a major U.S. troop offensive into Cambodia to clear out sanctuaries used by North Vietnamese and Viet Cong forces in waging the war in South Vietnam. The thrust, which was under way as the President addressed the nation on TV, involved several thousand American soldiers in the Fishhook area of Cambodia 50 miles northwest of Saigon. Nixon called the area a "key control center" for the enemy and its "headquarters for the entire Communist military operation in South Vietnam."

More than 20,000 U.S. and South Vietnamese troops launched the 2-pronged drive into Cambodia Apr. 29 and May 1 in an effort to destroy Communist sanctuaries along the border. The drive against Communist bases in the eastern border regions of Cambodia concentrated in the Parrot's Beak, which jutted into South Vietnam, about 33 miles from Saigon, and the Fishhook area, about 70 miles north of the South Vietnamese capital along Binhlong Province. By May 4 neither force was reported to have made any substantial contact with the enemy. Cambodian residents in both areas reported that thousands of Communist troops had fled to the west before the invasion began. Allied forces in both missions uncovered large caches of small arms, food and medical supplies.

At the same time, large-scale bombing raids were conducted by the U.S. over 2 North Vietnam provinces May 1-2.

The raids, the largest since the bombing halt declared by the U.S. in Nov. 1968, were acknowledged in Washington May 2 after a Hanoi radio broadcast charging that more than 100 U.S. planes struck "yesterday and today" in Quangbinh and Nghean Provinces, killing or wounding "many civilians, including 20 children." Washington sources cited by the *N.Y. Times* said the raids by 128 fighter-bombers were "protective reaction" against antiaircraft guns to protect unarmed reconnaissance aircraft. Defense Secy. Melvin R. Laird had warned earlier May 2 that bombing of North Vietnam would be resumed if Hanoi reacted to the Cambodian thrusts by moving troops across the demilitarized zone into South Vietnam. He also indicated that the Cambodia border with South Vietnam would be subject to air and ground attacks and that air raids were being conducted against 3 such areas.

Nixon Policy Under Attack

The U.S. military drive into Cambodia evoked surprise and considerable criticism in the Senate. Opposition to the action, while centered in the Senate Foreign Relations Committee, headed by Sen. J. W. Fulbright, extended beyond the regular dove ranks. The conflict was aggravated by the Administration's failure to consult Congressional leaders. There was also growing concern about a Constitutional conflict between the President and Congress over whether the chief executive had the authority to engage in such a military venture without the consent of Congress.

The first announcement of U.S. involvement in the Cambodia incursions, supporting the South Vietnamese thrust into the Parrot's Beak sector Apr. 29, 1970, drew angry Senate responses, some from those who generally supported the Administration's Vietnam policy. Sen. George D. Aiken (R., Vt.) said Apr. 29 that he "did not think the President would do what he reportedly has done." Sen. John Sherman Cooper (R., Ky.) called the action a "U-turn" in the Administration's Southeast Asia policy. Senate Democratic Leader Mike Mansfield (Mont.)

announced his backing of a move to bar Congressionally appropriated funds for military operations in Cambodia. Other criticism came from New York GOP Sens. Jacob K. Javits, who said it meant "the President's decision to expand the war," and Charles E. Goodell, who said it "demonstrates how the strategy of Vietnamization has failed and how it pulls us inexorably into a wider war."

On the Senate floor May 1, Mansfield, with rising anger, said the "vital" concern of the nation "must be to end our involvement in the war in Vietnam. It is not to become bogged down in another war in all of Indochina." Senate Republican Leader Hugh Scott (Pa.) defended the President's action as a "courageous" decision that could shorten the war.

The next day, informed of the new U.S. bombing of North Vietnam, Mansfield said "events are piling upon events in a way which indicates that there is without question a step-up in the fighting, which means, in plain English, an escalation of the war." "It is a difficult situation to reconcile one's mind to," he said, "because the outlook seems to be getting grimmer by the day." Fulbright said "it looks as if the President is following what he has been urged to do by many members of Congress —to seek a military decision and knock North Vietnam out of the war."

Antiwar forces across the country reacted to Nixon's decision to use U.S. troops in Cambodia with calls for a nationwide student strike, demands for impeachment proceedings against the President and plans for massive demonstrations. On many campuses, administrations sanctioned student strikes and demonstrations were peaceful; but elsewhere violence erupted. The worst outbreak occurred at Kent State University in Ohio, were 4 students were killed by National Guard troops May 4. The Ohio deaths and reports of a widening war in Indochina added impetus to the student strike movement, and student leaders joined with antiwar groups to plan a march on Washington May 9. Governors in a number of states called out National Guard troops to meet violence by protesters. A student strike center at Brandeis University (Waltham, Mass.) reported as of May 10 that 448 universities and colleges were on strike or closed.

In Paris, the Communist delegations to the peace talks boycotted the 66th plenary session May 6 in protest against the resumption of U.S. bombing attacks on North Vietnam.

In Peking, Prince Norodom Sihanouk, deposed Cambodian chief of state, announced the formation of a government in exile May 5. The regime was promptly recognized by Communist China as the "sole legal" government of Cambodia. As a consequence of its action, China May 6 severed diplomatic relations with the Cambodian government of Premier Lon Nol, as did North Vietnam and North Korea. Rallies were reported May 8 to have been held throughout China, hailing Sihanouk's government and pledging full support to him and all the Indochinese people in their struggle against the U.S. The Chinese news agency Hsinhua reported that Premier Penn Nouth had sent a message May 6 urging U.S. Sen. Mike Mansfield to use his influence as Senate majority leader to make "the great American people understand that they are being dangerously dragged by their President into a war spreading to the whole of Indochina." Penn Nouth was said to have expressed thanks to Mansfield and other U.S. senators for opposing President Nixon's move into Cambodia.

U.S. ROAD TO PEKING (1971-2)

Quiet Diplomacy

The incursions into Cambodia dramatized the linkage between the Vietnam War and the U.S. relations with China. State Secy. William P. Rogers said July 13, 1970 that the Chinese Communists had "increased their influence with Hanoi as a result" of the incursions. Rogers' remarks were recorded in a radio interview in London before he returned to Washington the following day from a 2-week tour of Asia. The secretary's statement was an amplification of a comment he had made in Tokyo July 9 that China was the "key to the future of Indochina" and that if Peking would "talk sensibly," Washington believed that an Indochina peace settlement could be achieved "very quickly."

Aware of the linkage, the Nixon Administration had been exploring, through private channels, ways to improve its relations with Peking as part of its broad-guaged policy to restore peace in Vietnam. Pres. Nixon gave an account of the behind-the-scene efforts in his State-of-the-World message to Congress in Feb. 1972 as follows:

Both political and technical problems lay in the way of such a search. When this Administration assumed responsibility, there had been virtually no contact between mainland China and the American people for 2 decades. This was true for our governments as well, although sterile talks in Geneva and Warsaw had dragged on intermittently since 1955. A deep gulf of mistrust and non-communication separated us.

We faced 2 major questions. First, how to convey our views privately to the authorities in Peking? 2d, what public steps would demonstrate our willingness to set a new direction in our relations? Within 2 weeks of my inauguration we moved on both of these fronts. I ordered that efforts be undertaken to communicate our new attitude through private channels, and to seek contact with the Peoples Republic of China.

This process turned out to be delicate and complex. It is extremely difficult to establish even rudimentary communications between 2 governments which have been completely isolated from one another for 20 years. Neither technical nor diplomatic means of direct contact existed. It was necessary to find an intermediary country which had the full trust of both nations and could be relied upon to promote the dialogue with discretion, restraint and diplomatic skill.

The 2 sides began clarifying their general intentions through mutually friendly countries. After a period of cautious exploration and gathering confidence, we settled upon a reliable means of communication between Washington and Peking.

In Feb. 1969 I also directed that a comprehensive National Security Council study be made of our policy toward China, setting in motion a policy review process which has continued throughout these past 3 years. We addressed both the broader ramifications of a new approach and the specific steps to carry it out.

Drawing on this analysis, we began to implement a phased sequence of unilateral measures to indicate the direction in which this Administration was prepared to move. We believed that these practical steps, progressively relaxing trade and travel restrictions, would make clear to the Chinese leaders over time that we were prepared for a serious dialogue. We had no illusion that we could bargain for Chinese good will. Because of the difficulties in communication, we deliberately chose initiatives that could be ignored or quietly accepted; since they required no Chinese actions, they were difficult to reject. We purposely avoided dramatic moves which could invoke dramatic rebukes and set back the whole carefully nurtured process.

More specifically, the "phased sequence of unilateral measures"—again to quote directly from the President's report— consisted of the following:

In July 1969, we permitted noncommercial purchases of Chinese goods without special authorization by American tourists, museums and others. We also broadened the categories of U.S. citizens whose passports would be validated automatically for travel to China.

In Dec. 1969, we allowed subsidiaries of American firms abroad to engage in commerce between mainland China and third countries.

In January and February 1970, the 2 sides held ambassadorial meetings in Warsaw, which in turn had been set through private exchanges. These sessions underlined the handicaps of this formal discourse. The 2 sides' representatives had minimum flexibility; they could do little more than read prepared statements and refer back to their capitals for instructions for the next meeting. This cumbersome exchange between wary adversaries reinforced the need for a new approach.

In Mar. 1970, we announced that U.S. passports would be validated for travel to mainland China for any legitimate purpose.

In Apr. 1970, we authorized selective licensing of non-strategic U.S, goods for export to mainland China.

In Aug. 1970, we lifted certain restrictions on American oil companies operating abroad so that most foreign ships could use American-owned bunkering facilities on trips to and from mainland Chinese ports.

By the end of 1970, therefore, we had laid out a careful record of unilateral initiatives. Throughout these 2 years we had accompanied these steps with a series of public statements which delineated our general attitude.

Secy. [of State William P.] Rogers, in a speech in Canberra, Australia on Aug. 8, 1969, noted the barriers between our countries but added, "We nonetheless look forward to a time when we can enter into a useful dialogue and to a reduction of tensions."

In my Feb. 1970 Foreign Policy Report, I stated that ". . . it is certainly in our interest, and in the interest of peace and stability in Asia and the world, that we take what steps we can toward improved practical relations with Peking . . . we will seek to promote understandings which can establish a new pattern of mutually beneficial actions."

On Oct. 26, 1970, in a toast to visiting Pres. [Nicolae] Ceausescu of Romania, I deliberately used Peking's official title, "the Peoples Republic of China." This was the first time an American President had ever done so.

By the time of my 2d Foreign Policy Report in Feb. 1971, we had reason to believe that our moves were being noted and evaluated by the Chinese. In that report, I cited the importance of China's participation in world affairs, reiterated that we were ready for a dialogue with Peking, and stated that we hoped to see the Peoples Republic of China assume a constructive role in the family of nations. I looked toward the immediate future:

"In the coming year, I will carefully examine what further steps we might take to create broader opportunities for contacts between the Chinese and American peoples, and how we might remove needless obstacles to the realization of these opportunities. We hope for, but will not be deterred by a lack of, reciprocity."

U.S. Pingpong Team Tours China

Peking began to respond positively to American overtures in the fall of 1970. The spring of 1971 saw the United States and Communist China engaged in a process that was to bring about a rapprochement.

The U.S. Mar. 15, 1971 discontinued the requirement that its citizens obtain specially validated passports for travel to Communist China. In announcing the policy change, Charles W. Bray 3d, a State Department spokesman, said the action was in conformity with a resolve expressed by Pres. Nixon in his State-of-the-World message in February to "carefully examine what further steps we might take to create broader opportunities for contacts between the Chinese and American peoples." Bray said the measure did not affect the ban on travel to North Korea, North Vietnam and Cuba, which the State Department extended for an additional 6-month period Mar. 15.

Shortly after this announcement, a U.S. table tennis team competing in Nagoya, Japan for the world championship received Apr. 6 an invitation from the Chinese Communist team to visit Communist China.

Sung Chung, a spokesman for the Chinese team, said the invitation to 9 U.S. players, 4 officials and 2 wives had been made "so that we can learn from each other and elevate our standards of play. We have also extended the invitation for the sake of promoting friendship between the peoples of China and the U.S."

Reversing a policy maintained since 1949, Peking Apr. 10 granted visas to 7 Western newsmen to cover the U.S. team's visit. Those affected were John Roderick of the Associated Press; John Rich and Jack Reynolds of the National Broadcasting Co. (NBC); Hiromasa Yamanaka and Masaaki Shiihara, Japanese TV technicians employed by NBC; and English correspondent John Saar and cameraman Frank Fischbeck, both of *Life* magazine. Tillman Durdin, chief of the *N.Y. Times* Hong Kong bureau, and Mark Gayn, a Canadian correspondent, were authorized to enter Communist China Apr. 13. No known restrictions were made on the length of their stay.

A direct phone connection between Britain and Communist China was scheduled Apr. 14 to reopen the following day after an interruption of 22 years, the British Post Office reported. There was no official explanation of how the resumption had been arranged.

Following several days of travel through China, the U.S. players were defeated in exhibition matches in Peking Apr. 13. They were received Apr. 14 by Premier Chou En-lai, who also received teams from Britain, Canada, Nigeria and Colombia, which had been invited at Nagoya. Chou told the U.S. team that "with your acceptance of our invitation, you have opened a new page in the relations of the Chinese and American people." After a week-long tour of the Chinese mainland as guests of the Peking government, the U.S. team returned to Tokyo Apr. 17. A U.S. official announced Apr. 20 that Communist China had accepted an invitation to send a team to the U.S.

Pres. Nixon received the U.S. team in an informal reception at the White House Apr. 21. Graham B. Steenhoven, president of the U.S. Table Tennis Association, said that the

President had assured him that he "certainly will cooperate" with the table tennis association's invitation to the Chinese team.

Pingpong Diplomacy & Other U.S.-Chinese Relations

On the day the U.S. table tennis team was received in Peking by Premier Chou En-lai, Pres. Nixon ordered a relaxation of the 20-year embargo on trade with Communist China.

Nixon's announcement said that he was asking the National Security Council for "a list of items of a nonstrategic nature which can be placed under general license for direct export to the People's Republic of China. Following my review and my approval of specific items on this list, direct imports of designated items from China will then also be authorized."

The statement said that U.S. firms would be allowed to trade with China in dollars and that the U.S. was "prepared to expedite visas" for visitors or groups of visitors from China. U.S. oil companies were to be allowed to supply fuel to ships or planes proceeding to or from mainland China with the exception of Chinese-owned or Chinese-chartered carriers going to or from North Vietnam, North Korea or Cuba. U.S. carriers were to be allowed to transport Chinese cargos between non-Chinese ports, and U.S.-owned carriers under foreign flags could call at Chinese ports.

Nixon said Apr. 16, 1971 that his Administration was prepared to take other steps in trade or exchange visits with China but that the next step was "up to them." Citing the U.S. moves a year previously and 2 days previously to improve travel and trade conditions between the U.S. and the People's Republic of China, Nixon said "now it is up to them." "It takes 2, of course," he said. "We have taken several steps. They have taken one. We are prepared to take other steps in the trade field and also with regard to the exchange field, but each step must be taken one at a time."

While it was "premature" to talk about diplomatic recognition or admission of Communist China to the United

Nations, Nixon said, "we are going to proceed in these very substantive fields of exchange of persons and also in the field of trade. That will open the way to other moves, which will be made at an appropriate time." The President emphasized that "normalization" of relations between the 2 countries and "the ending of the isolation of mainland China from the world community" were the "long-range goals" of his Administration. He cautioned, however, that "we can't go that far in one chunk" and "cannot do it now."

Speaking to newsmen Apr. 29 about the new developments in U.S.-Chinese relations, Nixon said: "What we have done is broken the ice. Now we have to test the water to see how deep it is." Taking a "long-term" view, he expected to visit mainland China "sometime in some capacity—I don't know what capacity," and he hoped to contribute to a policy for a "new relationship" with that country.

The apparent thaw in Sino-U.S. relations drew comments by American and foreign officials. At a Washington news conference Apr. 23, State Secy. William P. Rogers said he hoped that recent events signaled "the beginning of new relations" between the U.S. and Communist China. Rogers declared: "I think it was the prime minister of the People's Republic of China who said that it was a new page in our relations. We would hope that it becomes a new chapter, that there would be several pages to follow." Rogers said that a review of U.S. policy on the admission of Communist China to the UN was "actively under way" and was being discussed with "many other governments."

Charles W. Bray 3d, a State Department spokesman, said Apr. 28 that it might be possible to resolve the status of Taiwan by negotiation between Nationalist China and Communist China. Bray, who denied that he was articulating a new policy, said that the U.S. "must deal with the practical situation as we find it." There was on the one hand "a treaty commitment to the defense of Taiwan and the Pescadores Islands," but on the other hand "mainland China has been controlled and administered by the People's Republic of China for 21 years and for some time we have been dealing with that government on matters affecting our mutual interest."

What Rogers referred to was a report being prepared by a special Presidential commission headed by Henry Cabot Lodge Jr., former chief U.S. delegate to the UN. The report, made public Apr. 26, recommended that the U.S. try to obtain the admission of Communist China to the UN without the expulsion of Nationalist China from that body. The report explained: "However difficult the People's Republic of China's membership in the UN might become, the commission believes there is more hope for peace in its interaction in the organization than in its continued isolation from the UN and from the U.S." The commission emphasized that admission of Peking and retention of Nationalist China were "equally important" and that "under no circumstances" should Taiwan be expelled. "This is not a question of dual representation for one China but the provision of 2 seats for 2 governments," it said. The panel recommended that "firmly established governments" such as the 2 Germanys, the 2 Koreas and the 2 Vietnams be admitted to the UN because "logic argues both for admitting such established governments to the UN as are not members and for retaining in the UN such established governments as are already members."

Peking May 4 accused the U.S. of "brazen interference" in China's internal affairs. The statement, published in the Communist party newspaper *Jenmin Jih Pao,* took exception to Bray's remark that differences between Nationalist and Communist China over the status of Taiwan could be settled by direct negotiation between the 2 governments. The article spoke of continued friendship between the Chinese and American people but said Nixon's expressed desire for better relations with Peking became "fraudulent" in the light of Bray's remarks. Peking also criticized the report of the U.S. commission that recommended that the U.S. seek to have both Communist and Nationalist China represented in the UN.

Mao Tse-tung was reported in the Apr. 30 issue of *Life* magazine, however, to have said that Nixon would be welcome in China either in his official capacity or as a tourist. Mao's remarks were made in an interview with Edgar Snow, the U.S. writer.

Generalissimo Chiang Kai-shek, head of the Nationalist Chinese government on Taiwan, commented on the U.S. table tennis team's visit to mainland China in an interview with CBS-TV telecast Apr. 27 but filmed the previous week. Chiang said: "Such Chinese tactics of external infiltration and subversion have borne their first fruit. If all of us are aware of this, I think there should be no substantial change in the relationship between the U.S. and the Chinese Communists."

Washington sought to assure other governments, friends as well as adversaries, that its new China policy was not directed against any other country and was not being pursued at the expense of other governments. White House Press Secy. Ronald Ziegler told newsmen Apr. 15 that the U.S. effort to improve its Chinese relations was "in no way related to our relations with the Soviet Union." It was, he stressed, "simply not the purpose of the moves" to embarrass or put pressure on the Soviet Union.

But this U.S. effort failed to persuade the skeptics. The Soviet foreign affairs weekly New Times accused Peking Apr. 21 of playing a "diplomatic game" with the U.S. The journal asserted that China's foreign policy was designed to "win a place for China as a world power capable of imposing its decisions on other states." New Times added: "The political practices of the Maoists have shown that they can easily betray friends and quickly come to terms with those whom they had just called enemies, and that they can repudiate the principles they once proclaimed if they consider it in the great-power nationalistic interests of Peking."

The Soviet Union May 5 accused the Nixon Administration of pursuing "anti-Soviet objectives" in allowing the U.S. table tennis team to visit China. The accusation, expressed in the foreign affairs weekly Za Rubezhom, held that the U.S. government, "true to its rabid anti-Communist policy," had "long been trying to weaken the positions of the Socialist camp, striving to set Socialist countries against each other, and first of all against the Soviet Union."

Nixon Announces Plans to Visit China

Amidst speculations about the nature of the U.S. policy, every new development in Sino-American relations made a headline.

U.S. Treasury Secy. John B. Connally announced May 7, 1971 a general license for the use of dollars in transactions with the People's Republic of China. State Department spokesman Charles W. Bray 3d said that "in coming weeks, after completion of a high-level review, there will be further announcements with regard to direct trade with the People's Republic of China, in particular the designation of export and import programs."

In a related development, 2 U.S. biologists and a geophysicist were reported May 11 to be on their way to Communist China or planning to visit there shortly. The biologists, Dr. Arthur W. Galston of Yale University and Dr. Ethan Signer of the Massachusetts Institute of Technology, were said to be *en route* to China from Hanoi, North Vietnam. Dr. Robert Coe, a geophysicist from the University of California at Santa Cruz, was said to have received permission to visit Peking, where his father had been living.

The *N.Y. Times* said May 22 that James Reston, a *Times* columnist, had become the 3d writer for that newspaper to obtain a visa to visit China in recent months. Seymour Topping, also of the *Times,* and Robert I. Keatley of the *Wall Street Journal* were reported May 20 to have been granted visas.

Pres. Nixon June 10 released a list of 47 categories of items considered exportable to China and announced that Chinese exports to the U.S. would be treated in the same manner as items from other Communist countries. The President's list included such nonstrategic goods as farm products, household appliances, automobiles and basic metals. Among items omitted were locomotives, trucks, high-grade computers, petroleum products and commercial aircraft. The announcement said, however, that "consistent with the requirements of national security" such items could be deemed exportable under special licenses following a review by the Commerce Department and other government agencies.

The most startling U.S. move in the effort to improve relations with Communist China, however, was made public less than a week later.

Nixon announced to an astonished American public July 15, 1971 that he would visit Peking before May 1972 to confer with Communist Chinese leaders "to seek the normalization of relations between the 2 countries and to exchange views on questions of concern to the 2 sides." A follow-up announcement by the Western White House in San Clemente, Calif. July 16 said the President's trip might be made as early as late 1971 and that he would confer with both Communist Party Chairman Mao Tse-tung and Premier Chou En-lai. No American President had ever been received by a Chinese government.

In his July 15 address, broadcast from Los Angeles, Nixon disclosed that arrangements for the projected meeting with Chinese leaders had been worked out in secret talks held in Peking July 9-11 by Henry A. Kissinger, his national security affairs adviser, and Chou En-lai. Kissinger, on a fact-finding tour of Asia, had made a secret flight to Peking from Pakistan, one of his stop-over points. During his visit to the Chinese capital, Kissinger had been publicly reported to be resting in Nattria Gali, a Pakistani mountain resort, temporarily incapacitated by a stomach ailment.

Nixon said that the plan for the proposed trip was being announced simultaneously in the U.S. and Peking. Alluding to the Nationalist Chinese government on Taiwan, the President emphasized that "our action in seeking a new relationship with the People's Republic of China will not be at the expense of our old friends." Nixon called his forthcoming visit "a major development in our efforts to build a lasting peace in the world."

He said that it was in accord with his oft-stated belief that "there can be no stable and enduring peace without the participation of the People's Republic of China and its 750 million peoples."

The text of the President's announcement:

Good evening:

I have requested this television time tonight to announce a major development in our efforts to build a lasting peace in the world.

As I have pointed out on a number of occasions over the past 3 years, there can be no stable and enduring peace without the participation of the People's Republic of China and its 750 million people. That is why I have undertaken initiatives in several areas to open the door for more normal relations between our 2 countries.

In pursuance of that goal, I sent Dr. Kissinger, my assistant for national security affairs, to Peking during his recent world tour for the purpose of having talks with Premier Chou En-lai.

The announcement I shall now read is being issued simultaneously in Peking and in the United States:

"Premier Chou En-lai and Dr. Henry Kissinger, Pres. Nixon's assistant for national security affairs, held talks in Peking from July 9 to 11, 1971. Knowing of Pres. Nixon's expressed desire to visit the People's Republic of China, Premier Chou En-lai on behalf of the government of the People's Republic of China has extended an invitation to Pres. Nixon to visit China at an appropriate date before May, 1972.

"Pres. Nixon has accepted the invitation with pleasure.

"The meeting between the leaders of China and the United States is to seek the normalization of relations between the 2 countries and also to exchange views on questions of concern to the 2 sides."

In anticipation of the inevitable speculation which will follow this announcement, I want to put our policy in the clearest possible context. Our action in seeking a new relationship with the People's Republic of China will not be at the expense of our old friends.

It is not directed against any other nation. We seek friendly relations with all nations. Any nation can be our friend without being any other nation's enemy.

I have taken this action because of my profound conviction that all nations will gain from a reduction of tensions and a better relationship between the United States and the People's Republic of China.

It is in this spirit that I will undertake what I deeply hope will become a journey for peace, peace not just for our generation but for future generations on this earth we share together.

Thank you and good night.

The White House briefing disclosed these facts about the Kissinger mission to Peking that had arranged Nixon's trip:

• Preparations for the mission and the mission itself were shrouded in such secrecy that only Nixon, Kissinger, State Secy. William P. Rogers and "a very few White House staff members" knew what was going on. The arrangements were drawn up between April and June. Nixon did not work out plans for the project in his office "for fear that papers would be left behind and people might walk in and see [the President and Kissinger] working on the papers. So they usually met in the Lincoln sitting room [of the White House]. . . . "

• Kissinger flew to Peking from Islamabad, Pakistan aboard a U.S. Air Force plane. (He had conferred with Pres. Mohammad Agha Yahya Khan in Rawalpindi during his visit July 8-9.) Kissinger was accompanied by 3 members of his staff—John Holdridge, Winston Lord and Richard Smyser. During their 49-hour stay, the officials conferred with Premier Chou and 4 unidentified senior Chinese officials in 2 places: a state guest house where the Americans were lodged and the Great Hall of the People, used by Chou for receptions and dinners.

• The negotiations leading up to the Kissinger trip were accomplished in 2 stages. The first required the establishment of a framework for negotiations and success in convincing the Chinese leaders that Americans were flexible and were "not prisoners of history." "The 2d phase started in April when we moved from this general framework to a more specific exploration of where we might go from here. Then in April, May and June this meeting was set up through a series of exchanges." (The officials declined to say through whom the contacts with China were made.)

Nixon briefed Congressional leaders July 19 on his plans for the visit to China. White House Press Secy. Ronald L. Ziegler said Nixon had told the 8 Senators and 9 Representatives present that he would not speculate on "the effect of these discussions [in Peking] on any other matters," including the war in Indochina, and that "general speculation on the matter would not be helpful." The President's plans were discussed later at a Cabinet meeting attended by Nixon, Rogers and Kissinger.

Rogers held separate meetings July 19 with the envoys of 9 countries to acquaint them with Nixon's plans for talks with the Chinese leaders. Rogers told them that despite Washington's move toward a rapprochement with Peking, the U.S. was still seeking ways of keeping Nationalist China in the UN. Rogers met with the ambassadors of Nationalist China, Japan, Australia, Britain, New Zealand, Thailand, France and West Germany and the charge d'affaires of Italy.

The announcement of Nixon's intention to visit China drew generally favorable comment, mainly within Congress, from U.S. political figures.

Senate majority leader Mike Mansfield described himself July 15 as "flabbergasted, delighted and happy" that Nixon had accepted the Chinese invitation and said he was "looking forward to a new day" as a result of the decision. Sen. Hugh Scott, the Republican leader from Pennsylvania, called the planned visit "an extremely important step in producing world peace." Sen. Hubert H. Humphrey (D., Minn.) said the President's move was "a dramatic turn in American foreign policy and, in my mind, one that can lead to constructive developments." Sen. George S. McGovern (D., S.D.) said he hoped the trip would "mark the end of a long period of nonsense in our relations with China and the beginning of a new era of common sense." A similar view was taken July 16 by Sen. John Sherman Cooper (R., Ky.), who said the planned trip was "a step that may help bring stability and peace to Southeast Asia." Cooper added, however, that "the prospects for an international settlement will be enhanced by a firm declaration on the part of the U.S. that it will remove all its forces from Indochina in order to bring about a political settlement and an end to all hostilities there." Sen. Edmund S. Muskie (D., Me.) remarked: "We should not, in the glow of this symbolic step, forget the 2 crucial questions . . . First, how are we going to end the fighting and the killing in Indochina at the earliest possible moment? And, 2d, how are we going to stop the arms race before it gets completely out of control?" While commending the President's move, Rep. Paul N. McCloskey Jr. (R., Calif.) noted that the announcement "in itself does not mean that we are any closer to getting out of Vietnam."

Ex-State Secy. Dean Rusk said July 17 that he thought the
visit might bring a period in which "things can be talked out a
little more clearly," since "in a nuclear world, 2 big countries
like mainland China and the U.S. ought to have regular channels of contact with each other, even though there may be some
important points on which they disagree."

Sen. Jacob K. Javits (R., N.Y.) said July 19 that Nixon
would not have planned the visit to China unless the 2 powers
"were already on the way to agreement" on major issues. Javits
also declared that he hoped Nationalist China would be given
a UN General Assembly seat if Communist China took the
Chinese seat in the Security Council. Expressing approval of
Nixon's move, Sen. Edward M. Kennedy (D., Mass.) remarked:
"Rarely, I think, has the action of any President so captured
the imagination and support of the American people as Pres.
Nixon's magnificent gesture last week of the improvement in
our relations with China."

Strong opposition to the move was voiced July 16 by Sen.
James L. Buckley (R., N.Y.), who said he was "deeply concerned" over its possible results. Buckley added: "At home it
will inevitably strengthen the hand of those seeking accommodation with the Communist world at almost any price,"
and in Asia "the grand scale of this overture to Peking will be
anything but reassuring to those who have to live with the aggressive reality of mainland China." Sen. John G. Tower (R.,
Tex.) said he was "disturbed" by the scheduled visit, which he
said might be a result of "our steadily diminishing capability
to cope with Soviet expansionism and . . . military might."
Rep. John Schmitz (R., Calif.), who represented the President's
home Congressional district, charged that Nixon was "sur-
rendering to international communism."

Addressing a meeting of the American Bar Association in
London July 19, ex-State Undersecy. George W. Ball accused
the President of "flamboyant diplomacy" and said that the
likelihood of the trip's having an influence on the Indochina
war was not great because "one cannot reasonably expect

Peking to twist the arm of Hanoi on a basis less than Hanoi would like to see."

Gov. George C. Wallace (D., Ala.) said July 20 that he had been "shocked" by the announcement but hoped that Nixon's visit "pays off in world peace" although he had "my doubts." Wallace added that he found it difficult to believe the Communist Chinese were truly interested in peace as long as they were "exporting heroin [and] subversion."

Nationalist China expressed shock and dismay at the prospect of closer U.S.-Communist Chinese ties. Amb. James C. H. Shen delivered a strong protest to the State Department in Washington July 15. Shen said "I couldn't believe my ears" when he heard of Nixon's announcement. He complained that his government was "getting a shabby deal." U.S. Amb. Walter P. McConaughy July 16 was called into Tapei's Foreign Ministry, where Vice Foreign Min. Yang Hsi-kun lodged a vehement protest. Premier C. K. Yen expressed regret in Taipei July 16 that the U.S. had been "deceived by the Chinese Communists." He warned that "this could lead to a tragedy far more serious than that involved in the fall of the Chinese mainland" to the Communists in 1949. Despite the apparent improvement in Peking-Washington relations, Nationalist China had "the faith and determination to recover the Chinese mainland and to resist any external adverse tide," Yen said. "Under no circumstances shall we relax or weaken our stand." A senior official of Nationalist China's ruling Kuomintang party July 17 expressed his government's continued irreconcilable stand against an agreement with Peking. He said: "We want to liberate the mainland, and they want to liberate Taiwan. I don't see any time when there is a possibility of negotiations between the Chinese Communists and us."

Communist China treated the news of the Nixon visit with a studied reserve. In a dispatch from Peking July 17, visiting *N.Y. Times* correspondent James Reston reported that the Chinese news media had devoted little attention to the announcement of Nixon's planned visit. The Communist Party newspaper *Jenmin Jih Pao* carried only 7 lines on the story on its front page July 16, Reston wrote. He said the journal made no further mention of the event in its July 17 issue and ignored further comments by Nixon and Kissinger. Peking radio July 16 had limited its report to a reading of the official communique on the visit and ignored the topic in its July 17 news programs, broadcasting instead its usual denunciations of "American imperialism" and "Japanese militarism," according to Reston.

Communist China Enters UN

The dramatic turn in the U.S. policy produced the most visible impact on the UN General Assembly with regard to the representation of Communist China. The U.S. Aug. 2, 1971 ended 20 years of opposition to Communist China's presence in the UN by announcing that it would "support action at the General Assembly this fall calling for seating the People's Republic of China." At the same time, the U.S. emphasized its continued resistance to any move to expel Nationalist China "or otherwise deprive it of representation in the United Nations."

The announcement came at a State Department news briefing by State Secy. William P. Rogers, who said the change in policy had occurred because "in Asia and elsewhere in the world we are seeking to accommodate our role to the realities of the world today." Rogers said the move was "fully in accord with Pres. Nixon's desire to normalize relations with the People's Republic of China in the interests of world peace and in accord with our conviction that the continued representation in the United Nations of the Republic of China will contribute to peace and stability in the world." He praised Nationalist China for the "loyal and conscientious role" it had played in the UN "since the organization was founded."

Rogers' Aug. 2 statement drew criticism from both Taipei and Peking. In a statement released shortly after Rogers' announcement, the Nationalist Chinese Foreign Ministry called on all member states Aug. 2 to uphold its "unquestionable" right to membership in the UN. The dispatch warned that if Communist China were represented, "this organization would surely be confronted with the ever-increasing danger of infiltration, subversion and eventual destruction," and it urged "the majority of member-states" to "distinguish between friend and foe, between right and wrong with greater moral courage, to struggle along with us to save the UN from its present crisis."

On the other hand, the official Communist Chinese news agency Hsinhua accused the U.S. Aug. 4 of playing a "clumsy '2 Chinas' trick" that was "absolutely illegal and futile." Hsinhua declared that in promoting a seat for Peking while asking that one be retained for Taipei, the U.S. was continuing "to obstruct the restoration to the People's Republic of China all of her legitimate rights in the UN and insists on being the enemy of the Chinese people." Rogers was accused of practicing sophistry by asserting that Nixon's policies were based both on the heritage of the past and the realities of the present. "Everybody knows clearly that the 'legacies of the past' Rogers talked about mean the Chiang Kai-shek clique, which has long been spurned by the Chinese people, and this was created single-handed by U.S. imperialism through occupying China's Taiwan Province and the Taiwan Strait by armed forces," the agency said. Rogers' "so-called realities of '2 Chinas' " were described as "his sheer fancy." The article concluded: "We are deeply convinced that the justice-upholding countries and peoples of the world will also never allow anyone under the signboard of '2 Chinas' to continue to forcibly occupy China's territory Taiwan and obstruct the restoration to the People's Republic of China of her legitimate seats in the UN."

After complicated parliamentary maneuvers, the UN General Assembly Oct. 25 adopted a resolution, sponsored by Albania and 20 other nations, calling for the seating of Peking as the sole legitimate representative of China and for the expulsion of Taiwan. The resolution was adopted by 76-35 vote, with 17 abstentions. The result was greeted with cheers and jubilation from many of the delegates in the Assembly. The

Assembly earlier had defeated the U.S. resolution to declare the expulsion of Taiwan an important question requiring a 2/3 majority. That vote was 59-55 with 15 abstentions. The U.S. had predicted victory, and its defeat precipitated the landslide victory for the Albanian resolution. *The text of the Albanian resolution:*

The General Assembly,
Recalling the principles of the Charter of United Nations.
Considering that the restoration of the lawful rights of the People's Republic of China is essential both for the protection of the Charter of the United Nations and for the cause that the United Nations must serve under the Charter.
Recognizing that the representatives of the Government of the People's Republic of China are the only lawful representatives of China to the United Nations and that the People's Republic of China is one of the 5 permanent members of the Security Council.
Decides to restore all its rights to the People's Republic of China and to recognize the representatives of its Government as the only legitimate representatives of China to the United Nations, and to expel forthwith the representatives of Chiang Kai-shek from the place which they unlawfully occupy at the United Nations and in all the organizations affiliated to it.
Sponsored by Albania, Algeria, Ceylon, Congo [Brazzaville], Cuba, Equatorial Guinea, Guinea, Iraq, Mali, Mauritania, Nepal, Pakistan, Rumania, Somalia, Southern Yemen, Syria, Sudan, Tanzania, Yemen, Yugoslavia and Zambia.

The UN action created considerable repercussions in Washington. Official reaction was restrained. In a statement approved by Nixon and read to newsmen by State Secy. Rogers Oct. 26, the Administration welcomed Communist China's admission to the UN as "consistent with the policy of the U.S." but said that "at the same time, the U.S. deeply regrets the action taken by the UN to deprive the Republic of China of representation in that organization." The statement added: "Although we believe that a mistake of major proportions has been made in expelling the Republic of China from the United Nations, the U.S. recognizes that the will of a majority of the members has been expressed. We, of course, accept that decision."

Congressional reaction was a different matter. Immediately after the UN vote Oct. 25, Sen. Buckley said he had asked his staff to prepare legislation for "a major reduction" in the U.S. financial contribution to the UN. He told reporters that "the action taken by the General Assembly may well be recorded as the beginning of the end of the UN, as marking that clear moment when a majority of the member nations decided to abandon principle in order to curry favor with a government which still remains branded by the UN as an agressor; a government which by precept and action repudiates provisions of the UN Charter." Buckley and Sen. Peter Dominick (R., Colo.) announced Oct. 27 that they were working on legislation to reduce the U.S. contribution to the UN in conjunction with the $3.2 billion foreign aid authorization bill on which debate began in the Senate Oct. 26. Their proposed reductions covered not the annual UN membership dues but U.S. donations to UN specialized agencies.

Sen. William Saxbe (R., O.) insisted Oct. 26 that any decisions about cuts should be taken in a "calmer mood." He moved to recommit the foreign aid authorization bill to allow a "cooling off period" before beginning the vote on the bill. Saxbe's motion was withdrawn when opposed by Senators who argued it would hold up Senate business.

Both Senate majority leader Mike Mansfield and Senate minority leader Hugh Scott said Oct. 26 that they supported a cut in U.S. contributions to the UN but stressed that their positions were not based on the vote on China. Mansfield suggested a possible reduction of U.S. support for the UN budget from 33% of the total to about 25%. He said that any cut that had a "crippling" effect on the organization would be unacceptable. Scott said he had long believed that a reduction in the U.S. share of UN costs was required and added that he was "extremely disappointed" by the vote and the fact that "a good many nations we've helped very generously over the years have shown a classic lack of appreciation . . ."

Sen. Hubert Humphrey said Oct. 26 that the General Assembly's action "was regrettable" but added that it should "in no way . . . prejudice our active support of the UN." Humphrey criticized the Buckley proposal as an act of "irresponsibility and immaturity." He said the Assembly's vote "represents the diplomatic backlash of a long misguided U.S. policy relating to China."

Sen. J. William Fulbright, chairman of the Senate Foreign Relations Committee, said that rather than reduce U.S. contributions to the UN, Congress might reduce aid to countries that had voted against the U.S. position on China.

Few Senators called for U.S. withdrawal from the world organization. Sen. Barry Goldwater (R., Ariz.), however, said "the time has come to recognize the UN for the anti-American, anti-freedom organization that it has become. The time has come for us to cut off all financial help, withdraw as a member, and ask the UN to find a headquarters location outside the U.S. . . . , someplace like Moscow or Peking."

In the House, several representatives deplored the expulsion of Taiwan. Speaker Carl Albert (D., Okla.), while criticizing the action, said Oct. 26 that "It would be heaping one irresponsibility on another to diminish our support of the UN because of our displeasure with this vote."

The Committee of One Million, the leading U.S. pro-Nationalist group, claiming 40,000 dues-paying members, said Oct. 26 that the UN "must be prepared for an outcry from the American people for a reduction and even the elimination of U.S. support for the world organization." The group's chairman, ex-Rep. Walter H. Judd, denounced the UN action as "an ominous blow to international justice and a cynical affront to human justice."

Lin Piao Falls from Power

During the General Assembly's debate on the China question, Dr. Henry A. Kissinger, Pres. Nixon's national security adviser, was in Peking reportedly making arrangements for Nixon's forthcoming visit. Kissinger stayed in the Chinese capital Oct. 20-25, 1971. Prior to Kissinger's departure for Peking, there had been persistent rumors that China was in the grip of a political crisis. These rumours were touched off by the cancellation of the National Day parade Oct. 1.

Thousands of persons, including several hundred visiting foreigners, watched the activities in the city's Tienanmen Square.

The customary huge parade did not take place. The Communist Party newspaper *Jenmin Jih Pao* failed to carry its usual editorial marking the founding of the Chinese Communist government and did not publish the customary large photographs of Chairman Mao Tse-tung and Deputy Chairman Lin Piao. Premier Chou En-lai and other high-ranking officials witnessed performances in Tienanmen Square by theater and dance groups. Absent were Mao and Politburo members of the armed services —Huang Yung-sheng (army), Wu Fa-Hsien (air force) and Li Tso-peng (navy). The service officials had not been mentioned or seen in more than 3 weeks. Chou and other top-ranking officials had not attended a National Day eve reception Sept. 30, adding to the speculation that China was faced with some kind of unrest. The reception was attended by Tung Pi-wu, a deputy chief of state, and Deputy Premier Li Hsien-nien.

U.S. State Secy. William P. Rogers said Oct. 2 that Washington was "not sure" what was occurring in China but hoped that the events there "do not signal any change in the possibility of Pres. Nixon's" visit to Peking.

The Soviet news agency Tass had said Sept. 24 that Peking was beset by "a number of grave internal political developments." Describing the situation as "rather unusual," Tass accused the Chinese leadership of "seeking to extricate itself from the tangle of internal difficulties by fanning another anti-Soviet hysteria" by accusing Soviet forces of threatening China. Tass reported that the foreign press had quoted Chinese officials as explaining that the National Day parade had been canceled because of "the alleged threat to China on the northern frontiers, where an attack on Chinese territory is allegedly planned and therefore it is impossible to celebrate National Day as usual."

Etienne Manac'h, French ambassador to Peking, said Oct. 3 that "something has happened in China. I cannot tell you anything more." Manac'h made the remark while traveling in France with a visiting Chinese trade delegation.

The Mongolian press agency reported Sept. 30 that a Chinese air force plane had gone off course and crashed deep inside

Mongolia, near the Soviet border the night of Sept. 12-13 with the loss of 9 persons. The report said Mongolia had protested to Peking about the intrusion.

Tass and other Soviet newspapers, carrying a version of a report filed by the French news agency Agence France-Presse, said Nov. 13 that "in many diplomatic circles in Peking, even among persons closest to the Chinese government, there is growing doubt of Lin Piao remaining the 'Number 2 man' in China." The newspaper said it was becoming more difficult "to find in Peking's bookshops the Chinese edition of the party statutes adopted by the 9th Party Congress in 1969." These statutes, Tass noted, referred to Lin "as the successor" of Chairman Mao Tse-tung.

In a further comment on the alleged turmoil in China, Tass reported Nov. 19 that "although the Chinese leaders persist in keeping a veil of secrecy over the nature and causes of the events that took place in China recently, information reaching here from Peking and the press reports indicate the existence of a grave crisis in the Chinese leadership."

A Washington dispatch Nov. 16 said U.S. intelligence sources had been receiving reports that Communist Party groups throughout China were being informed by top party leaders that Lin "no longer holds power." According to the U.S. specialists, further evidence of Lin's downfall was manifested in the UN Nov. 15 when China's new delegation was welcomed by representatives of other Communist states and "3d world" nations close to Peking in speeches that failed to mention Lin. The U.S. intelligence sources were reported as saying that the crisis in Peking had come to a head about Sept. 11 when Lin and his followers were forced out by Mao and Chou En-lai. Lin and some military leaders were said to have advocated economic priorities favorable to the armed forces while the Mao-Chou faction preferred to have the country's economic resources allocated largely for non-military use, according to the U.S. report. Lin also was said to have opposed Peking's new policy of detente with the West.

The apparent but still unconfirmed fall from power of Lin and other top military leaders was reported to have resulted in a major reshuffling of the government hierarchy. The upheaval was said to have included Mao Tse-tung's takeover of the armed forces and Chou En-lai's elevation to the No. 2 spot in the party Politburo. The *N.Y. Times* Nov. 27 quoted numerous radio broadcasts and newspapers in China as saying that Chinese military units were now "under the direct leadership and command of Chairman Mao." One recent broadcast, from Chengtu, in Szechwan Province, stated: "The party commands the gun, and the gun must never be allowed to command the party, so we must place the army under the absolute leadership of the party, carry out whatever Chairman Mao instructs and go wherever the party directs." A *Times* report Nov. 28 said that Premier Chou, formerly listed 3d after Lin in the Politburo standing, was in 2d place, directly behind Mao. The advancement of Mao's wife, Chiang Ching, from 6th to 3d place, was said to have been brought about by the purging of Chen Po-ta and the disappearance from public view of Kang Sheng, both former top Politburo members.

Nixon Goes to Peking

Lin's fall, which was later confirmed, removed an obstacle to Nixon's visit to Peking. At the end of Nov. 1971, it was announced in Peking and Washington simultaneously that the President would visit China during the week Feb. 21-28, 1972. At a White House news conference Nov. 30, Press Secy. Ronald L. Ziegler and Henry A. Kissinger, Nixon's adviser on national security affairs, announced further details of the trip: Mrs. Nixon would accompany the President; the party would fly directly to and from China with refueling and rest stops only in American territory; the President and Mrs. Nixon would stay with a small working party at a Chinese government guest house on the edge of Peking during a 4-day stay in Peking; the President also would visit Shanghai and Hangchow, but sightseeing was only a "peripheral feature" of the visit; the trip would end Feb. 28; and Nixon would meet with Premier Chou En-lai.

Kissinger said that discussions would be of "a free-wheeling nature" permitting either side to raise any topic it considered urgent. He said the "major thrust" of the talks would be on bilateral issues, that "no agreement will be made about 3d-party problems" but that 3d-party issues could be broached if either side "considers something of crucial importance."

Kissinger specified that the trip was not expected to result in the establishment of formal diplomatic relations between the U.S. and China, a settlement of the differences between Peking and the Nationalist Chinese on Taiwan, nor an end to the war in Southeast Asia. "We're not sentimental about this," he said. "We recognize that the People's Republic is led by highly principled men whose principles are diametrically opposed to ours." It was in the interest of both countries, Kissinger said, "that we understand what we are about and that on those matters that are in our common interest we know how to cooperate." The minimum objective of the trip, he said, would be to establish a system of communication on opposing views and thus avert "very dramatic, set-piece encounters."

Anticipating Nixon's visit, Communist China Dec. 12 freed 2 Americans from prison. A dispatch Dec. 13 from Hsinhua identified the former prisoners as Richard G. Fecteau and Mary Ann Harbert. Hsinhua said Fecteau, of Lynn, Mass., and John T. Downey, of New Britain, Conn., had been shot down in a military aircraft over China in 1952 after dropping espionage agents trained in Japan into Manchuria. Downey's life sentence was being reduced to 5 more years because "both men had admitted their crimes during the trial and their behavior was not bad while serving their terms." Miss Harbert had strayed into Chinese waters off southern Kwangtung Province in 1968 while sailing from Hong Kong in a yacht with Gerald R. McLaughlin, a family friend. Hsinhua declared that McLaughlin had "behaved badly" during detention, "resisted investigation and, taking the warders unawares, committed suicide on March 7, 1969." Both arrived in the U.S. Dec. 13.

The President conferred with the leaders of France, Britain, West Germany, Japan and Canada in the intervening months prior to his trip to Peking. Meanwhile, technical preparations for the Presidential trip proceeded apace.

A party of 61 U.S. radio and TV technicians flew into Peking Feb. 1, 1972 and were joined by 18 others Feb. 14. A new communications satellite, *Intelstat 4*, which would broadcast reports of Nixon's visit to China, went into operation Feb. 14, and a temporary receiving station in Peking, built by the Hughes Tool Co., was reported to have been leased to the Chinese government. RCA Global Communications, Inc. announced Feb. 15 that it was installing a permanent station in Shanghai, which would be purchased by China for $2.9 million.

The White House announced Feb. 12 the members of Nixon's official party. They were: State Secy. William P. Rogers; Kissinger; H. R. Haldeman, assistant to the President; Ziegler; Brig. Gen. Brent Scowcroft, military assistant to the President; Marshall Green, assistant state secretary for East Asian and Pacific affairs; Dwight L. Chapin, deputy assistant to the President; John A. Scali, special consultant to the President; Patrick J. Buchanan, special assistant to the President; Rose Mary Woods, personal secretary to the President; Alfred L. Jenkins, State Department director for Asian Communist affairs; John Holdridge, staff member of the National Security Council, and Winston Lord, special assistant to Kissinger.

Ziegler also said that an "unofficial" party of "approximately 21" would include Gerald L. Warren, deputy White House press secretary; Brig. Gen. Walter R. Tkach, the President's physician; Ronald Walker, staff assistant to the President; Timothy Elbourne, a press aide, and a number of "secretarial assistants." The total press contingent was to number 168, including 87 newsmen, 13 satellite ground station technicians and 68 other communications personnel.

Pres. and Mrs. Nixon left the U.S. Feb. 17 on their way to China, with scheduled stops in Hawaii and Guam. 3 days before departing, the President had further relaxed barriers to trade with China and had talks with Andre Malraux, the French writer and specialist in Chinese affairs. In a farewell statement made during ceremonies at the White House, Nixon described himself as being "under no illusions that 20 years of hostility between the People's Republic of China and the U.S. are going to be swept away by one week of talks that we will have there." Referring to the words of a toast given by Chinese Premier Chou En-lai to Henry A. Kissinger during Kissinger's Oct. 1971 visit to Peking, Nixon said that both the U.S. and the Chinese were "a great people" and that their separation by "a vast ocean and great differences in philosophy should not prevent them from finding common ground." He noted "that if there was a postscript that I hope might be written with regard to this trip, it would be the words on the plaque which was left on the moon by our first astronauts when they landed there. We came in peace for all mankind."

The Presidential party stopped Feb. 17 and 18 at the Kaneohe Marine Corps Air Station in Hawaii. The party then flew to Guam, crossing the international dateline, for another overnight stay Feb. 20. After landing at Shanghai to pick up a Chinese navigator for the last leg of the 11,500-mile journey, the Presidential jet touched down at Hung Chiao Airport in Peking.

Nixon arrived in China Feb. 21, 1972. On hand to greet the U.S. visitors were Premier Chou En-lai, several other Chinese dignitaries and a 500-man military honor guard. There were no crowds, no apparent efforts to decorate the city and no speeches.

Although the airport reception was restrained, Nixon later in the day met with Chairman Mao Tse-tung, an event that had not been announced beforehand. Nixon's visit with Mao, which took place at Mao's residence in the old Forbidden City, lasted one hour and was described afterwards as "frank and serious." Spokesmen for both sides declined to say what had been discussed. Nixon was accompanied by Kissinger. Mao was accompanied during the talks by Premier Chou, by Wang Hai-jung, deputy director of protocol, and by Tang Wen-sheng, an interpreter.

The Chinese were hosts at a banquet the evening of Feb. 21 at the Great Hall of the People. Chou offered a toast to the Nixon party in which he said that Nixon's visit "provides the leaders of the 2 countries with an opportunity of meeting in person to seek the normalization of relations between the 2 countries and also to exchange views on questions of concern." Calling the trip a "positive move," he said that Sino-U.S. "contacts" had been suspended "owing to reasons known to all." The social systems of the 2 countries were "fundamentally different, and there exist great differences between the Chinese government and the U.S. government." Nonetheless, Chou said, "normal state relations" could still be established "on the basis of the 5 principles of mutual respect for sovereignty and territorial integrity; mutual nonaggression; noninterference in each other's internal affairs; equality and mutual benefits, and peaceful coexistence."

Nixon responded by noting that "more people are seeing and hearing what we say than on any other occasion in the whole history of the world." He said: If the 2 countries could "find common ground to work together, the chance for world peace is immeasurably increased." The U.S. and China had "at times in the past been enemies. We have great differences today. What brings us together is that we have common interests which transcend those differences." There was "no reason for us to be enemies. Neither of us seeks the territory of the other. Neither of us seeks domination over the other. Neither of us seeks to stretch out our hands and rule the world."

In the central portion of his toast, Nixon referred to the legendary Long March of 1934-5, in which Mao's army broke through an encirclement by the forces of Chiang Kai-shek and traveled some 6,000 miles from their base in Kiangsi Province to the caves of Yenan, in Shensi Province, where they lived for more than a decade. Nixon declared: "And so let us, in these next 5 days, start a long march together. Not in lockstep, but on different roads leading to the same goal: the goal of building a world structure of peace and justice in which all may stand together with equal dignity and in which each nation, large or small, has a right to determine its own form of government free of outside interference or domination."

Nixon and Chou met Feb. 22 for 4 hours of policy discussions. Accompanying the President were Kissinger and John H. Holdridge and Winston Lord of the National Security Council. Those attending with Chou were: Yeh Chien-ying, deputy chairman of the Communist Party Central Committee's military commission; Li Hsien-nien, a deputy premier; Wang Hai-jung; Chiao Kuan-hua, a deputy foreign minister; and Chang Wen-chin, head of the European, American and Australian section at the Foreign Ministry.

State Secy. William P. Rogers and Foreign Min. Chi Peng-fei held a separate conference.

In the evening, after a private dinner, the Nixons attended a special performance of "Red Detachment of Women," a revolutionary opera fashioned by Chiang Ching, Mao's wife and a member of the Politburo. Chou and his wife, Teng Ying-chiao, also attended the performance.

Nixon and Chou met Feb. 23 for 4 more hours of talks. They were followed in the evening by exhibitions of gymnastics and table tennis. Mrs. Nixon visited the Evergreen People's Commune, an agricultural cooperative near the capital, and the Peking Glassware Factory. *Jenmin Jih Pao*, in an article at the bottom of the front page, printed 4 photos showing aspects of the Nixon trip.

Nixon Feb. 24 made excursions to the Great Wall of China, a fortification built in pre-Christian times to keep out barbarian invaders, and to the Ming Tombs, which had been constructed by members of a dynasty that ruled China from the 14th to the 17th centuries. Some of Nixon's comments to newsmen were taken as an indication that his talks with Premier Chou had explored the prospect of Sino-U.S. tourist exchanges. Speaking informally to reporters for the first time during his visit,

Nixon said: "I think that you would have to conclude that this is a great wall and it had to be built by a great people. Many lives, of course, were lost in building it. There was no machinery or equipment at the time. It had to all be done by hand. But under the circumstances it is a certain symbol of what China in the past has been and what China in the future can become. . . . As we look at this wall, we do not want walls of any kind between peoples." He hoped one result of the journey to Peking might be that "peoples, regardless of their differences and backgrounds and philosophies, will have an opportunity to. communicate with each other, and to share with each other those particular endeavors that will mean peaceful progress in the years ahead."

According to the *Washington Post* Feb. 25, Nixon remarked on his way to the Ming Tombs that one outcome of his talks with Chou might be, "apart from relations between governments, that people will be able to come here and that, of course, Chinese people would be able to come to the U.S."

Nixon held talks for 3 hours again Feb. 24 with Chou. The session was followed by a private dinner, which was also attended by Rogers and Foreign Min. Chi, whose meetings be continuing.

In its last full day in Peking Feb. 25, the group visited the Forbidden City, where the Nixons viewed the palaces and courtyards of ancient Chinese emperors. Later in the afternoon Nixon and Chou met for about an hour of private talks. That night at the Great Hall of the People, Nixon gave a banquet for Chou at which their mutual toasts suggested the substance of the communique released Feb. 27. The President remarked that the U.S. and China had "begun the long process of removing that wall between us" and he ended his toast with a quotation from George Washington's farewell address: "Observe good faith and justice toward all nations, cultivate peace and harmony with all."

Chou said the two sides had exchanged views on "the normalization of relations," although there existed "great differences of principle" between them. He added: "The times are advancing and the world changes. We are deeply convinced that the strength of the people is powerful and that whatever zigzags and reverses there will be in the development of history, the general trend of the world is definitely toward light and not darkness."

The Nixons went Feb. 26 to Hangchow, a resort city 100 miles southwest of Shanghai, where they were the guests of Nan Ping, chairman of the Revolutionary Committee of Chekiang Province, of which Hangchow was the capital. The following day, in the company of Chou En-lai, the Nixons flew to Shang-hai. At a banquet, Nixon declared that "our 2 peoples tonight hold the future of the world in our hands." He said the talks with Mao and Chou had been "characterized by frankness, by honesty, by determination and above all by mutual respect." The President noted that both the Chinese and the American people were dedicated to the principle "that never again shall foreign domination, foreign occupation, be visited upon this city or any part of China or any independent country in this world."

Nixon and Chou released a joint communique Feb. 27 indicating that their talks had resulted in agreement on the need for increased Sino-U.S. contacts and for eventual withdrawal of U.S. troops from Taiwan.

The 1,800-word communique had been reached after several nights of intensive negotiation and was divided into 5 sections. The first was a general account of the President's stay in China. In the 2d part, each nation recorded separately its views on Asian policy issues.

The U.S. emphasized its support for an 8-point proposal advocated in January by itself and South Vietnam for an end to the Indochina war. It added that "in the absence of a negoti-ated settlement the U.S. envisages the ultimate withdrawal of all U.S. forces from the region consistent with the aim of self-de-termination for each country of Indochina." The statement also said: The U.S. would "maintain its close ties with and sup-port for the Republic of [South] Korea." Washington "places the highest value on its friendly relations with Japan; it will continue to develop the existing close bonds." Regarding the India-Pakistan dispute, the U.S. favored a continuation of the cease-fire and "the withdrawal of all military forces to within their own territories and to their own sides of the cease-fire line in Jammu and Kashmir."

In its statement, China announced its support for the revised 7-point Viet Cong proposal elaborated in February. It favored North Korean proposals for the "peaceful unification" of Korea. It opposed the "revival and outward expansion of Japanese militarism." The first part of the Chinese statement on the India-Pakistan dispute was virtually identical to that of the U.S., but Peking emphasized that it "firmly supports the Pakistan government and people in their struggle to preserve their independence and sovereignty and the people of Jammu and Kashmir in their struggle for the right of self-determination."

The 3d section of the communique pointed out that although there were "essential differences" in the "social systems and foreign policies" of the U.S. and China, "the 2 sides agreed" on general rules of international relations. These were that countries "should conduct their relations on the principles of respect for the sovereignty and territorial integrity of all states, nonaggression against other states, noninterference in the internal affairs of other states, equality and mutual benefit, and peaceful coexistence." (These principles had been enunciated by Chou En-lai as early as 1955 at the Bandung Conference of Asian and African Peoples.)

The 2 sides further agreed that progress toward "the normalization of relations" between them was "in the interests of all countries." The statement said: Both sides wished "to reduce the danger of international military conflict"; neither "should seek hegemony in the Asia-Pacific region, and each is opposed to the efforts by any other country or group of countries to establish such hegemony"; neither "is prepared to negotiate on behalf of any 3d party or to enter into agreements or understandings with the other directed at other states."

The 4th part of the communique was given over to separate statements on Taiwan. The Chinese declared that the "Taiwan question is the crucial question obstructing the normalization of relations" between Washington and Peking. In the remainder of the passage, China reaffirmed its traditional claims to the island, emphasizing that the "liberation of Taiwan is China's internal affair." The communique said: "The Chinese government firmly opposes any activities which aim at the creation of 'one China, one Taiwan,' 'one China, 2 governments,' 2 Chinas' and 'independent Taiwan,' or advocate that 'the status of Taiwan remains to be determined.'" The U.S. said: "The U.S. acknowledges that all Chinese on either side of the Taiwan Strait maintain there is but one China and that Taiwan is a part of China. The U.S. government does not challenge that position. It reaffirms its interest in a peaceful settlement of the Taiwan question by the Chinese themselves. With this prospect in mind, it affirms the ultimate objective of the withdrawal of all U.S. forces and military installations from Taiwan. In the meantime, it will progressively reduce its forces and military installations on Taiwan as the tension in the area diminishes."

In the communique's final section, the 2 sides said they had discussed joint contacts "in such fields as science, technology, culture, sports and journalism" and that they planned to "facilitate the further development of such contacts and exchanges." The desirability of increasing "bilateral trade" was stressed. It was agreed to send "a senior U.S. representative to Peking from time to time for concrete consultations to further the normalization of relations between the two countries and continue to exchange views on issues of common interest."

Kissinger held a news conference in Shanghai Feb. 27 on aspects of the communique. Kissinger was accompanied by Marshall Green, assistant state secretary for East Asian and Pacific affairs, who had been with State Secy. Rogers in his talks with Chinese Foreign Min. Chi Peng-fei.

In explaining how the communique was produced, Kissinger said both sides had tried to insure that the document "would not pretend to an agreement that did not exist and which would have to be interpreted away in the subsequent implementation." To assemble materials for the text of the communique, he said, "issues of general principle" were first discussed in meetings between Nixon and Premier Chou. Then the discussions were transferred "to the meetings chaired by" Rogers and Chi. If "any additional issues arose," they were sent back to Nixon and Chou. Kissinger said that for the previous "few nights" this process had gone on until "the early hours of the morning." He remarked that the document "ought to be seen in 2 aspects: first, in terms of the specific principles and conclusions it states, and secondly, in terms of the direction to which it seeks to point."

Green explained that the meetings he attended had been notable for their "candor, friendliness and courtesy" but that participants had been "out-spoken" with "no effort to cover up or paper over differences."

Responding to questions from newsmen, Kissinger declared that the portion of the text promising a gradual reduction of U.S. forces on Taiwan was "a general statement of our policy which we have enunciated on innumerable occasions in innumerable forms." He said the communique was "a fair characterization of the basic positions" of both sides regarding the issue of U.S. prisoners of war in Vietnam.

Asked what features of the communique indicated significant steps by China since its 1971 invitation to the U.S. table tennis team, Kissinger replied: "The formalization of exchanges encouraged by the 2 governments, the opening of trade encouraged by the 2 governments, the establishment of a diplomatic mechanism for continued contact, the joint statement of some general principles of international relations, the joint statement of some basic approaches to the view of the world with respect to, for instance, the section which includes the reference to hegemony—these, I believe, are matters that most of us would have considered unthinkable at the time of the invitation to the ping-pong team."

Nixon and his party left China for the U.S. Feb. 28. Arriving at Andrews Air force Base, Md. Feb. 28, the President said in a nationally televised address that his trip had shown "that nations with very deep and fundamental differences can learn to discuss those differences calmly, rationally and frankly without compromising principles" and that this amounted to "the basis of a structure for peace." Nixon said he and his Chinese hosts had "agreed on some rules of international conduct which will reduce the risk of confrontation and war in Asia and the Pacific" and had "set up a procedure whereby we can continue to have discussions in the future." They had also decided, he said, "that we will not negotiate the fate of other nations behind their back and we did not do so in Peking. There were no secret deals of any kind." The President described the Shanghai communique as "unique in honestly setting forth differences rather than trying to cover them up with diplomatic double-talk." He explained: "We did not bring back any written or unwritten agreements that will guarantee peace in our time. We did not bring home any magic formula which will make unnecessary the efforts of the American people to continue to maintain the strength so that we can continue to be free."

Reaction to Nixon Trip

The President's trip and final communique drew criticism from conservative Republicans, who objected to the U.S. withdrawal from Taiwan and the absence in the communique of any mention of the mutual defense pact with the Nationalist Chinese. According to Sen. James L. Buckley Feb. 28, the communique was "being widely interpreted both at home and abroad as signaling the ultimate abandonment of Taiwan" by the U.S. "If we permit doubts about our intentions to persist with respect to our security agreement with Taiwan," he said, "we will undercut the credibility of our arrangements with Japan, South Korea and our other Asian allies as well." Buckley criticized the Nixon trip Feb. 29 as "a disastrous adventure in American diplomacy" and the communique as having done "enormous damage to American credibility."

The Senator's brother, William F. Buckley Jr., publisher of the *National Review,* joined in the criticism. Buckley, a member of the press party accompanying the President to China, objected Feb. 29 to the Nixon assertion that the Peking-Taiwan dispute was an internal matter and to the U.S.' making it clear it was "pulling out of that area and yielding to Red China's dominance in that area." "His desire for the spotlight in China," Buckley said, "transformed, subtly, his analysis of what was going on into a desire for maximum political publicity." By so doing, he said, concessions had been made that undermined the "whole moral basis" of U.S. treaty commitments in Asia.

Buckley made the comments in Manchester, N.H., where he endorsed Rep. John M. Ashbrook (R., O.) in his campaign against Nixon in the Presidential primary election. Ashbrook, with Buckley in agreement, deplored the Taiwan aspect of the communique as a "sellout of principle." Ashbrook had said Feb. 27 that he was "shocked and dismayed at Pres. Nixon's decision to accept Communist China's central demand of the past 22 years—unilateral withdrawal of all U.S. forces from the Republic of China on Taiwan."

Reassuring statements that Nixon had not undermined basic conservative positions concerning Taiwan were issued Mar. 1 by GOP Sens. Barry M. Goldwater (Ariz.) and Gordon Allott (Colo.), chairman of the Senate Republican Policy Committee. Goldwater expressed satisfaction "we have not given away one single thing to the Red Chinese." Allott said there was "no basic change in policy regarding Taiwan involved in the joint communique."

Only a few of the many Democratic Presidential contenders criticized the Nixon trip to China. Sen. Henry M. Jackson (Wash.) observed Feb. 28, "It appears that we are doing the withdrawing and they are doing the staying." He said "that does not strike me as a good horse trade." Sen. Hubert Humphrey (Minn.) said Feb. 28 that on first interpretation it appeared that Nixon had made concessions but the Chinese had not. Many of the Democratic candidates, however, considered the Nixon trip and communique a step forward diplomatically. Sen. Edward M. Kennedy (Mass.) called the communique "one of the most progressive documents" in the history of American diplomacy and hailed "the bridge that has now been built to Peking."

The White House announced Feb. 29 that Senate leaders Mike Mansfield (D., Mont.) and Hugh Scott (R., Pa.) would visit China at the invitation of Premier Chou En-lai. White House Press Secy. Ronald L. Ziegler said that the invitation, which had originated with Chou, had been extended to the leaders by Nixon when he met with Congressional leaders Feb. 29 to brief them on his China trip. Other members of Congress also were briefed Feb. 29 by Kissinger, and the President briefed his cabinet Feb. 29. Mansfield commented after the briefing that the group meeting with the President had been "unanimously in favor of the President's trip and what he accomplished." Scott said he had "no doubt whatever ... that we have in no way by this visit altered our treaty commitments to Korea, Taiwan or Japan." Scott also said Nixon had stressed that the promise to withdraw U.S. troops from Taiwan, as mentioned in the final communique, was not to be considered a separate item and was not unrelated to a decrease in tensions in Asia, particularly in Vietnam. Scott indicated that the current U.S. force of 8,000 men on Taiwan would be reduced to 2,000 with total withdrawal contingent upon a peaceful settlement of differences between Taiwan and Peking.

The Nationalist Chinese Foreign Ministry issued a statement Feb. 28 denouncing the Sino-U.S. communique. Taiwan newspapers joined in condemning the document. The Foreign Ministry dispatch repeated the government's earlier warning that it would consider "null and void" any agreement "which has been and which may not have been published, involving the rights and interests of the government and people of the Republic of China, reached between the U.S. and the Chinese Communist regime." It said: The "so-called 'question of Taiwan'" would be "solved only when the government of the

Republic of China, the sole legitimate government elected by all people of China, has succeeded in its task of the recovery of the unification of China and the deliverance of our compatriots. There is definitely no other alternative." These efforts "have as their objectives not only the salvation of China but also that of Asia and the world."

The Taipei daily newspaper *Chung-kuo Shih Pao* said Nixon had "gained nothing in return for his statement about the withdrawal. Not even a specific commitment that the Chinese Communists will not resort to the use of force in the Taiwan area." *Lien Ho Pao,* the largest paper on the island, said the Nixon journey had been a "complete failure."

James C.H. Shen, Nationalist Chinese ambassador to the U.S., said in Washington Mar. 2 that State Secy. Rogers had assured him that day of the U.S. commitment to the 1954 Taiwan defense treaty. Shen, who had gone at Rogers' invitation to a special briefing on Nixon's visit, remarked: "I understand a little more now but I have no comment on my personal feelings."

Marshall Green, U.S. assistant state secretary for East Asian affairs, and John H. Holdridge, an Asian specialist for the National Security Council staff, went to Tokyo from Shanghai Feb. 28 to reassure officials of the Japanese government about Nixon's trip. Green and Holdridge met Feb. 28 with Foreign Min. Takeo Fukuda, who had told newsmen the previous day he thought the President's visit had been fruitful. Fukuda said he regarded the portion of the Shanghai communique advocating a progressive reduction of U.S. troops on Taiwan as "just another way of expressing the Nixon Doctrine. What this means is that U.S. armed forces will be pulled out, not only from Taiwan but from Japan and other Asian countries in the event that tensions can be relaxed."

Green told South Korean Foreign Min. Kim Yong Shik in Seoul Mar. 1 that Nixon had made no secret deals during his China visit. Green repeated his message the following day in interviews with Premier Kim Chong Pil and Pres. Chung Hee

Park. Foreign Min. Kim had told newsmen Feb. 28: "We welcome the American support for our position on the Korean problem, opposing Communist China's stand." Kim said his people regarded the Shanghai communique as "reaffirmation of the U.S. pledge to stand with us for the defense of our nation." Lee Dong Won, chairman of the National Assembly's foreign affairs committee, had declared that day: "I am afraid that there must be some tacit agreements in the U.S.-Chinese summit talks that were not officially revealed."

In Taipei Mar. 2, Green had lunch with Nationalist Chinese Foreign Min. Chow Shu-kai but did not meet Pres. Chiang Kai-shek. In a news interview that day, Chow declared that there was now less prospect than ever of a negotiated settlement between Peking and Taipei because in the Shanghai communique Peking had mentioned its determination to "liberate" Taiwan. This seemed to Chow to rule out any "sensible" discussion of the matter.

(Andre Malraux, the French writer, who had attended a White House conference before Nixon's departure for China, said in an interview with Agence France Press in Paris Mar. 2 that he believed there was a secret Peking-Taipei accord under the terms of which Taiwan would be controlled by the mainland government after Chiang Kai-shek's death. Malraux asserted: "I don't think Nixon gave up anything over Formosa because there has been for at least 5 years an agreement between Peking and Taipei, linked with the death of Chiang Kai-shek.")

The official Soviet news agency Tass Feb. 28 had given a long account of the Sino-U.S. communique, noting with approval Peking's support for the Viet Cong peace proposal and mentioning that the communique had stressed "essential differences between China and the U.S." The Soviet trade union newspaper *Trud* declared Feb. 29, however, that the Chinese leaders had "broken all records to curry favor" with the U.S. It added: "The entire progressive world, along with the condemnation of the activities of American imperialism against the peace and freedom of peoples, also condemns the Maoists for having entered a dangerous plot with the ruling circles of the U.S." *Trud* cited favorably what it claimed were evaluations of the Nixon trip made by U.S. newsmen, who "jokingly called it the show of the century because it was well-rehearsed, combed and sleek." A Feb. 25 statement by the Soviet Defense Ministry, appearing in the armed forces newspaper *Krasnaya Zvezda,* had said China was annually setting aside approximately 1/3 of its budget ($8 billion to $8.5 billion) for military expenditures. It asserted that Peking was intensifying "purely military measures to prepare for war, such as the development and stockpiling of modern weapons, widespread military construction in border districts, and military training of the population through the system of people's volunteers functioning even in peacetime." The paper said of China's trade with capitalist countries that "a greater and greater proportion consists of goods of a strategic character: nonferrous and rare metals, equipment and materials necessary for the production of nuclear weapons and the means of their delivery, and even military equipment."

South Vietnam's first official comment on Nixon's visit to China came Mar. 1 in remarks by Foreign Min. Tran Van Lam, who said he was not upset by the Sino-U.S. communique's reference to the ultimate withdrawal of U.S. forces from Indochina. Lam declared: "It has already been agreed between our two governments that when Vietnamese troops are fully trained and equipped the American troops will go home." He also said: "We fully approve of Mr. Nixon's trip. No one can deny that it helped create an atmosphere of eased tensions. . . . The U.S. has been very correct and faithful in its commitments to Vietnam, and we especially appreciate the mention of our eight-point peace proposal."

Aftermath

The polemical contest between the U.S. and China was resumed soon after the conclusion of Nixon's visit, but a number of developments of a less bellicose nature indicated that a

genuine improvement in Sino-U.S. relations—and in the lessening of associated international tensions—may have taken
place.

China denounced the U.S. Mar. 10, 1972 for recent air
strikes on North Vietnam, and it reiterated support for Communist forces in Indochina. The statement was Peking's first
attack on Washington since Nixon's visit to China. The statement by the Foreign Affairs Ministry demanded that the U.S.
halt the bombings and other attacks, withdraw unconditionally
"before a set terminal date" and "cease to support the puppet
cliques in the Indochinese countries."

Chinese Premier Chou En-lai Apr. 5 vowed continued
support to the Vietnamese Communists in their struggle against
the U.S. "war of aggression." His statement was made in a
filmed interview in Peking with British journalist Felix Greene
and was broadcast over NBC TV Apr. 19. The premier pledged
that if the U.S. "war of aggression against Indochina does not
stop. . . . and the bombings are expanded, the free Indochinese
peoples can only fight on to the end and the Chinese people
will certainly support them to the end." Chou characterized
Nixon's trip to China in February as "at least a start" toward
the understanding of each other's views. "The most outstanding question in the Far East remains that of the United States
war of aggression against Vietnam and Indochina," he said.

The USSR accused China Apr. 19 of rejecting a Soviet
proposal for joint support of the Vietnamese Communists. A
Moscow broadcast beamed to China said Peking had "refused
to issue a joint statement denouncing U.S. crimes" in Vietnam and had turned down "any step for united action in support
of the Vietnamese patriots." The broadcast noted that the
Soviet Union had provided North Vietnam with material and
political assistance, while China, it charged, merely issued
statements on Hanoi's behalf. The broadcast added: "The authorities in Washington have long treated such statements ca-
sually, especially since Nixon's China visit, because the U.S.
ruling clique is well aware that the Chinese ruling clique, to

carry out its selfish political conspiracy, is prepared to sacrifice the interests of the people of various countries in Asia."

Nixon announced May 8 that he had ordered the mining of North Vietnamese ports and interdiction of land and sea routes to North Vietnam in a move to prevent the delivery of war supplies to that country. "Rail and all other communications will be cut off to the maximum extent possible," the President said, and "air and naval strikes against military targets in North Vietnam will continue." The President stressed that the actions were not directed against other nations, such as allies of North Vietnam. "Their sole purpose," he said, "is to protect the lives of 60,000 Americans who would be gravely endangered in the event that the Communist offensive continues to roll forward and to prevent the imposition of a Communist government by brutal aggression upon 17 million people" of South Vietnam.

An article appearing May 11 in the Chinese Communist party newspaper *Jenmin Jih Pao* and distributed by the official news agency Hsinhua called Nixon's action a "dangerous move" and a "flagrant provocation against the people of Vietnam and the world over." The statement declared: "The Chinese people express the gravest indignation at and the strongest condemnation of this grave act of war escalation of U.S. imperialism." As long as the war "against Vietnam and Indochina continues in any form," the article said, "we shall firmly support the Vietnamese and other Indochinese peoples . . . to the end and final victory."

Soviet and Chinese officials met with North Vietnamese and Mongolian representatives in Peking May 19 to map plans to speed up war assistance to North Vietnam in view of the American mining of its harbors. China and the Soviet Union were said to have known in advance of the North Vietnamese offensive that had begun Mar. 30 and were prepared for possible U.S. response. A North Vietnamese source in Peking was quoted as saying that Hanoi was "very, very satisfied" with China's assistance efforts. "We have received everything we have sought from the Chinese," the source said. The statement was in comment on the continuing visit of a North Vietnamese delegation headed by Deputy Foreign Trade Minister Ly Ban that had arrived in Peking May 3. The presence of the Mongolian ambassador in the Peking talks was an indication of his country's role in the transshipment of Soviet goods through China to North Vietnam.

Diplomatic sources in Peking reported May 21 that the Chinese were diverting trains to carry increased war aid to North Vietnam from the Soviet Union and other Communist countries. Train engines and freight cars that normally operated between north and south China on the Peking-Canton line had been shifted to the Nanking-Hanoi link. Different gauges, however, required unloading and reloading trains at the Chinese-North Vietnamese border. Another report by diplomatic sources in Peking May 23 said China had begun to prepare its railways for the new aid program to North Vietnam not long after the mining of its ports. Prior to the mining of North Vietnam's ports, about 80% of Soviet supplies was reaching North Vietnam by sea, according to U.S. estimates.

Sens. Mike Mansfield and Hugh Scott visited mainland China Apr. 15 May 9. They filed separate reports with the Senate May 11 on conclusions reached as a result of their trip. Mansfield said he thought it "illusory" to hope that, out of a desire to improve relations with the U.S., China would influence North Vietnam to end the war or release American prisoners. He also declared that "the new sorties into North Vietnam have tarnished the significance of the President's visit to China and, of course, the visit of the Senate's joint leadership. They have thrown into at least temporary eclipse the possibilities of Chinese-U.S. rapprochement." Scott said the U.S. and China should "normalize relations to the greatest extent possible. At the same time we must remain alert to the fact that there are basic philosophical differences in our views of man and society."

2 U.S. House of Representatives leaders visited China for 10 days and then reported July 8 that Chinese officials had

expressed concern to them about the possible combination of a Soviet arms buildup and U.S. disarmament and withdrawal from the Pacific and other regions. Democratic leader Hale Boggs (La.) said the concern had been expressed in conversations with Premier Chou and other Chinese officials. "As they put it," he reported, "there are 2 superpowers—the United States and Russia—and if Russia becomes the greater superpower then much of the world is in difficulty." Republican Leader Gerald R. Ford (Mich.) said the Chinese officials had shown "a great deal of interest" in "the sufficiency of our military capability and what our direction might be in the future with respect to the Defense Department funding and its programs." "They don't want the United States to withdraw from the Pacific or the world at any point," Ford said.

The Soviet Communist Party newspaper *Pravda* July 16 published an attack on the Chinese leadership on the basis of the Boggs and Ford remarks, which were categorically denied by Chinese sources July 17. The sources denied that China desired a continued U.S. presence in the Far East and said Chou had protested to the visiting Congressmen about the apparent strengthening of U.S. forces in other areas, particularly in Thailand and off the coast of Vietnam, while the U.S. withdrew its troops from Vietnam.

The 2 major U.S. political parties, in the platforms they issued during the 1972 Presidential election campaign, took up the subject of the changing Sino-U.S. relationship.

The Democratic platform, adopted July 11-12, said on this subject: "The beginnings of a new U.S.-China relationship is welcome and important. However, so far little of substance has changed, and the exaggerated secrecy and rhetoric of the Nixon Administration have produced unnecessary complications in our relationship with our allies and friends in Asia and with the USSR. What is needed now is serious negotiation on trade, travel exchanges and progress on more basic issues. The U.S. should take the steps necessary to establish regular diplomatic relations with China."

The Republican platform, adopted Aug. 22, said: "In the 1960s it seemed beyond possibility that the United States could dispel the ingrained hostility and confrontation with the China mainland. Pres. Nixon's visit to the People's Republic of China was, therefore, an historic milestone in his effort to transform our era from one of confrontation to one of negotiation. While profound differences remain between the United States and China, at least a generation of hostility has been replaced by frank discussions. In Feb. 1972 rules of international conduct were agreed upon which should make the Pacific region a more peaceful area now and in the future. Both the People's Republic and the United States affirmed the usefulness of promoting trade and cultural exchanges as ways of improving understanding between our 2 peoples. All this is being done without affecting our mutual defense treaty or our continued diplomatic relations with our valued friend and ally on Taiwan, the Republic of China."

The establishment of a new department in the Chinese Foreign Ministry dealing with U.S. and Pacific affairs was disclosed by Hsinhua Aug. 12. Chen Teh-ho was named deputy director of the department.

Pentagon officials reported Aug. 24 that U.S. fighter bombers, in an effort to choke off the flow of war supplies to North Vietnam, had attacked railroad bridges within 25 miles of the Chinese border on several occasions during the past 4 months. U.S. officials had previously disclosed the existence of a 25-mile buffer zone in which U.S. warplanes were normally forbidden to strike. Pentagon officials said that in 2 or 3 instances, planes strayed very close to Chinese air space before being warned back by U.S. air controllers in large radar planes. In at least one such case, an official said, the Chinese sent aircraft into the area. The officials stressed that special permission from Washington was necessary before planes could attack in the buffer zone. They asserted that no U.S. plane had ever violated the Chinese border. Peking however, had charged on several previous occasions that U.S. planes had violated Chinese air space.

China said Aug. 24 that it had lodged a strong protest with the U.S. over what it described as an attack by U.S. aircraft against a lifeboat of a Chinese merchant ship, resulting in the death of the ship's captain, a deputy political commissar and 3 seamen. The alleged attack reportedly took place Aug. 22 off Honngu Island, near the North Vietnamese port of Vinh, where the merchant ship *Hung Chi No. 151* was reportedly anchored. The U.S. command acknowledged Aug. 25 that Navy jets had sunk "one 30-foot supply water craft" in the area Aug. 22 but said "we have no evidence to indicate that we attacked a lifeboat." U.S. spokesmen said pilots and operations officers believed the boat was carrying supplies from a Chinese freighter anchored near Honngu Island in an attempt to circumvent U.S. mining of Vinh harbor.

Despite the Vietnam disputes, the Sino-U.S. reapprochement had apparently made considerable progress. U.S. Agriculture Secy. Earl L. Butz said Sept. 14 that China had placed an order for wheat with the U.S. subsidiary of a French-based company. Butz made the announcement before the opening of hearings by the House Subcommittee on Livestock & Grains investigating possible windfall profits by international grain operators arising out of a $750 million U.S.-Soviet grain transaction. Later Sept. 14, an official of the Louis Dreyfus Corp., the New York branch of the French firm Societe Anonyme Louis-Dreyfus et Cie., said the Chinese had agreed to purchase 18 million bushels of soft red wheat. The U.S. firm would "de-Americanize" the grain by selling it first to the parent firm in France for "business reasons."

Another apparent effect of the Sino-U.S. development was a shift in Sino-Japanese relations. Japan and China agreed Sept. 29, 1972 to end the legal state of war that had existed between the 2 countries for 35 years and to establish diplomatic relations. Japan immediately notified Nationalist China of its decision to recognize China and broke relations with the Taiwan government. Taipei followed suit and severed ties with Tokyo Sept. 29. The Sino-Japanese accord was contained in a joint

communique signed in Peking by Premiers Chou En-lai and
Kakuei Tanaka at the conclusion of a summit meeting that had
started Sept. 25. Among other principal points of the joint
statement were Japanese acceptance of China's position that
"Taiwan is an inalienable part" of the People's Republic of
China, Chinese renunciation of war indemnities from Japan
and an agreement to negotiate a "treaty of peace and friendship" and accords on trade and other bilateral arrangements.
On his arrival in Peking Sept. 25, Premier Tanaka had declared
in an address at a banquet in the Great Hall of the People that
Japan expressed regret and repentance for past aggression
against China. Holding that both countries "should not forever
linger in the dim blind alley of the past," Tanaka said: "It is
important now for the leaders of Japan and China to confer in
the interest of tomorrow. That is to say, to conduct frank and
sincere talks for the common goals of peace and prosperity in
Asia and in the world as a whole." Referring to Japan's history
of militarism and aggression, Premier Chou declared in a toast
that "the past not forgotten is a guide for the future." But he
said "the Chinese people make a strict distinction between the
very few militarists and the broad masses of the Japanese
people."

China, however, issued a warning that it would continue
to oppose major U.S.-supported causes. In a policy statement
to the UN General Assembly Oct. 3, Chinese representative
Chiao Kuanhua asserted that "war is inevitable so long as society
is divided into classes and the exploitation of man by man still
exists." He pledged China's support for "just wars." So long
as "imperialism, colonialism and neocolonialism" used force
to commit aggression against "a majority of the countries of
the world," Chiao said, it would be a "betrayal to the people
of the world to advocate non-use of force in international relations indiscriminately, without regard to conditions and in an
absolute way." Chiao cited the Middle East conflict, repeating
China's pledge to "always stand together with the Arab and
Palestinian peoples in their just struggle against aggression."

Despite U.S. support for "Israeli Zionism" and implicitly weak opposition to Israel by the Soviet Union, Arab countries were "fully capable of recovering their sacred territories and the injured Palestinian people [of] regaining their national rights," Chiao asserted.

Chinese Acting Pres. Tung Pi-wu and Premier Chou En-lai sent a note Dec. 19 congratulating the Viet Cong, on its 12th anniverssary, for having "waged protracted and indomitable struggles against the U.S. aggressors and their running dogs and won splendid victories." The Chinese leaders promised support "so long as the U.S. does not stop its war of aggression."

Celebrations were held throughout China Oct. 1, 1972, marking the 23d anniversary of the founding of the People's Republic. In addition to the festivities, major government journals published an official National Day editorial. The editorial, reviewing the events of the previous year, cited China's entry into the UN and its new diplomatic relations with the U.S. and Japan. The article, however, was highly critical of the U.S. and of the Soviet Union, accusing both of causing tensions in Southeast Asia and the Middle East. The statement appeared in *Jenmin Jih Pao,* the party journal; *Hung Chi,* the ideological journal, and *Chieh Fang Chun Pao,* the military daily.

The Sino-U.S. rapprochement ended the 2-decade suspension of almost all trade between the U.S. and mainland China. U.S. exports to China rose from an official total of zero in 1971 (when only illegally transshipped goods from the U.S. reached China) to $60.2 million in 1972, $689.1 million (not counting an additional $50.6 million worth of wheat, corn and soybeans by way of Canada) in 1973 and an estimate of perhaps $1.15 billion in 1974. During this period, mainland Chinese exports to the U.S. rose from $4.9 million in 1971 to $32.2 million in 1972, $63.7 million in 1973 and an estimate of possibly $100 million in 1974. The U.S. shipments, however, included probable "one-time-only" items such as $290 million worth of fertilizer plants bought by China in 1973. And fertilizer plants, of course, would make it possible for China to reduce its purchases of U.S. fertilizers. The Chinese also made it clear to the Americans that their large purchases could not continue unless the U.S. increased its purchases from China.